We've a Story To Tell

We've a Story To Tell

A History of First Baptist Church
Orlando, Florida, 1871–1996

Patricia J. Birkhead

PROVIDENCE HOUSE PUBLISHERS
Franklin, Tennessee

Printed in the United States of America

00   99   98   97   96   5   4   3   2   1

Library of Congress Catalog Card Number: 96–70690

ISBN: 1–57736–020–6

Dust jacket by James Hansen and Bozeman Design

Unless otherwise indicated, photographs are provided courtesy of the archives of First Baptist Church, Orlando, Florida. Photographs courtesy of the Florida State Archives are noted by FSA; those courtesy of the Orange County Historical Museum are noted by OCHM.

PROVIDENCE HOUSE PUBLISHERS
238 Seaboard Lane • Franklin, Tennessee 37067
800-321-5692

This book is lovingly dedicated to the Lord Jesus Christ to glorify his name. It is also dedicated to three distinct groups: the eighteen saints who saw a vision of establishing a Baptist church in the very remote and beautiful settlement that came to be known as Orlando and those who made up the church during its early years; the saints who currently work within the First Baptist Church of Orlando striving to do God's will in a variety of ministries; and finally the saints who will follow us, continuing on this rich foundation until the coming of our Lord.

Contents

Foreword

Genesis 16 tells the story of Hagar, a handmaiden of Sarai. During a time of crisis, Hagar fled into the wilderness to a spring on the road to Shur. There, the angel of the Lord confronted her with two very appropriate questions, "Where have you come from, and where are you going?" Such questions are so intertwined that they cannot be separated. And they are so continuously relevant that they are appropriate today and for all generations to come.

As First Baptist Church, Orlando, Florida, reaches another milestone in its history, the answer to these questions may well represent the labor of Patricia Birkhead in researching and writing WE'VE A STORY TO TELL. In reminding the members and others who are interested in the history of this significant Southern Baptist church, Birkhead and the Ad Hoc History Committee members also have provided a foundation upon which to build for the present and future generations of members of First Baptist Church.

As a church historian, I have frequently stated that every generation has a debt to the past to remember the accomplishments of those who came before it and a debt to future generations—to provide them a record from which to trace their lineage. Birkhead and the committee have led the way for First Baptist Church to pay both of these debts to generations past and future. They are to be commended for their dedication and effort.

As the author of the centennial history of my home church in Shawnee, Oklahoma, I can assure you that there are two great joys in researching and writing an anniversary history of a church. First, there is the joy of discovery. There are few greater thrills for a researcher than to uncover some significant or interesting event from the past and to find oneself thirsting for more information, more answers to questions that arise out of the discovery, and more insights into who we are today as we know more about who we were and where we have been. Second, there is the joy of excitement in sharing our discoveries with others. There is no greater compliment to a writer than having a reader say, "I loved the story about . . . ," or "I didn't know that about . . . ," or "Well, that explains that."

Unfortunately, there are no eyewitnesses left to tell the story of the beginnings of First Baptist Church, Orlando, some 125 years ago. But there are records which create in our minds the visions of those early days and the years that followed. There are minutes, official documents (such as constitutions and covenants), and stories that have been passed down from earlier generations. There are records and stories about the community and the early associational work which provide insights into the people and the church. And there are events, such as wars, financial crises, and cultural trends, that impact the church, community, state, nation, and world.

Readers of this book can imagine, through the words of Birkhead, the way that things were, or in the words found in Genesis, "Where have you come from?" And each member who takes the time to read the stories that follow will have the opportunity to dream dreams for the future. The most important contribution of this history may well be a renewed commitment of this congregation to "write" its own pages of history for the generations that follow—to play a significant role in determining "where" First Baptist Church, Orlando, is "going."

Beginning in 1871 under the leadership of George C. Powell as the first pastor of the congregation and continuing through the pastoral guidance of Jim Henry, president of the Southern Baptist Convention from 1994 to 1996, this church has an inspiring story to be absorbed by its members and to be shared with others. Enjoy this rich heritage.

As you read this record of the history of First Baptist Church, never forget that its earthly history belongs to a greater heritage of God's work in his world. This church has not existed in isolation. It is simply, yet significantly, another part of the history that quietly began with the life and ministry of a carpenter from Nazareth who taught us and showed us how to live and who sacrificially gave his life that those who believe in him might have eternal life. The answer to the questions posed to Hagar must ultimately and continually find their way back to our understanding of the place of Jesus in our past and in our future.

Slayden A. Yarbrough, Executive Director
Historical Commission of the Southern Baptist Convention

Preface

For several years, I have been interested in family history. I began with a research project to discover more about my mother's people in Vermont. I concentrated my efforts on the quaint dairy farm in North Pomfret, on whose canvas might be painted raspberry and rose bushes, Jersey cattle, energetic children, hard-working adults, and a ramshackle farmhouse, circled by a stone fence reminiscent of Robert Frost's poem "Mending Wall." After five years of interviews with my mother, her siblings, and others, and after wading through a surprising avalanche of family papers, letters, and journals, a one-hundred-page history was written, and a reunion was held.

Next, as an educator, I decided to use what I had learned and developed a writing course to introduce college freshmen to the joys of family research. Some of our projects included storytelling, journal keeping, family medicine, photograph albums, tradition exploration, birth order studies, basic genealogy, library research, ethnic cuisine, family trees, ethnic costumes, family jokes and expressions, interviewing techniques, cemetery research, computer searches, and reunions.

My curiosity about family and history naturally made another turn and extended to my church. Since I was not raised in the Baptist faith, I found I knew very little about Baptist origins. And as a fairly recent member of First Baptist Church of Orlando (having joined in 1983), I wanted to know more about this particular church's history. A visit to our church library uncovered a gold mine of information from books on the Baptist faith but very little written about our particular church's history. I talked with Wayne Johnson, our minister of media, about the possibility of my researching our church's history and writing a book about my findings. He did a quick calculation of an upcoming church anniversary, our 125th, and said with his usual enthusiasm, "Let's do it." He suggested I interview Mildred Talton, the church's former historian. Pastor Jim

Henry also gave me his endorsement and directed me to Jimmy Dusek, the pastor representing our history and archives.

A visit to Talton proved very valuable. She graciously loaned her extensive albums and notes and gave me her blessing and encouragement. Jimmy Dusek, already wearing many "hats" in the church, nevertheless wholeheartedly endorsed the project and suggested several members to comprise an ad hoc history committee. That summer I visited Nashville to study church history books at the Southern Baptist Historical Library and Archives. I discovered our convention has wonderful literature on nearly every subject, including how to write a church history. A trip to the Florida State Archives in Tallahassee also proved helpful, as did numerous visits to the Orange County Historical Museum and the Orlando Public Library.

In February 1994, our ten-member Ad Hoc History Committee began meeting once a month and continued to do so until the publication date. The committee developed a questionnaire which was sent out to some of the members of the church. Committee members have also proven to be a very congenial group with multiple talents. Many of the members have been affiliated with the church for decades, and all have been willing participants in the research and editing of the manuscript.

As the research progressed, I became enamored with our city and its colorful history as well as our church and its precious members. As I drive through the streets of Orlando, I am reminded of the city's past and its founders. I turn onto Gatlin Avenue and imagine the fort that stood there so very long ago. Delaney Avenue calls forth that pioneering Delaney family, many of whom were members of our church. Summerlin Avenue takes me back to Jacob and Samuel, cattlemen in the early days. While strolling the beautiful walkways of Lake Eola, I seem to hear the laughter of sunbathers from long ago and witness the solemn baptisms which used to take place within its water. The sense of place, to me, seems to be so important in the study of a church's past and present.

And as I walk the halls of our present church buildings, the walls seem almost to echo the sounds of the past. If we could hear these echoes, Mattie Hart's strike of her ruler would sound to keep up the pace of the week's Scripture verse to the recitations of her young Sunday School pupils. William Miller would call out in the night to those inside the William Hull home waiting for his arrival. Construction sounds would echo as different buildings of the church are erected. Voices would lift in song, as thousands upon thousands of hymns are offered to the Lord as a sweet fragrance. Laughter and love would ring out with the wedding bells, and soft sobs would be heard as tears course down cheeks of those seated near a casket. The voices of thirty-five pastors, along with hundreds of guest speakers, would break the word of God and feed the saints.

Although the book in your hands has been read by the watchful eyes of many editors, some errors will inevitably remain. We ask your forgiveness, for they were not intended. Second, an effort has been made to give thumbnail sketches of various members and ministries of First Baptist Church, Orlando. Because of time and space constraints, many worthy and talented people and some ministries have not been mentioned or have been recorded very briefly. Perhaps a future work might include those people and events which may come to your mind. Finally, as in many books dealing with history, the most recent events often receive the most coverage. This should in no way diminish the many wonderful accomplishments, ministries, and people of the more distant past.

It is the hope of the author and the Ad Hoc History Committee that you enjoy reading WE'VE A STORY TO TELL. We further desire that it may inspire you to even greater works on behalf of our loving Creator, the Lord Jesus Christ. In John 21:25 we read, "Jesus did many other things as well. If every one of them were written down, I suppose that even the whole world would not have room for the books that would be written."

Acknowledgments

First and foremost, Mildred Talton and Pat Hanson deserve to be mentioned. Mildred was the historian for First Baptist Church for approximately twenty-five years. Educated with a degree in history, she was instrumental in writing brief histories of the church for its various publications and events, including its one hundredth anniversary. A lover of accurate details, she kept meticulous notes and wrote and compiled various binders and other materials about the church, which she freely loaned to the author. She has made herself available to the Ad Hoc History Committee and has come to some of its meetings. Most of all, she has become a friend to the author and a respected colleague, working tirelessly with the author toward the completion of this book. Now a member of Downtown Baptist Church, Mildred's ministry has continued there. In addition, she has been working on a history of the Wekiwa Association.

Pat Hanson has continued Mildred's tradition as church historian for the past twelve years. Whenever the author had a question, her first call was to Pat. The author knew that if Pat did not have the answer at her fingertips, she almost always would be able to find it in a short time. Pat joined the church in 1954 and began to work there shortly thereafter. Because of that longevity, she began to be known as the one to be called by any church member or staff. Most recently, she helped in the technical accuracy of the murals in Faith Hall. Pat, too, has become a valued friend and colleague in the project of this book.

And then the author's appreciation and respect go to the Ad Hoc History Committee: Jimmy Dusek, Ralph and Martha Edfeldt, Louise Gouge, Carol Hansen, Pat Hanson, Loren Mallory, Emily Meiner, and Murl Morrow. Only the Lord could have arranged such a congenial group. We have all become friends and colaborers in this task. All have assembled their special and varied talents to work on this very interesting

Mildred Talton

and yet challenging journey.

Charles Deweese and the staff of Providence House Publishers in Franklin, Tennessee, have greatly contributed to the many technical aspects of the book. They labored in its proofreading, editing, layout and design, publishing, and other varied work.

Of course, various staff and members of the First Baptist Church of Orlando, Florida, have been of great help. In no particular order, they include Jim Henry, Sandi Mathis, Henry Meiner, Gene and Barbara Kelsey, Ruth Moses, Gennivee Rich, Charles Bell, Gail Brown, Shirley Dusek, Bill Silkman, Dot Hawk, Barbara Hawxwell, Wayne Johnson, Jimmy Knott, Bill Mitchell, Jerry Montgomery, Art Murphy, Scott Randlett, David Taylor, Kyle Wall, Nancy Nutting, Ann Richardson, Grace Sanford, Steve Smith, Ragan Vandegriff, Terry Winch, J. B. Collingsworth, Tim Grosshans, Mike McKee, Jean King, Sharon Cooper, Kitty Denson, Glenda Mowdy, Karick Price, Randall James, Marshall Wilson, Kathy McRae, Virginia McClellan, Helen Lawrence, Don McKenzie, Barbara Hawxwell, Sandy Epperson, Shirley Mallory, F. Ray and Helen Dorman, Richard and Beverly Downes, Bob Vickery, Lisa Hale, Bob and Donna Marrero, Todd and Dora Mae Pemberton, Charles and Frances Skinner, Fran Roycroft, members of the 8:15 A.M. singles' Sunday School class, Barbara Wellington, Anita Crews, Darla Driggers, Virginia Taylor, Nancy Jones, Alan Rasmussen, Mac McKinney, Pat Shackelford, Nancy Hull, Mac and Doris McCully, Millard and Margaret Smith, Frances Williams, Edna Sanders, Ralph Cottrell Jr., Alene Gatch, James L. and C. Jane McKinney, Bruce Ogden, Doris Morgan, and Henry Meiner.

Two very talented First Baptist Church members and artists are James Hansen, who designed the book's cover, and David Naquin, the photographer for some of the work within the book, most notably the pictures of the committee and the photograph titled "Christ Crucified."

Several members of Downtown Baptist also helped a great deal. A few of them include Ed and Missy Moses, Betty Lassiter, Howard and June Dobson, George Shearouse, Alex Marsh, and Barbara Thigpen.

Other helpful Baptists have been Virginia Parker, Josephine Kesler, Charles Moses, Gerry Leonard, George Tucker, Betty Carow, Bonnie Verlander of the *Florida Baptist Witness*, Bill Sumners and Slayden Yarbrough of the Historical Commission of the Southern Baptist Convention, Kay Brooks and Aronelle Lofton of First Baptist Church of Apopka, Earl Joiner and Pat Nordman of the Florida Baptist Archives, Melanie Mueller, Diane Ciavarra, Patsy Powell, and Hampton Dunn.

Several librarians have been extremely helpful. Those from Orlando Public Library would include Steve Gataletta, Margaret Wells, Dan Kennedy, and Nancy Bond. Those from the Florida State Library in Tallahassee would include Karen Southwell, Synthia Wise, and Mary Ann Cleveland. The staff of Orange County Historical Society Library were very generous with their time and expertise. They include Sara van Arsdel, director; Frank Mendola, librarian; and Hayley Fensch, photographs. Joanna Norman of the Florida State Archives was very prompt in her assistance with archival photographs.

Orlando and Orange County are blessed with talented historians and employees. Some who have been most helpful include Jean Yothers, Ileta Spitzer, Ruth Kursman, Orville R. Davis, Jack Lemmon, Brenda Elliot, Grace Chewning, Peggy Jo van den Berg, and Fran Carlton.

Some of the descendants of past pastors and early church members have also given of their time. They are Dorothy H. Shaw (William and Emily Hull), Jewell Powell Fillmon, Helen Alderman, Mrs. R. E. Gustafson, and Sharon Tate (G. C. and Patience Powell).

The following have also given help. They are Donald C. Hurst of the Health and Human Services Board, Richard Adicks of the University of Central Florida and a Florida historian and author, Mark Andrews and Jim Robison of the *Orlando Sentinel*, Robert Hopkins of the St. John's River Cruises, and talented artists Michael W. and Deborah D. Smith.

Finally, friends and family of the author have given much encouragement and support. They include

Pat Hanson

Melissa and Mark Welch; Paul and Dana Birkhead; Marge Wallace and Bill Wallace; Mary Beth Daugherty; Joe and Katrina Wallace; Ed, Irene, Stephen, and Cathy Welch; Ian, Brenda, Paul, and Michael Brownlow; Shirley Brewer; Nancy Chiaro; Gail Calcutt; Bill and Bettye Davis; Neal, Kathy, Brandt, and Blair Erickson; Mary Easter; Mike Glaspy; Max and Joyce Holman; Barbara and Leanne Knowles; Paul and Saundra Kraus; Gary and Kim Parks; John and Leslie Puik; Jim and Marion Russell; Laura Ross; Leslie Castle; Gary Minor; Beverly Bailey; the staff of Seminole Community College Hunt Club campus; Kathleen Bell; Carolyn Wilson; Maxine McKenzie; Judy Wall Townsend; Victoria Antonacci; Ron Greene; Lorna Hallal; Russ Kesler; Nancy Marshall; and Catherine Schutz.

If any have been inadvertently left out, please accept the author's apologies. Of course, God—the Lord Jesus Christ, the Holy Spirit, and the Father—is acknowledged as the prime mover in all these endeavors. The glorification of the Name which is above every name is the ultimate purpose of this volume.

The Ad Hoc History Committee Members

Jimmy Dusek came to First Baptist Church on January 1, 1982, from the pastorate of First Baptist Church, Franklin, North Carolina. He first served as assistant pastor of senior adults. Then in the early 1990s, he moved to his present position as assistant pastor of pastoral care. However, he energetically serves in a variety of other areas, most notably in baptism and as the pastor on several committees. His wife Shirley has served as director of the Child Enrichment Center of the church for ten years, and she is currently the preschool associate. Jimmy and Shirley have two children and three grandchildren.

Martha and Ralph Edfeldt joined First Baptist Church in 1957. Since that time they have both served the Lord in many areas, such as Sunday School in the Cradle Roll, Youth, College Age, Young Married, and now Senior Adult Departments. Ralph was Sunday School superintendent for four years. He has sung in the choir since 1957, and Martha, since 1959. Ralph twice has been chairman of the deacons serving a total of three years. He has also served on the Stewardship, Nominating, Budget, and other committees as well as being secretary of the trustees. Martha started helping count the Sunday offerings on Mondays in 1961 and has continued to serve in that area. She was music secretary to Edwin Irey from 1963 until he retired, and then she moved to the Finance Office until her retirement in 1988, having worked on the staff at the church for twenty-five years. At the present time, Ralph is the state president of Campers on Mission, and Martha is the state treasurer. Martha and Ralph have three grown children who were all brought up in First Baptist Church. The Edfeldts have been blessed with seven grandchildren and one great-grandchild.

Louise Gouge joined First Baptist Church in 1987 along with her husband David and their four children. She has been active in the music ministry as a soloist, Ladies' Ensemble member and director, director of the Girls' Ensemble, and adult choir member, taking part in both the Twin Singing Christmas Trees and the Easter program called "The Light." Louise has also been a drama cast member in "The Light" for nine years. In addition to working as a television marketing coordinator and producer, Louise has published a Christian novel, *Once There Was a Way Back Home*, with Crossway Books. Louise and David are currently taking a break from teaching Sunday School and their leadership duties, where they served for seven years. They have four children.

Carol Hansen enjoys a rich legacy of connection to First Baptist Church reaching back to 1925. Her daughter completes the fourth generation of family ties with the church, beginning with Carol's grandmother, Gennivee Rich, and Carol's mother, Carolyn Trumbo. Carol joined First Baptist Church in 1979 and has been an active member in several areas of the children's ministry: children's Sunday School, Training Union, Vacation Bible School, Mission Orlando, and children's altar counseling. In addition, she has served in the women's ministry, discipleship ministry, adult Sunday School ministry, and on the Missions Committee. Her husband Jim is a well-known local artist, specializing in architectural renderings and residential design. Their family, which includes two sons and a daughter, has been involved in local and home missions since 1980.

Pat Hanson joined First Baptist Church in 1954. Several months after joining, she was called to be youth director and served in that capacity until 1957. She returned to the staff in 1965 as secretary in the Finance Office and remained in that area until early in 1996 when she joined the Facilities Department as secretary. She has served under Pastors Tucker, Parker, and Henry, and worked with five different business administrators. Because of her years on staff, she has a broad knowledge of the history of First Baptist Church. Her desire has always been to be available for any needs of the church's members or visitors who either call or come into the church office. For over twelve years she has been the church historian and is often called upon for information from the church's safe and archives. Most recently she has worked with the artist for the four historical murals in Faith Hall and with the Ad Hoc History Committee in the work on this book. As well as being on staff, Pat continues to be an active member of First Baptist Church in several key areas. She has four children who were raised and came to know the Lord in this church. They and her granddaughter are her greatest gifts from God.

Loren Mallory vacationed in Florida after leaving the air force and decided to stay. He joined First Baptist Church in 1947. He served in the Sunday School Youth Division for over twenty-five years as teacher and department director. His tours as a sponsor of youth choirs included the Holy Land, two trips to Jamaica for evangelistic crusades, and services in the United States. Loren served on a number of committees including Trustees, Properties, Ordinances, Budget Planning, Personnel, Operations, and Nominating Committees. He was ordained as a deacon in 1960 and served one year as chairman. Loren was business administrator for First Baptist Church for over eight years, retiring in 1984. Since then he has been serving as a volunteer wherever needed. His ministry included prisons around the state. He currently presents the gospel each week to the homeless who come to the thrift shop for clothing. Loren married Jean Parker in 1950. She served with him in the Sunday School and choir programs and was junior high department director. The Lord called Jean home in 1983. They have a son, daughter, and granddaughter. Loren married Shirley Yaros in 1985. Shirley's first husband, Andrew Yaros, had been called home to be with the Lord in 1982. Andrew was a prominent businessman and was active in the growth of First Baptist Church. Shirley was Sunday School director of senior high and served on the Personnel, Building, and Pastor Search Committees. Her children and grandchildren live in the Orlando area. Loren and Shirley currently serve on the Year of the Church Committee and help maintain the archives.

Emily Meiner holds the distinction of being the committee member with the longest membership at First Baptist Church. She moved to Orlando from Tifton, Georgia, with her parents Ivan and Marguerite Morgan when she was four years old. Her parents' active involvement in this church prompted her own lifelong association. In 1932, at age twelve, she was baptized by Pastor Adcock. During her sixty-plus years of membership, she has taught children's Sunday School, been a leader of the Sunbeams (a mission organization for preschoolers), served on the Hospitality Committee, and spent several years visiting members who were physically unable to attend church services. She and her husband Henry T. were married by Pastor Tucker in 1942, and they have three daughters who were raised at First Baptist Church and six grandchildren. Husband Henry was a prominent businessman in the catering business in the Orlando area for a number of years. Emily is presently a member of the Peacemakers Sunday School Class.

Murl Whorton Morrow was born in Hollis, Oklahoma, but in 1953 Orlando became her home. She and her husband John attended First Baptist Church from 1953 until his death in 1975. At that time, Murl formally joined the church and became an active member, serving in several capacities in Sunday School. She was an outreach leader for five years and worked with senior adults in Baptists Extra Years of Zest (BXYZ), now called Saints Alive! She was president of this organization for eight years. She served for two years as a worker in the archives. Currently, she enjoys traveling on mission trips and with the senior adults on trips throughout the United States and foreign countries.

Pat Birkhead's biography appears on the book jacket.

History Committee—Front row (l/r): Carol Hansen, recorder and research; Pat Birkhead, author; Jimmy Dusek, pastor in charge; Emily Meiner, research and hospitality; and Pat Hanson, church historian and research. Back row (l/r): Murl Morrow, research; Martha Edfeldt, research; Ralph Edfeldt, research; Loren Mallory, leader, archives, research, and hospitality; and Louise Gouge, editor and research.

We've a Story To Tell

CHAPTER ONE

A Brief Baptist History

"If my people, who are called by my name, will humble themselves and pray and seek my face and turn from their wicked ways, then will I hear from heaven and will forgive their sin and will heal their land."

—*2 Chronicles 7:14*

THE GATHERING
THE EIGHTEEN CHARTER MEMBERS ASSEMBLE

"'On the first day hold a sacred assembly.'"
Exodus 12:16

The air seemed to stir with excitement as John Wofford climbed out of bed that morning. He quietly moved about the makeshift cabin so as not to disturb Caroline. He heard a bobcat worrying their cattle, so he reluctantly opened the door and felt a blast of unusually frigid air hit him. The cold penetrated to his bones. At sixty-two, he was feeling his age, although he still imagined himself as able-bodied. Trying to eke out a living in the pine forest required him to be energetic, and he felt the activity kept him young. He called softly to the animals to comfort them while he gripped his rifle and walked to the pen.

Caroline, age thirty-nine, hadn't slept much the night before because the children were coming down with colds. Perhaps Doctor Levy wouldn't mind taking a look at them later in the day. She walked slowly to the corner of their small home. Feeling chilled, she stirred up the fire and put on a pot of ground sweet potato coffee. The supply of canned food on the shelf was dwindling fast. For a moment she felt alarmed, but she quickly reminded herself of the Lord's provision in the past and whispered the verse, "When I am afraid, I will trust in Thee." Her fears pushed aside, she assembled a quick breakfast for her family. They would need to get an early start if they hoped to meet the others on time.

Levy C. Whitted, forty-six, had decided to stay up. Although it was still early, there would be no time to go back to bed. He had been up nearly all night tending to the needs of a new mother. Being a physician meant he was on call at all hours, but he didn't mind. He felt God had called him to this remote settlement. His wife Sarah, thirty-two, appeared to be flourishing in spite of the hardships. Now, where had he placed his Bible? Perhaps he should be ready to read a few passages of Scripture if Reverend Powell asked him to. He paused to look over some notes he had jotted down concerning the constitution and decorum he and the others would be drawing up that day.

A few miles away, Jeptha Purvis, thirty-four, took one more look at his wife Martha before heading out the door. Try though he might, he just couldn't convince her to go with him. Even though he couldn't read or write, he still thought he could make an important contribution to the gathering. After all, the earth that he tilled was the Lord's, wasn't it? Perhaps the others might have need of some of his winter's store. He ducked back inside and filled a bag with beef strips, flour, syrup, coffee, and other foodstuffs.

John, seventeen, and Sally, fourteen, were arguing again. Sally wanted to get an early start, and John, like most brothers, was teasing her. He joked about her dress, saying she looked like she was trying to impress William. Did she really need to wear those ribbons? For some strange reason, their parents wouldn't accompany them to the service. Sometimes John just couldn't understand the "older generation."

William Hodges, sixteen, was glad to have the day off from his farm laborer duties. He had finally persuaded his boss to let him go to the meeting. Maybe Sally would be there. He certainly hoped so. Clemuel Tiner, twenty-five, had promised to meet him at the clearing. They would travel the rest of the way together.

Patience Powell, fifty-nine, was very proud of George, sixty-one. While the memory of their son's crime and awful death would always cause her husband to have furrows in his brow, he still felt inspired and motivated by the Lord to plant churches. The people in this little community seemed especially committed to forming a group of believers. Now that the war was finally over, it was time to begin anew. Today, George would put away his blacksmith tools and forge a new endeavor, the forming of the Bethel Church. How Patience loved that name. Bethel, a sacred area. "And Jacob awoke from his sleep, and he said, 'Surely the Lord is in this place, and I did not know it.' He was afraid, and said, 'How to be feared and reverenced is this place! This is none other than the house of God, and this is the gateway to heaven!' And Jacob rose early in the morning, and took the stone he had put under his head, and he set it up for a pillar, and he poured oil on its top. And he named that place Bethel [the house of God]" (Gen. 28:16–19, The Amplified Bible).

And so it was that on March 5, 1871, eighteen charter members—John and Caroline Wofford, Levy and Sarah Whitted, John and Sally Hughey, William Hodges, Clemuel Tiner, Jeptha and Henry Purvis, Malintha Yates, John Brook, John Roberson, Narcissa and Mary Lovell, Josepene McClane, Julia Garott, and Winford Griggs—came together with George C. and Patience Powell to form the first permanent church in Orlando—Bethel Missionary Baptist Church.

Some may ask, why study history as it relates to the church? George W. Truett, venerable pastor of the First Baptist Church of Dallas, Texas, had an answer. He said we should be like the ancient Hebrews and take an "occasional backward look" to give ourselves "poise and patience and courage and fearlessness and faith." With that in mind, let us begin.

The small band of believers who began First Baptist Church of Orlando (formerly known as Bethel Baptist Church) were no different from those early pioneers of the Baptist faith. "Soul-liberty is cherished by Baptists as a distinctive principle, with no one—priest, parent, pope, or potentate—coming between him and God. Every soul should have direct access to God" (Routh 7).

The early churches of New Testament times had pastors, deacons, and two memorials or symbols: baptism and the Lord's Supper. These churches were independent of each other but cooperative in their efforts to do good with every individual accountable to God. No one could "act for another in the spiritual realm." They taught that sinners were saved only by "faith in the Lord Jesus Christ; not by good works." They believed that the act of baptism did not save but was practiced by the believer as a profession of faith. The churches made no "alliances with earthly rulers," and the only priest was Jesus Christ (Routh 9–11).

Not much later, heresies plagued these early churches, many of which still plague the church today. For example, bishops and pastors began to extend their oversight and authority beyond their own individual churches; baptism began to be regarded as having "saving efficacy" and was no longer just a symbol, which led to infant baptism and the replacement of immersion by sprinkling; the Lord's Supper was linked to salvation rather than serving only as a memorial, and the doctrine of transubstantiation was given official sanction; and the deity of Jesus was put under question (Routh 13–17). State churches were established, with much persecution suffered by nonconformists. Out of this dissension sprung many groups and schisms, such as the Montanists, Novatianists, Anabaptists, and Mennonites. For several centuries, evangelistic groups would form and then face persecution and suppression.

In the 1500s, many Christians were so shocked by their church's corruption that they demanded purification. As the Bible was translated into a language the common people could understand, and as the beliefs of Martin Luther and John Calvin electrified England, the stage was set for a great era of change.

In England—One militant group which sought to cleanse the Church of England from within was the Puritans. A second group, the Separatists, branched off from the Puritans. They believed the only way to achieve true reform was to leave the state church and work from outside. A few of these Separatists, or Independents, became Congregationalists, with a continued belief in infant baptism. A second group of these Separatists, after studying the Bible, began to accept the concept of believer's baptism. Their opponents, in a derisive way, called them "Anabaptists," which later became the word "Baptists."

As the movement grew, distinctive Baptist beliefs and practices emerged, such as the authority and sufficiency of the Scriptures; the priesthood of the believer; the view of salvation as God's gift of divine grace received by man through repentance and faith in Jesus Christ; a regenerated church membership; baptism by immersion, only given to believers; two ordinances, baptism and the Lord's Supper, viewed primarily as symbols and reminders; each church as an independent, self-governing body, the members possessing equal rights and privileges; religious liberty for all; and separation of church and state (May pamphlet).

Some notables in the Baptist faith on the world's stage must include John Bunyan, the famous preacher and writer confined to jail for twelve years for preaching without a license and failing to attend the Anglican Church; John Gill; and William Carey, who is considered by many to be the first missionary to India. "Within the heart of William Carey—cobbler, teacher, student, pastor—burned the flames of evangelism in the light of which he saw the whole world in need of the Gospel. He had great difficulty in breaking down the walls of hyper-Calvinism, but, reinforced by Andrew Fuller and John Sutcliff of Northampton Association, the way was opened for the formation in 1792 of the Baptist Missionary Society . . ." (Routh 40–41).

The modern Sunday School can be traced to William Fox, a Baptist deacon living in London, who encouraged voluntary, rather than paid, teachers to teach the Bible instead of secular studies. Three outstanding Baptist pastors in England were Charles Haddon Spurgeon, a remarkable evangelist ranked with Wycliffe, Wesley, and Bunyan; Alexander Maclaren, one of the greatest expository preachers of his day; and John Clifford, called the "Apostle of Soul Liberty."

One group of Congregationalists, now known as the Pilgrims, set sail for the new world in 1620. They established a colony at Plymouth. In 1630 another group traveling in seventeen ships sailed from England and began the Massachusetts Bay Colony. Ironically, these Puritans became intolerant of others, insisting on infant baptism. Much later, in 1905 in London, the Baptists held their first World Congress, now called the Baptist World Alliance.

In the United States—Just as Baptists were persecuted for their faith in England and elsewhere, they also found a hostile reception in the New World, most notably from the Established (Congregational) Church in New England. Strangely enough, seeking religious freedom in this new land was not easy for those who arrived after the founders of the colonies.

While Roger Williams, an early Baptist, later called himself a "seeker," he was instrumental in promoting the faith in Rhode Island. "Forced to leave Massachusetts because of his radical views, Williams founded the colony of Rhode Island and led in forming the First Baptist Church of Providence in 1638/39. Most historians point to that congregation as the first Baptist church on American soil" (Hastey pamphlet). John Clarke organized a Baptist church at Newport, and William Screven, in 1682, set up a Baptist church in Kittery, Maine. There he and his congregation faced such persecution that some of them later resettled in Charleston, South Carolina. A group of Baptists was located in the Philadelphia area in 1688, led by Elias Keach. Of all those Baptists suffering persecution, the areas of strongest opposition were felt in Massachusetts and Virginia.

In 1707, five small churches organized the first Baptist association, called the Philadelphia Baptist Association. A few years later, the Great Awakening, which had its beginnings from messages by Jonathan Edwards and George Whitefield, increased to a remarkable degree the numbers of churches and members in the Baptist faith. Yet persecution continued, most notably in New England and Virginia. Many Baptist preachers were jailed for their beliefs. Also, after the Great Awakening, Baptists divided themselves into Regulars (conservatives) and Separates (revivalists).

Brown University, the first Baptist college, was opened in 1765. During the American Revolution, several notable Baptists became worthy of mention. John Gano was a chaplain in high favor with George Washington (Routh 55). Other valiant Baptist preachers during the Revolution were Richard Furman, Jeremiah Walker, John Williams, Hezekiah Smith, and Samuel Rogers (Routh 55).

When Americans began expanding westward, Tennessee and Kentucky received many Baptist pioneers. Revivals and frontier preachers were instrumental in the increase in numbers of Baptists. Foreign missions also began to grow. Some divisions among Baptists occurred over what has been termed the "Three Crises": the missions crisis, the racial crisis, and the landmark crisis. Even so, the faith continued as it broke off into several branches. Northern and southern Baptists were split over several concerns. One of these was called "the slavery issue." Another problem was the distance the southern churches had to travel to attend the northern convention. Finally, the southern mission boards felt they were being neglected by the mission boards of New York and Boston (Routh 65).

On May 8, 1845, Southern Baptists withdrew from the General Missionary Convention; met in Augusta, Georgia; and formed the Southern Baptist Convention (SBC) with William B. Johnson as the first president. Later, the SBC began two mission boards: the Foreign Mission Board in Richmond, Virginia, and the Domestic (Home) Mission Board in Marion, Alabama.

China was the first foreign field entered by Southern Baptists. Samuel C. Clopton, the J. L. Shucks, Matthew T. Yates, R. H. Graves, E. Z. Simmons, and J. B. Hartwell were early missionaries there. Africa's early missionaries were T. J. Bowen, Lott Carey, W. H. Clarke, Moses Stone, the J. M. Hardens, and W. J. David, to name a few. In Italy were the George B. Taylors and the John H. Eagers. W. D. Powell pioneered the efforts in

Mexico while the W. B. Bagbys and the Z. C. Taylors were at work in Brazil. Japan was reached in the early years by the J. W. McCollums and the E. N. Walnes.

Not to be overlooked, Baptist women organized their auxiliary organization called the Woman's Missionary Union (WMU) on May 11, 1888, at Broad Street Methodist Church in Richmond, Virginia. One of their first endeavors was to respond to Lottie Moon's appeal for funds for China. Their first Christmas offering was approximately three thousand dollars. The WMU pioneered many areas of mission work for Southern Baptists, such as work among American Indians (the beginning of Home Mission Board language work) and the establishment of a Church Building Loan Fund. WMU's sub-organizations (namely Baptist Women, Baptist Young Women, Acteens, Girls in Action, and Mission Friends) continue to remain major vehicles for missions education in Southern Baptist churches. The youth in the Baptist faith also were not without representation. In 1895 the Baptist Young People's Union (BYPU)—later Training Union—was formed.

With the missionary effort expanding, adequate training for these men and women was needed. In 1859, the Southern Baptist Theological Seminary was established in Greenville, South Carolina.

Southern Baptists' most important areas of concentration are evangelism, missionaries, and missions. Revivals and crusades have marked their 150-year history. Southern Baptists pride themselves in the total autonomy of each Baptist church (*One Sacred Effort* video).

Prominent names in a list of United States Baptists in America are John Clark, William Screven, Luther Rice, Isaac Backus, John Leland, Lottie Moon, Annie Armstrong, W. B. Johnson, and Billy Graham.

In Florida—Any study of Baptist history in Florida must begin with the presence of other religious influences. "For more than three centuries [beginning with Ponce de Leon's landing near St. Augustine on April 2, 1513] the Catholics enjoyed a monopoly of religious privileges in Florida. Here first, they exploited their advantage. They tolerated no rivals" (Rosser 1). Spanish authorities and Seminole Indians were a constant threat. Following the Catholics were the Episcopalians and Methodists, to name two denominations. Official Methodist records date from approximately 1821, when a circuit rider traveled in north Florida.

Some think the first Baptist preacher on Florida soil was Wilson Conner, a Baptist traveling with General John Houston McIntosh in 1812. Later, Conner died at a Baptist pulpit in Hawkinsville, Georgia (Rogers 4). Fleming Bates and Isom Peacock organized the first Baptist church constituted in Florida, Pigeon Creek Baptist, in 1821 (Baker 133). Bates is believed to be the first full-time Baptist preacher. "Pioneers frequently brought their church affiliations with them and organized congregations. . . . The Baptists' congregational form of church government made it easy to form congregations, choose lay preachers, and use the services of itinerant ministers until the churches could afford one of their own" (Tebeau 196). Believing that in numbers there is strength, the Suwannee Association was formed in 1835 by the eight Baptist churches in Florida. Another name in early Florida Baptist history was James McDonald who came in 1836 to east Florida as a missionary of the American Baptist Home Missionary Society of New York and formed three churches. He often preached at funerals during one of the Seminole wars.

Other early Florida associations were Florida Association (1841), West Florida Association (1845), Alachua Association (1847), Santa Fe River Association (1857), South Florida Association (1867), St. Johns River Association (1869), Wekiwa Association (1870) [Joiner has this as 1869 (301)], New River Association (1874), and Peace River Association (1875) (Rogers 8–9).

While pioneers coming into Florida braved many hardships and began meeting in their homes for worship, much of the credit for establishing the faith belongs to the preachers who braved Indian and wild beast attacks. Scattered settlements were also a problem. Mildred Talton, our church's historian for over twenty-five years, wrote, "These early preachers were dedicated and thought little of their own comfort. Many walked miles, swam rivers and lakes, and received practically no compensation for their services. Through their individual efforts, Christianity was spread through Central Florida." And from Baker: "Before Florida became a state, Florida Baptists were led by outstanding pioneer missionaries like John Tucker, William B. Cooper, Richard L. Mays, Joshua Mercer, James MacDonald, and J. M. Hayman" (186). Baptists would open their homes to ministers from Alabama and Georgia who traveled to Florida on mission trips. If discovered, the home owners were sometimes imprisoned by Spanish authorities.

The first Florida Baptist State Convention was held in 1854 with R. Fleming as its first president. He served from 1854 to 1857. The first Florida State Board of Missions was held in 1881 in Lake City. In 1882, this body employed N. A. Bailey as one of its missionaries.

As worshipers traveled to church, it was necessary to carry guns. MacDonald helped organize the Bethel Baptist Church (now First Baptist

Church of Jacksonville) in 1838 with four white members and two black slaves. Some of the earliest settlers of south Florida were Baptist preachers. When Florida became a state in 1845, Baptists numbered 644 between the Chattahoochee River and the Escambia Bay.

The Civil War caused most, if not all, of the churches to disband. At the war's end, the slow process of organization resumed. For a while, services were held outdoors or in people's homes. Since the meetings were infrequent but eagerly anticipated, people traveled long distances, using any means available. "The early churches served not only as places to worship God but also as places for social gatherings. Dinners on the grounds were festive occasions and ice cream socials and quilting parties helped to raise much needed funds" so that church structures could be built (*Pioneer Days Magazine* 16). At first, brush arbors were constructed, followed by pine buildings. Sometimes a common building was designed to educate children during the week and to hold church services on Sundays for alternating denominations. Baptisms were performed in nearby lakes and creeks. It is often joked that present-day Baptists love to eat. Our ancestors were no exception. Food such as wild turkey, venison, swamp cabbage, sweet potatoes, and various desserts were shared after services, along with gossip and games.

In 1869 or 1870, the Wekiwa (sometimes spelled Wekiva) Baptist Association was formed as a welcomed meeting forum for central Florida Baptists. It is believed that two churches (Oviedo and Apopka) were members in the beginning year, although there has been some uncertainty about Apopka Church's founding date. Bethel Baptist became a member in 1871 along with Umatilla. By 1882, there were approximately twenty-one churches in this association.

Whether worldwide or statewide, Baptists have a common heritage. Two recurring themes that come to mind in a study of Baptist history are religious liberty and religious persecution. While there have been numerous Baptist confessions of faith, these are not generally believed to be binding over an individual's conscience. Baptists take great store in an individual's liberty as long as it is aligned with Scripture. Additionally, "Baptists are not creedal in the traditional sense" (Bush 18). The whole, infallible word of God is our creed. While others might scoff and persecute members of our faith, we should be reminded of Christ's example.

The stage was set for a great stirring of the faith in Orlando.

CHAPTER TWO

A Brief Central Florida History

By day the Lord went ahead of them in a pillar of cloud to guide them on their way.

—*Exodus 13:21*

THE INDIAN PRESENCE
COACOOCHEE

"The heavens declare the glory of God; and the skies proclaim the work of his hands."
Psalm 19:1

C oacoochee stared up in the night sky. The stars were unusually bright that early spring evening. As he contemplated the vastness, he recognized from nature that there was a Spirit greater than he.

His moccasined feet made no sound as he descended the valley leading to the lake. The area around it was marshy, and the lake itself was swollen from the recent rains. A snake slithered underneath the water as he approached. He began to fish and was soon rewarded for his efforts. He stopped when his line held six large bass.

Coacoochee (also known as Wild Cat) returned to his village with his catch. From this vista, he clearly saw the ravages of the recent war and the devastations of the great sickness upon his people. Their numbers

34

were dwindling at an alarming rate. To make matters worse, representatives from the white man's government had sent a message calling for a meeting with leaders of his tribe. They would gather under the huge live oak tree, which much later would come to be called the "Council Oak." Coacoochee remembered the site as his former meeting ground with another Indian warrior, King Philip. Fort Gatlin would later be built in this area. Situated on a small triangular piece of land formed by three lakes—Gatlin, Gem Mary, and Jennie Jewell—this fortification would prove to be practically impregnable.

After giving the fish to the women, he dressed deliberately in his ceremonial clothing and joined the others as they made their way to the clearing. A feeling of dread filled his heart as he thought about the future of his people. It was not the first of such meetings. The white man had often made a promise but delivered something different, always to the disadvantage of Coacoochee and his tribe.

Years later, Coacoochee stared up into the same night sky. He and his people were aboard ships commissioned to take them away from their beloved Florida. As the coastline became distant, then disappeared altogether, his thoughts traveled backward. He remembered his companion Louis, a black slave. His heart ached as he relived the scenes of Indian families torn apart, the stoic fathers watching as their children were led away crying. Wild Cat's own little daughter had been captured and held for ransom. He idolized this only child, and once again, under the white flag of truce, surrendered to General Worth. How often had the promises made by the military and others been tossed aside. He remembered that, as he approached the camp, Hoke-Ti-Chee (little girl with bright eyes) ran to him and embraced his neck. He recalled every word of his speech to the general:

> The whites dealt unjustly with me. I came to them when they deceived me. I loved the land I was upon. My body is made of its sands . . . legs to walk over it, eyes to see it, hands to aid myself, a head with which I think. The sun which shines warm and bright brings forth our crops. . . . The white man comes and my people grow pale and sickly; why can we not live in peace? They steal our horses and cattle, cheat us and take our lands. They may shoot us, chain our hands and feet, but the red man's heart will be free. I have come to you in peace and have taken you by the hand. I will sleep in your camp, though your soldiers stand around me thick as pine trees. I am done. When we know each other better, I will say more.

Coacoochee—Courtesy FSA

And they truly did come to know each other better. While General Worth and Wild Cat became ardent friends, the ability to live side by side, for most white men and red men, was not to be. Convinced that peaceful coexistence was impossible, the stalwart former warrior had boarded the ship to travel to a new land. Coacoochee set his face westward and stared into the distance, into the future.

As we travel down Interstate Highway I-4, we may often have time to reflect as the traffic comes to a standstill. Some of us may wish for "the good old days," but were they really all that good? What was it like to come to this area? What did our forefathers use for travel? Was crime as rampant as it is now? What did people eat, wear, and think? Fortunately, a number of books, some written many years ago, can answer these questions.

In *Early Settlers of Orange County Florida*, a book published in 1915, Mrs. J. N. Whitner wrote, "Whatever of pride and enjoyment we citizens of Orange County may feel in her present-day achievements, our sentiment cannot be praiseworthy till we shall have paused and paid our tributes of respect and honor to those of a generation ago, who, by their Christian faith and practice, their sterling characteristics and ability, overcame primitive conditions and made possible within a lifetime the civilization we now enjoy" (quoted in Howard 3). This rosy picture was not always the case, however.

The earliest accounts of life in Florida go back to the Indians, most notably the Muskogans, Tomokans, Caloosas, Creeks, and Seminoles. For years, many of them lived in the pine forests and fished the lakes of central Florida. According to French and Spanish records, present-day Orlando was once an Indian hunting ground. There were probably several large Indian settlements in an eighteen-mile radius of the area (Breakfast 5). When Ponce de Leon came to the New World in 1513 and

Juan Ponce de Leon at the Fountain
of Youth—Courtesy FSA

named the peninsula Florida, meaning feast of flowers, present-day Orlando was occupied by the Acueras, who were farmers.

The Spanish explorers who followed de Leon in a quest for gold were plagued by harsh conditions, such as overflowing lakes, deep sands, stagnant water, wild animals, and vicious mosquitoes. Florida was also labeled a breeding ground for "refugees and renegades." Nevertheless, a little over three hundred years later, in 1821, the United States purchased Florida from Spain. In 1824, Mosquito County was established from St. Johns County. Seven years later, in 1831, John James Audubon made his first visit to Florida in order to provide models for his paintings, most notably his flamingo.

Then because of the growing "Indian problem," Fort Gatlin was established in 1838 between present-day Orlando and Pine Castle. The fort was one in a chain of several along the Indian trail extending from Lake Monroe to Tampa. The fort remained until 1849, when it was abandoned.

The Armed Occupation Act of 1842 introduced new settlers into the area, eager to take advantage of the act's land provisions. Many of these people settled in and around the old fort. One of the first white settlers was Aaron Jernigan, a cattlemen who, with his brother Isaac, came to the Lake Holden area. In 1845, Florida entered the United States, and part of Mosquito County became Orange County. Then in 1850, a post office was established. It was called Jernigan since it was set up in the Jernigan store. Martha Jernigan Tyler wrote that "Orlando was woods and the deer and turkeys fed all about where the city now stands" (quoted in Kendrick 6).

In the 1854–1855 school year, the number of children ages five to eighteen in school in Orange County was recorded as 105. In 1855, William B. Hull moved his family to the area from Cobb County, Georgia. He would prove instrumental in the founding of the Baptist church. In 1857, the village's name was given as Orlando. Several legends surround the naming of the town. So much controversy exists that most historians throw up their hands at ever finding the truth. Later, Florida seceded from the Union in 1861 at the time of the Civil War. Seven years later the state was readmitted.

The best way to imagine Orlando after the Civil War would be to envision a wild west town. Cattle raising and farming were the chief occupations. Although there was a town sheriff, much lawlessness reigned. In 1868, the courthouse was burned down, probably to destroy evidence for an impending trial. "It was conjectured at the time that the fire was of incendiary origin, the intention being to destroy inconvenient, and perhaps incriminating records" (Blackman 32).

"Postwar central Florida was an open-range cattle frontier of the type most often associated with the American west. Cattle rustling and range wars were common. Self-reliant frontiersmen protected their rights—as they understood them—with direct and sometimes violent action. Range disputes led to frequent shootings and killings. Confrontations on the streets of Orlando between feuding cowmen became common, and efforts to bring about justice through the courts were rarely successful" (Shofner, *Orlando* 34).

Of course, not all settlers were violent. Much of their time was spent in merely surviving. They became practically self-sustaining. They "lived chiefly on pork, beef, grits, sweet potatoes, syrup, milk, and butter. They distilled a considerable quantity of whisky, there was an abundance of fish and game, and practically the only foodstuffs they had to buy were wheat flour and salt" (Breakfast 18). In addition to the constant mosquitoes, the pioneers had a running feud with wild hogs that roamed the countryside. Called razorbacks, they were "dangerously vicious, had long heads, very long noses, small ears, tusks three to four inches long, and all would fight when any member of the herd was molested" (Breakfast 18–19).

Our forefathers were industrious and made do. Taking what they found, they fashioned most of what they needed. For example, hollow logs were used to make beehives. Other wood became spinning wheels, looms, chairs, tables, and bed frames. Most of their livestock ran loose and fed in the woods. Domestic hogs were slaughtered, then smoked to preserve the meat against the semi-tropical temperatures. Gourds became containers for the lard and were also used for other kitchen storage and as ladling implements. Lye made from oak ash removed the hair from butchered cattle. "Tan ooze" from oak bark went into the tanning process. Cattle hides became boots and shoes, and softer dress shoes were fashioned from deerskins.

Store-bought clothes were only for the wealthy. Our pioneers made their attire. Cotton fared well in the climate and became the chief material for clothing, with a feed sack thrown in for variety. Cotton was also used for most domestic necessities like "tablecloths, sheets, pillowcases, quilts, counterpanes, suits for husbands and sons, stockings, socks, gloves and sunbonnets" (Kendrick 9). Plants, particularly palmettos, were fashioned into hats to protect all members of the family from the sun. There were few trips to the barber. Most hair dressing was done at home, so most hair was worn long, with head lice a constant problem. Ingenious housewives used sweet potatoes, much like the biblical manna, as a staple. Once the potatoes were ground, they could be made into a passable coffee (Kendrick 10–11).

Not all their time was devoted to hard work. "In the early days Saturday was known as 'Cracker Day' in Orlando and the country people for miles around came to town to do their weekly trading. . . . They had to have some amusement and Bud Yates with his large pet alligator would get out in front of Sinclair's real estate office . . . and wrestle with the alligator, much to the amusement of the crowd that always gathered to watch. Bud used to hold the alligator's mouth open and let the boys look into its throat" (Gore, *Sand* 87).

In 1869, a frame courthouse was built to replace the one that had burned down a year earlier. It is felt this was the site of the first official meetings of the Baptist church. Earlier, in 1858, some twelve Baptists had joined forces to meet together, possibly in the William Hull home, pastored by the visiting William Miller, but this congregation had to disband during the Civil War when the men went off to fight. During the year and a half surrounding the officially recognized founding of the church in 1871, Orlando faced several outbreaks of violence, both man-made and from weather.

In 1870, what became known as the Barber and Mizell feud erupted. David Mizell was sheriff and Moses Barber Jr. was a cattleman. In a

Alligator wrestling—Courtesy OCHM

complicated set of circumstances, the sheriff tried to serve papers to Barber against some of Barber's cattle as payment for a crime against the community. Mizell was gunned down and killed. His death brought about several bloody episodes between the two families.

Then, a few months after the church's founding in March 1871, a storm of hurricane force rained down on the community. "In August of 1871, an unprecedented storm of wind and rain occurred. For forty-eight hours, the tempest raged without intermission; then followed a week of calm weather; and then for another forty-eight hours, 'the rain descended and the floods came, and the winds blew. . . .' Thousands of cattle were bogged down and drowned on the prairies, and . . . countless numbers of pine trees were prostrated. Fortunately most of the houses of that time were built of heavy logs, and so withstood the onset, but the property loss was great" (Blackman 74–75).

In 1872, thirty children attended school three months of the year, and Orlando continued to be a turbulent place to live. Forty-one people were slain that year, and the town's first jail was built. (See expanded chronology in Appendix I.)

As we come out of our reverie and traffic begins to move, we can see that in many ways our city has changed and in many ways it has stayed the same. Ox carts have been replaced by instruments of another kind of power, our clothing is softer and store-bought, the deer and other wildlife have retreated or died out, concrete and steel have replaced dirt paths and log structures, food is purchased in well-stocked stores and, unfortunately, occasional crime and violence still erupt. However, much of the good remains. The sunshine and warm weather continue to draw visitors, and the beauty of the landscape and the perfume of the flowers attract others to set down roots. Orlando has grown and has changed, but many find it a great place to live.

With the preceding as a backdrop, and some of our questions answered, let's explore church records and other bits of history to weave a tapestry of the early years of First Baptist Church.

CHAPTER THREE

First Baptist Church
The Very Early Years, 1858–1881

"'But for their sake I will remember the covenant with their ancestors whom I brought out of Egypt in the sight of the nations to be their God. I am the Lord.'"
—*Leviticus 26:45*

A WEARY TRAVELER
WILLIAM MILLER'S TREK

"Be joyful in hope, patient in affliction, faithful in prayer."
Romans 12:12

Because he was so tired, the Reverend William Miller struggled to remain on Betsy's back. The mule had proven to be a faithful friend in spite of the blacksmith's warning about her cantankerous nature. Only God's persuasion could have convinced Miller to leave the relative warmth of the Lodge (later renamed Apopka) for this trek through the swamps and pine forests.

For a second time, he studied the map Hull had sent to him. The newly named village of Orlando ought to be coming into his sight very soon. Although it was still March and relatively cold, the insects were a real bother. The odorous grease he had smeared on his face to ward off his tormenters proved ineffective. One big fly continued to buzz around him and bite his neck. William thought of Beelzebub, Lord of the Flies, and struck at the insect with renewed fervor. After a few more minutes, it left him to travel to another place and to another victim.

As he combed his long hair with his fingers, he felt the ever-present cooties and began to scratch. John Perry, a fellow circuit rider of the Methodist faith, had sent him a cure that so far had not taken effect. Perhaps the best remedy would be to cut his hair and really eradicate the vermin.

Suddenly, his nerves stood on edge. He felt his spine tingle as the noise intensified. It couldn't be Seminoles because they moved with no sound. The uproar grew louder as he traveled farther southeast. When he came to a clearing, he caught a glimpse of the beasts he had feared. Called razorbacks, they looked like a creative mistake. These were especially large and ugly. Their tusks measured at least four inches, their eyes held a vicious stare, and their long snouts were raised to pick up his scent. Gently and noiselessly, he maneuvered Betsy away from the path in an effort to detour around the hideous group. One false move on his part, and they all would charge at him. Once angered, they became a precision army.

In a few minutes, he was able to breathe another prayer, this time one of relief and thanksgiving. The Lord again had protected him from harm. Feeling hungry, he pulled out another piece of jerky, offered a brief prayer, and slowly began to chew. He already had decided to stop off at the Worthington store and post office. The last offering he had been given was unusually generous, and if he were careful he would be able to make a few necessary purchases.

As soon as he thought about the store, it appeared in a clearing. Smoke drifted lazily from an opening in the roof. He tied up Betsy at the post, stooped low to enter, and immediately paused. His eyes needed time to adjust to the dim light coming from several candles stuck in sand-laden cigar boxes. As he waited, he smelled a myriad of odors: cigars, venison, leather, oranges, whiskey, wheat flour, and sweat. From his jacket he retrieved a letter he had written and deposited it in the box for outgoing mail.

In a matter of minutes, with the small parcel of his purchases secured by twine tucked under his arm, he remounted and headed to Lake Fairview as the sun began to set. If he hurried, he would make the Hulls' home before it turned too dark. Worthington had verified the directions. William wondered how many families would be assembled. Whether it was one or a larger number really didn't matter. He was about the Lord's work. His duty was to remain faithful, diligent, and listening. The Lord would do the rest. As he made his way, a group of chimney swifts flew overhead and lifted their evening benediction announcing his arrival to the waiting and eager band of Baptist believers.

Against this backdrop, Bethel Baptist Church was organized. If a community needed a church, Orlando was such a place. Lawlessness reigned, and nature continued to challenge everyone. Eve Bacon, in the first volume of *Orlando: A Centennial History*, writes, "As early as 1856, members of the Baptist faith had been meeting in private homes for worship" (16). Our church's earliest existing records do not mention the meeting place, but it would seem logical that homes would serve as the first setting.

In his booklet about our church, renowned Orlando historian and church member E. H. Gore perhaps best summed up the Baptist presence in our city: "The earliest history of the Baptists in Orlando is clouded in obscurity. . . . About the year 1856 the Indian wars ended and the several forts hereabouts abandoned and the people began to seek homes, some in Oviedo, some in Apopka, and others in Orlando. . . ."

E. H. Gore—Courtesy OCHM

Our earliest official record book, titled "Church Record Book From 3/5/1871 to 12/1893 Book One," mentions the following on the last few pages: "Organization in 58 [1858] by Wm. Miller from Lake Eustis settlement. Ten or 12 included in list of members. First meeting was in log court house where all the churches first met."

Others feel these first meetings were held in the home of the William Benjamin Hulls, located near Lake Fairview. It is unfortunate no official records have been found that can give with certainty the true location. The Hulls' great-granddaughter, Dorothy H. Shaw, writes, "We don't have anything to indicate if church services were held in their home prior to completion of a church

William Benjamin and Emily Harriett (Watson) Hull

building, though it was entirely possible" (letter).

In 1858, James Buchanan was president; Lincoln and Douglas were enmeshed in their famous debates; and Longfellow's "The Courtship of Miles Standish" was published. An annular eclipse of the sun was visible on March 15; another eruption tore Mount Vesuvius; an impressive comet was sighted; the name "diphtheria" was given to a strange illness accompanied by a sore throat; and the first trans-Atlantic cable was laid. Nearer to home, John R. Worthington was postmaster, and the town was named Orlando. There was no mayor; the sheriff during the second half of the year was Jonathan Stewart; and the population of the county grew from 466 to 987.

Gore wrote, "In 1858 the Rev. Miller came over from Apopka and organized a church in Orlando consisting of a dozen members. One of these was Brother W. B. Hull. . . . The church remained intact until the Civil War and then was dissolved and not until March 5, 1871, was it revived again. Brother G. C. Powell came over from Oviedo and reorganized the church with eighteen members. The church was then called 'The Bethel Baptist Church of Orlando' and it is recorded that there were nine men and nine women as members" ("History of Florida Baptists: First Baptist Church" booklet).

Of course, the time during the Civil War was difficult for the nation. Most congregations in our area were discontinued after the men had gone off to war. Some of the women remaining behind relocated farther north. Jerrell H. Shofner, in *Orlando: The City Beautiful*, writes, "Once Florida joined the Confederacy, many Orange County residents supported their state, and a large number actually marched off to war. The county's sparse population and isolated location spared it from direct military conflict, but the Orlando area, nevertheless, felt the inconvenience, hardships, and privations of the war" (32). He continues by stating that residents became resourceful in providing for themselves and looking out for others. One store owner, James P. Hughey, made trips to Gainesville to help supply his neighbors and himself with necessary items. "Military wives learned to cultivate their own fields. When the post office was discontinued early in the war [March 1861], Mrs. W. B. Hull, who ran a rooming house while her husband was in the army, established an unofficial postal facility" (32). Some people went to the coast to collect and bring back much-needed salt.

Then in 1863 a log courthouse was built in Orlando, and in 1866 the post office was reestablished. In that year the Homestead Act was passed, and former slaves took up land in Orange County (34). After the war, many visitors came and then stayed in the area. Francis Eppes, a former mayor of Tallahassee and a grandson of Thomas Jefferson, arrived in Orlando. In 1868 the log courthouse was burned; in 1869 a frame courthouse was built. Some sources give the address of this building as Central and Court Streets. This was probably the place where our charter members met to reestablish the church on March 5, 1871. Our record book does not mention the place of meeting. E. H. Gore in *From Florida Sand to "The City Beautiful,"* writes about the courthouse reports:

> The men sat on one side of the room and the women on the other. The floor was covered with sawdust for the convenience of those who chewed tobacco or snuff and many brought their babies and dogs to meeting.
>
> One deacon had an old hound dog that disturbed the minister [we're not sure if this man was a Baptist, an Episcopalian, or a Methodist, since each denomination met in the courthouse on a rotating basis] by lying

down beside him and scratching fleas while he was preaching. One morning, this dog kept getting up and rubbing against the preacher's legs and it so annoyed him that he picked up the dog and threw him out of the window.

After service he went to the deacon to apologize for throwing the dog out but the deacon said, "That was all right parson for I would not have even my dog hear that sermon." (139)

This same courthouse had a problem with razorback hogs. The brutes would sleep and root under the floorboards. Their noise and fleas would often disturb the parishioners.

Thus, although the organization of the first Baptist church was really in 1858, the official starting date is given as 1871, the year that this church began its uninterrupted service. During 1871, Ulysses Grant was president; the country was beginning to recover from the Civil War; the United States census from the previous year gave the nation's population as 38,549,987; and Chicago experienced its great fire, in which one-third of the city was destroyed, over five hundred people perished, and one hundred thousand were rendered homeless (*Annual Register* 1871, 296–97). In Orlando, E. W. Speir was postmaster, and Isaac Winegord was sheriff. There were approximately 2,195 people living in Orange County.

The first few pages of the church's earliest book are as follows:

Church Record Book
From 3/5/1871 to 12/1893
Book One

Record of the Missionary Baptist Church
Beginning March 5th, 1871
At Orlando, Fla.

Constitution

Orange County Florida   March 5th 1871
by request of a No. of Baptist[s] being desirous of forming a constitution they were met by El. G. C. Powell after which the credentials were read of members to wit:

Males	Females
John Wofford	Caroline Wofford
Levy C. Whitted	Narcissa Lovell
Jeptha Purvis	Sarah Whitted
John Brook	Josepene S. McClane
Clemuel Tiner	Malintha Yates
Henry Purvis	Sally Hughey
Wm. Hodges	Mary Lovell
John Hughey	Julia Garott
John Roberson	Winford Griggs

And their credentials together with their standing being orthodox and orderly the articles of faith together with the Church Covenant was read and approved after which Brother G. C. Powell led in the constituting prair [prayer] and the brethren and sisters gave to each other the right hands in covenant agreement to keep house for the Lord and set to order the things that are wanting according to the gospel and Bro. G. C. Powell delivered a solemn charge pronouncing them a Church of Jesus Christ in Witness whereof we have set our hands.

[signed]

El. G. C. Powell

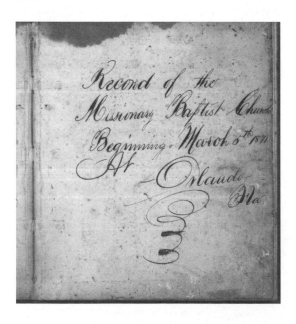

Church Covenant

As we trust we have been brought by divine grace to embrace the Lord Jesus Christ and by the influence of his spirit to give ourselves up to live so we do solemnly covenant with each other that God enabling us we will walk together in brotherly love, that we will exercise a Christian care and watchfulness over each other and faithfully warn, rebuke, and admonish one another as the case shall require—and we will not forsake the assembling ourselves together nor omit the great duty of prayer both for ourselves and for others—that we will participate in each other's joys and endeavor with tenderness and sympathy to bear each other's burdens and sorrows and that we will earnestly endeavor to bring up those under our care in nurture and admonition of the Lord, that we will seek divine aid to enable us to walk circumspectly and watchfully in the world denying all ungodliness and every worldly lust—that we will strive together for the support of a faithful evangelical minister—among us that we will endeavor by example & effort to win soles [souls] to Christ—& through evil as well as good report seek to live to the glory of Him who has called us out of darkness into His marvelous light.

How wonderful this document reads 125 years later. It is obvious the precious people who drew it up had a firm faith in the Lord and felt an awesome responsibility to themselves and to each other to live godly lives. The church decorum, which follows the covenant, continues to lend insight into the heart of these people.

Church Decorum

Article 1st—It shall be the duty of the church to hold monthly conferences [meetings]

Article 2nd—It shall be the duty of the church to call a pastor every year, and the pastor so chosen shall preside as Moderator and in the absence of the Moderator, the church shall appoint a Moderator Protem

Article 3rd—It shall be the duty of the Moderator to open the conference by singing or prayer

Article 4th—It shall be the duty of each free male member to attend their regular conferences and each brother failing to attend shall give the reason of his absence at the next conference, and any brother failing to attend for three successive meetings shall be cited [writing unclear] to give satisfaction, and in case of the cause of absence be not satisfactory he shall for the first time be admonished, for the second reproved, for the third time dealt with as the church may deem proper

Article 5th—No member shall absent himself from the conference without permission of the Moderator

Article 6th—Any member wishing to speak in conference shall rise from his seat and address the Moderator, and no member shall speak more than three times on the same subject without leave of the conference

Article 7th—The church shall commune [have communion] quarterly and oftener if they choose

Article 8th—It shall be the duty of each member to commune, and if they refuse, the deacon should inquire into the cause and, if proper, report to the church for consideration

Article 9th—In all private offenses, the case to be treated according to the [writing illegible] of the Moderator

Article 10th—In all cases of public offenses, a public acknowledgement shall be required

Article 11th—No member shall backbite or treat his brother or sister with disrespect

Article 12th—The officers of this church shall be two or more deacons & clerk & treasurer

Article 13th—It shall be the duty of the deacons to prepare the elements for communion & wait on the table, also to visit the sick and minister to their spiritual comforts, also to attend to the treasurer [writing illegible, possibly the word is treasury] of the church and report their temporal wants to the church, and attend to the wants of their pastor

Article 14th—It shall be the duty of the clerk to keep a correct record of all the proceedings of this church

Article 15th—It shall be the duty of the treasurer to keep a strict account of all money paid over to him and pay out to the order of the church taking a receipt for the same

Article 16th—In choosing officers, it shall be the duty of all male members to vote, and females if they choose

Article 17th—In time of conference, there shall be no private conversation or laughing, and in time of public debate, the speaker shall not be interrupted unless he depart from the subject

Article 18th—This decorum shall be read quarterly or oftener if required and church covenant every six months

Article 19th—This decorum shall be subject to alteration by a two thirds vote of the male members

Article 20th—The church may adjourn conference from time to time and from place to place as she may think best [Some punctuation has been added to make for easier reading.]

There are several elements in this decorum which seem especially noteworthy. First, the rules appear to be stated so that the business of the church might run in an orderly fashion. At the time of the writing of the decorum, the church only met once a month. A pastor was called on a yearly basis. This might be due to the transitory nature of many people living in central Florida at that time. For the first several years, this church had a number of pastors. Some of the reasons are based on health and moving patterns. Life seemed to be very uncertain. Another characteristic which comes through in the decorum is the importance placed on attendance, with the males being held accountable. Article 6 seems to help the members guard against long-winded and monopolizing speeches. Article 8 seems to mean that if some members have a hesitancy to take communion, there might be something wrong with their spiritual or personal life, and a deacon would respond with concern. Articles 11 and 13 appear to be especially touching. Everyone is to be kind to one another, and the deacons are to assume a servant attitude waiting on the needs of the sick and the needs of their pastor.

The next entry in the book is dated nearly a year later on February 3, 1872.

1872 Bethel Church
Feb 3 Saturday before the first Lord's Day in Feb met in conference
church doors were opened none came forward
called for business
it is moved and seconded that Brother W. J. Brack be appointed clerk—carried
a move for adjournment—carried
[signed]
W. J. Brack clerk—G. C. Powell moderator

W. J. Brack was elected the first mayor of Orlando three years later in 1875. He served for two years. G. C. Powell was a pastor who apparently felt called to establish churches. He came over from Oviedo to reorganize the church along with the help of nine men and nine women from Orlando. The 1870 census lists Powell as being sixty years old and a blacksmith. His wife Patience was fifty-eight.

William Jackson Brack—Orlando's first mayor

In 1872, the first jail was built, probably in response to the growing number of violent crimes in the area (forty-one people were slain that year). Also in that year, a happier place was constructed that had been much anticipated. This was called the Union Free Church. "The Union Free Church, planned in 1857, finally was built in 1872, financed by contributions and fund-raising social events. It did double duty as church and school house. The one-acre lot given by John Patrick was located on South Main Street [now Magnolia] between Pine and Church streets. . . . The Free church was built 150 feet south of Pine Street and 100 feet east of Main" (Bacon I, 46). In 1872, Cassius A. Boone, a descendant of Daniel Boone, came to Orlando. W. F. Blackman believed Boone to be the first teacher in Orlando schools (88). If this is so, Boone would have taught in the Union Free Church building.

On March 3, 1872, seven people were joined to the church by letter. They were William B. Hull, Emily Hull, Henry Meeks, Mary Meeks, Elvis [or Elius] Meeks, Martha Meeks, and Eldorada E. Meeks. It seems strange that the Hulls would not be 1871 charter members since they were instrumental in the 1858 organization of the church. Apparently something must have prevented them from attending the March 1871 charter meeting. W. J. Brack continued as clerk, and G. C. Powell continued as moderator.

Since our church was sharing space with other congregations, it appears that Bethel Baptist met once a month on Saturday for a business meeting and once a month on Sunday for a church service. In early September 1872, the church decided to have communion twice a year in May and October. There was a strong feeling for community and ecumenical accord, for "Brother Powell is requested to invite all or as many of our sister churches to commune with us as is convenient" ("Record Book One"). At this same meeting, two delegates were chosen to attend Deep Creek Association. They were John Wofford and W. J. Brack.

Brother Henry Purvis was granted a "letter of dismission."

At the October meeting a new pastor was called. He was Elder A. Tindall. Five people came forward: Sisters Mariah Smith and Jane Tiner at the beginning, and later, "colored sisters Rosetta Glover, Ellen Glover, Rachael Glover." On Sunday, three more came forward: G. W. Hesmith, Sister Laura Hesmith, and "young Glover colored." In November James M. Blitch placed himself under the watchcare of the church until his letter could be sent. He was to become a prominent member of the church.

In 1873, two years after the reorganization, something happened to cause dissension. The church records do not shed any light as to the problem, but three families, the Meeks, the Woffords, and the Russes, asked for letters to start a new church, which was called Fairview. The next year, perhaps in an attempt at a reconciliation, "mail [male] members unanimously agreed to go to a Union Meeting . . . at Fairview Church." In 1879, the Fairview group returned to the fold. These members were listed as A. Russ, Elizabeth D. Russ, Sarah Russ, A. L. Mills, W. W. Barber, Caroline Wofford, and Moriah Barber.

In the next few years, other names were added and deleted from the church. Some who came were Ezekiel Hull, Easter Raulerson, and Annie McDufee "colored." Some dismissals are interesting to note. In March 1873, "Brother G. W. Hesmith granted a letter of dismissal to join another church of the same faith and order." Sister Hesmith was "excommunicated for treating the church with contempt" in August 1873. In September 1874, "Brother Hodge called for a letter of dismissal on the grounds that he lived near the Fort Christmas church." In August 1879, "S. A. Lucky was in disorder before the church, charge: billiard playing and other public offenses." And in August 1880, "Walter Davis charged with drinking, swearing, and horse racing."

Another entry is interesting in a puzzling sort of way: "Motion by J. J. Davis that the house be opened only for worship and schools and that the key be delivered to E. A. Richards." Perhaps the Union Free Church and school was being unlawfully entered, making it necessary to put it under lock and key in a time when it was customary to keep everything unlocked. Unfortunately, some community problems never change.

In 1876, "Brethren from Fairview invited to sit with us. S. A. Russ acted as moderator. There were 17 members: 7 males and 10 females" (Talton notes).

An interesting list of members appears in April 1879, with notations made after some of their names. The notations probably were made at a later date. Males were listed first: Brick, *expelled*; Samuel Lucky, *excom;*

Samuel Summerlin; W. B. Hull; Newton Fearless; and Charles King. Females were listed separately: Malintha Yates; Sally Bown [or Brown], *exp*; Julia Buchan; Winford Griggs, *dis. by letter*; Emily Hull; Annie Brack, *dead*; Mary Self; Elizabeth Fearless; Ellen Johns; King [no first name given].

A "vigilant committee" was appointed August 1879, perhaps to oversee errant members. For the first time, a female was elected to a church committee: Emily Hull to the vigilant committee.

In September 1879, there was a committee on the "property case," consisting of S. A. Russ, A. Bass, and W. B. Hull. Apparently, the need for its own quarters was moving Bethel Church to look for some land. This endeavor continued in 1880 when a committee was appointed to "locate a church lot." On April 30, 1881, the building committee was "instructed and requested to proceed to collect sufficient amount of money subscriptions and purchase the lumber for the church building and the clerk instructed to write a copy of this order and forward to each of the members of the committee."

Sometime in 1881, G. W. Culbreth requested to hold a meeting with the church on the third Sabbath in each month. He was to be ordained by G. C. Powell, R. W. Lawton, and James Alexander Tyndall. For some reason, he was expelled upon examination. Also in 1881, J. B. Graves was licensed to teach the gospel. The associational meeting was held at Bethel Church on September 30, October 1, and October 2.

On November 5, 1881, it was "resolved that the building committee of this church be vested with full power to act as attorney in fact for said church in all matters pertaining to the building of a house of worship and the disposal of any property." A separate meeting place was nearing. Brother John Young was recorded as having died, the first to hold this dubious distinction.

"Sister Theodasher Tyner came forward and joined by restoration" on May 6, 1882. Also in 1882, the church decided to organize a Sunday school. Pastor Gove attended the state convention meeting at Lake City, Florida.

Although church records don't give an exact date, the church building was ready for occupancy some time probably in 1882 or early 1883, for on April 8, 1883, "The building committee was then discharged with a vote of thanks for their attention and labor in building a house of worship." Services were also changed to the second and fourth Sabbaths in 1883.

For several years, the church called pastors who served for a very brief time. Some had to resign due to poor health. Apparently, some preachers retired to Florida for health reasons and were enlisted into service until poor health or death claimed them. Other pastors were not recalled, some because of stringent enforcements or personal weaknesses. The matter of salary came up a few times. Reverend A. L. Farr was one of the first pastors whose pay was mentioned. He received forty dollars per month.

On one of the last pages in this first record book, members as of September 6, 1879, are listed, again with notations after some names. Once again, the males are listed first: W. B. Hull; J. M. Blitch; S. A. Lucky, *expelled*; Saml. Summerlin; William Lucy [Lucky?], *dismissed by letter*; Newton Lawless, *expelled;* ——King; Cabin Childens, *at Kissimmee*; Aaron Jernigan; W. Ryley Lee, *expelled*; Archibald Bass, *dismissed by letter*; Charles Russ, *dismissed by letter*; S. A. Russ, *dead*; L. Mills, *dismissed by letter*; and W. W. Babera. The female members included: E. H. Hull; Julia Buchan; Anna Brack, *dead*; M. F. Self; Elizabeth Lawless; Ellen Childens, *Kissimmee*; Mrs. King, *dead*; Malintha Yates; Amy Brack, *dead*; Mrs. Lee, *dead*; Anna Bass, *dismissed by letter*; Amanda Bass; Mary Jernigan; Martha Russ, *by letter*; Elizabeth Whited; Mrs. Jernigan, *dead*; Elizabeth Lucy [Lucky?]; Narcissa Lovell, *dismissed by letter*; Mary Lovell, *dismissed by letter*; J. D. Russ, *dismissed by letter*; Sarah A. Russ, *letter*; Moriah Barber; and Caroline Wofford.

While some call the church a building, the church is actually the members guided by the Holy Spirit. Two lists follow. The first is a list of the charter members, along with information about some of them. Our first members, for the most part, appear to have been rather obscure people with few facts about them able to be found. The second list contains early members of the church who were not charter members. For some of them, a few facts are given. For others, unfortunately, nothing was found in the few months that were allotted to this section of the research for this book.

CHARTER MEMBERS

John Wofford is listed in the 1860 census as being fifty-one and a farmer. That would make him sixty-two at the church's organization in 1871. A man named John Wofford, a jailer, was authorized to "hire out any prisoners he may have in custody for the best wages he can procure, provided the prisoners want to work" (Bacon I, 64). Bacon names him as an alderman in 1876 and 1878 (I, 383). He was listed as seventy-one and a fruit grower on the 1880 census. Blackman reports that Captain John W. Wofford came from Georgia to Marion County, and then in 1859 to Orlando. He had been a captain in the Mexican War and a lieutenant in the Seminole War. He also served in the Civil War (85). *Caroline Wofford* is listed as being twenty-nine in 1860 so is presumably the wife or, with the age difference, daughter of John. She would have been forty in 1871.

Levy C. Whitted, listed as Levi C. in the 1870 census, was listed as age forty-five and a physician in the 1870 census. In 1871 he was in Hawk's *Gazeteer* as a store owner (Bacon I, 42). *Sarah Whitted*, listed as Sallie in 1870 census, was listed as thirty-one and "keeping house."

Jeptha Purvis was listed as fifty in 1860 and a farmer. Another Jeptha Purvis was in the 1870 census with his age listed as thirty-three, a farmer who couldn't read or write and perhaps a son of the elder Purvis. His wife was listed as Martha, thirty-six, keeping house, but she wasn't a charter member.

John Brook (or *Brack* or *Braok*) was first thought to be W. J. Brack, the first mayor of Orlando. It appears by the faint handwriting on the record book, however, that the last name is Brook, not Brack, and the first name is John, not W. J. (William Jackson). W. J. Brack was, however, the church clerk in the following months.

Clemuel Tiner was on a list of registered voters for Orange County in 1876 as C. R. Tiner (Bacon I, 361). Clement, twenty-four, was described as a farm laborer on the 1870 census.

William Hodges was fifteen and a farm laborer in the 1870 census. There was a William Hodges listed in the 1880 Florida census as twenty-seven, a farmer, with a wife Mary, twenty-one. Mary was not a charter member.

John Hughey presents somewhat of a problem. Bishop writes, "Mr. John Hughey, ex-soldier, brought his family and slaves from Georgia and claimed his 160 acres along the Wekiva River. He built a house, planted orange groves and later acquired a large tract of land now comprising Sanford Heights and Markham Heights" (9). John Hughey and John Hughey Jr. were on a list of registered voters for Orange County in 1876 (Bacon I, 357). In the 1860 Census Population Schedules of Florida, a John Hughey was listed as sixty-seven years old and a farmer with a post office address in Mellonville (Sanford). There was a different John Hughey listed in the 1870 census. His father's name was given as James, his mother as Susan, and this John was sixteen with a sister Sallie, fourteen. It is unclear which John Hughey was a member of the church. There was a John Hughey listed as the teacher at Simmons School making a salary of $47.86 in 1874 (Bacon I, 36). There was a John Hughey listed as part of Captain Aaron Jernigan's Company, General Hopkin's Division of Florida troops in 1852 and beyond. It is unclear whether the charter member *Sally Hughey* is the same as Sallie Hughey, fourteen, listed on the 1860 Census Population Schedules of Florida, whose father was James, forty-six, mother Susan, forty-five (parents not members), and brother John, sixteen, who was possibly a charter member.

In 1882, a *John L. Roberson* was issued a license to sell merchandise (Bacon I, 94). He was also on a list of registered voters for 1876 (Bacon I, 360).

In 1881, when the Woman's Missionary Society was begun, *Narcissa Lovell* was its first president. She was listed in the 1860 Census Population Schedules for Florida as being twenty-eight and married to William A. Lovell, the first superintendent of Orange County schools in an 1871 directory. She would have been thirty-nine in 1871. In Blackman's book on page 56, William Lovell is listed as a store owner who owned a saw and grist mill and was the county superintendent 1869–1873. He was not a charter member. *Mary Lovell* was listed as Mary Jan Lovell age six in the 1860 census, so she would have been seventeen in 1871.

Malintha Yates was listed as fifty-three with no husband on the 1880 census, so she would have been forty-four in 1871. Other charter members include Henry Purvis, Julia Garott, Winford Griggs, and J. S. McClane, whose first name is uncertain because of the handwriting and ink in the church record book—it may have been Josepene.

OTHER EARLY MEMBERS
(FROM EARLY CHURCH MINUTES, 1871–1884)

Isaac O. Barber became an Orlando builder and in his early years was "a professional budder and budded many an orange tree in and around Orlando. He was a member of the Odd Fellows Lodge. . . " (Bacon II, 332). His wife was Elizabeth, daughter of William and Emily Hull (see Lizzie Hull below). *W. W. Barber* was an Orange County registered voter in 1876. *Moriah Barber* was one of the members of Fairview church who returned to Bethel Baptist in 1979.

Archibald Bass was listed as a road commissioner for district eight (Bacon I, 42). *Anna Bass* and *Amanda Bass* were also early members.

James D. Beggs was a clerk for the church in 1883. "Captain J. D. Beggs, a native Floridian, came from Madison in 1882 and opened a law office.

He became city attorney in 1883, and served as judge of the Orange County Court from June 1883 to January 1885, when he was appointed state attorney. He practiced law with W. L. Palmer under the firm name of Beggs and Palmer. Both men were shrewd politicians and their advice was often sought by candidates for political office" (Bacon I, 96).

James M. Blitch was on a list of registered voters in Orange County in 1876 (Bacon I, 355). He ran a real estate office in 1887 according to the *Gazetteer* on page 38. He was treasurer for the Wekiva Baptist Association for a number of years and was also on its executive committee. Other early members with the same last name, *Thomas L. Blitch*, *W. I. Blitch*, and *Sister Blitch*, were likely somehow related.

W. J. Brack, the first mayor of Orlando, was on the 1880 census as age forty-three, a farmer and fruit grower with no wife listed. It is unclear what his relation to *Amy Brack* or *Anna Brock* (or *Brack*) may have been.

Julia Buchan is believed to have begun the first private school in Orlando. She was a widow from Mississippi. "Her class had about thirty pupils who met in a room with a dirt floor in the county's first log courthouse in the pine woods near what would later be Church Street" (Robinson and Andrews 203).

S. B. Carter (possibly *Silas B.*) was on a list of registered voters (Bacon I, 356). Other members for which little is known include *Kevin Childrons*, *Ellen Childons* (or *Childrons*), *Miss* (or *Mrs.*) *Datson*, and *Walter Davis*.

*James A. Delaney and family
—Courtesy OCHM*

James Delaney came to Orlando in 1875. He was a leading merchant and a postmaster. He was selected as an alderman in 1877 and in 1878. In 1884, Orlando experienced a devastating fire which began in his store. All his stock was lost. In 1894, he was a member of the church's building committee. In 1895, he was elected to the city council. Delaney Street was named in his honor. The Delaney Street Baptist Church was named to honor his family. He was the father of eight children, two of whom were also listed as early members (Bacon I, 66ff.). *Claudia Delaney* was a Sunday School teacher for the church. She was a postmistress for Orlando from 1923 to 1930 (Bacon I, 66). *Eunice Delaney* (affectionately called "Miss Nune") became the Sunday School secretary for First Baptist Church in 1903. She was a maiden lady and a very devoted church member all of her life. A Sunday School class was named in her honor. She was also a teacher and later a principal of Orlando High School. She organized a meeting of PTA presidents which met once a month. In 1943, she retired after forty-nine years of an educational career. Orville Davis, Orlando historian and educator, remembered her as being a petite ball of fire. He also related a story told to him by Ken Guernsey about Miss Delaney: "Miss Nune had a cat that had kittens. A carpenter came to make holes in her kitchen door to let out the cats. He asked her what she wanted and she said she wanted him to make five holes. That startled him, thinking that one hole would be plenty. But she said she wanted five, explaining: 'When I say scat, I mean scat!'" (Davis interview).

J. L. Empie was another early member. His wife, *Mrs. J. L. Empie*, was a secretary for the Woman's Missionary Union. Other members included *Newton Farless* (or *Fearless*); *Elizabeth Farless* (or *Fearless*); *John Fullwood*; "young boy *Glover* Negro"; *Rosetta Glover*, "Negro"; *Ellen Glover*, "Negro"; and *Rachael Glover*, "Negro."

Sam F. Gove initiated a reorganization of the Baptist church in Apopka in June 1880. He was a traveling pastor and often spoke at Bethel Baptist, becoming its pastor for three years. He was also an educational supervisor. *J. B. Graves* (possibly *J. B. Greaves*, who was a registered voter in 1876) was a delegate to the Wekiva Association in 1883. *L. B. Greaves*, *L. C. Greves* (or *Greaves*), *G. W. Hesmith, Laura Hesmith, Charles Hinson*, and *Trinity Horney* were also members.

William Benjamin Hull (1829–1914) was on a list of registered voters in Orange County in 1876 (Bacon I, 357). He moved to Orlando from Cobb County, Georgia, and was in the Civil War and wounded twice, returning to Orlando in July of 1865 (Bacon II, 339). He was probably the first shipper of citrus on a commercial basis in central Florida (Bacon II, 339).

"William Hull, who began construction of his first home on Conway Road in 1875, shipped his first crop of oranges that year, a total of three barrels, on consignment. He received no returns, but, undaunted, continued to set out more trees. He became one of the largest grove owners in the area" (Bacon I, 64). He would have been forty-one at the church's organization in 1871. On the 1870 census he was listed as forty and a farmer.

The Hulls' first residence in the Orlando area was near Lake Fairview. Next the family, which eventually included eleven children, moved to a home on Orange Avenue, near the intersection with Central, which was turned into a boardinghouse. Finally, the Hulls moved in 1875 to the juncture of present-day Fern Creek and Conway Road. There they built a home and eventually developed an estate with twelve rooms finished in 1883. He bought land finally totaling 640 acres, some of which was used as an orange grove. At the time of the home's demolition, it was believed to have been one of Orlando's oldest at sixty-six years. Mrs. Shaw, a descendant, wrote, "Their first (Conway) home was at the corner of Fern Creek and Old Conway Road. Their 'new' house was at Hull Circle off Fern Creek" (letter).

Mr. Hull wrote an interesting article for the *South Florida Sentinel*, published on July 1, 1885, in which he described his life as a pioneer living in Orlando:

> When I first moved to [central Florida] on the 27 of November 1855, I left my home in Cobb County, Georgia, in company with four other families, thirty-six of us, white and black. We had horse and mule teams, and traveled every day, Sunday not excepted. On the 24th of December, we stopped within four miles of Melonville, and about the same distance from Sanford, but there was no Sanford there then. We had a pleasant time moving to Florida; the weather was fine; we all came through safely; we had good appetites and ate everything we could buy on the road. This country is quite different now, but few people and few settlements, and they were quite a long ways from each other then, yet we were all neighbors; and I was not here long before I knew every man in the county. . . . Our place of trade was Fort Reed, and the boat came to Melonville from there once a week. Fort Reed was one mile from the boat landing, and had one small store kept by Mr. Arthur Ginn. Our post office was at Melonville and as the boat came there almost every man in the county was there to get his mail and to trade, to sell his venison and cow hides, which were the principal articles of trade at that time. Our

boat was named the Darlington, owned by Captain Issachar Brock, Sr. Many a time have I stood on the wharf and watched for the Darlington; sometimes we could see her smoke several hours before she landed.

I remember the first court that was held at Melonville. A few months after I came here, I was summoned as a juror, for it took every man in the county to hold court. I attended. At ten o'clock the grand jury was empaneled; about two o'clock or three in the evening the jurors were dismissed; county business all attended to in less than one day; now it takes five and six weeks and more left undone than we had to do at that time. Judge Forward was our residing officer in 56, he was a nice, pleasant man.

In about a month after I landed here the Indian War broke out, and then I wished I was back in old Georgia, but I was here and not able to make my way back there. We soon had soldiers here stationed at Fort Gatlin, three miles South of Orlando, but there was no Orlando here then, all wild woods. In July, 56, I came out and took a look at this part of the country and moved out there, settling one mile and a half Northwest of where Orlando is. We had exciting times during our little Indian war which lasted two years. I remember one walk I took to Melonville. The weather was hot and as my shoes hurt my feet, I took them off and walked in my socks, not thinking that for my track was similar to those made by the Indians' moccasins; other parties traveled the road after me that day and reported that they had seen Indian tracks in the road at Soldier Creek swamp. This swamp was a frightful looking place at that time, and this caused quite an excitement; after a while I told people that I had walked through there that day in my stocking feet, but saw no Indians; I was the little Indian that created the big scare.

We over took but one Indian hunt. Eight of us took our guns and a two horse team; I was the driver; my old grandfather, then nearly 80 years old, went with us, taking his usual heavy stick. We went around South to Lake Jessup into a wild, lonesome country; the first evening we struck camp handy to wood and water; some of the men took their guns and went out to hunt deer and bee trees, returning at night and reporting seeing a smoke rising up in a swamp; we thought it might be an Indian camp, which caused us to be a little frightened; that night three of our men volunteered to go with the captain and see if they could find any Indians and on their return, reported that they found none; we then built a fire and some of our men got up a game of cards to pass away the time. I lassoed the horses that they might feed, and then I lay down to rest, but the mosquitoes would not permit of such indulgence; about midnight our horses commenced snorting and came running to the camp; some one said "Indians" the men dropped their cards, we seized our guns and got behind pine trees away from the firelight; our captain called for a volunteer to put out the fire, which I did by throwing a bucket of water on it and went back to my tree; a man close by me told me that a fox had passed close by him. I asked if it came from the direction that the horses ran from, and he said it did, then I knew the horses had got scared at the fox, for they did not like the scent of wild animals. That was the last scare we had on that hunt, my first and last Indian hunt.

I said I settled where Orlando is. The first Monday in October, 1856, the voters of this county held an election to decide the location of the county site, and we had a lively time of it, but the people of this district polled the greatest number of votes and we got the court house. It was claimed that some of the soldiers who had homes in other counties voted with us. James G. Speer was our leader, and if it hadn't been for his shrewd-ness, we should have lost it. He is now our State Senator and one of our members in the Constitutional Convention. Mr. Speer took the contract to build the court house; I worked 21 1/2 days on it at $1.00 per day and fed myself, and thought I was getting pretty good wages at that.

In 1860, I moved to Orlando; our Civil War broke out and I went into the service on the Confederate side. Was taken prisoner at the battle of Gettysburg, July 2, 1863, was carried to Fort Delaware where I remained until June 11, 65 when I was paroled and carried to New York City where I stayed seven days and then Uncle Sam paid my fare to Palatka, feeding me on bacon and hard tack on the journey. I think the old uncle was good to me considering I had been a little rebellious. I walked from Palatka and got home July 2, 1865. There were but two families here then, mine and a widow lady, named Mrs. Keene.

Blackman writes that when the Hull and other families moved to cen-tral Florida in 1855, "this influx of new settlers, it is said, nearly doubled the population of Orange County" (46). And further, "In 1862 Mr. Hull joined Captain Joshua Mizell's company of 'Home Guards,' and went to Tallahassee, where the company was mustered into the regular army and they were quickly hurried to Virginia, where they soon saw service. Mr. Hull was twice wounded slightly by partially spent balls and later sustained a badly sprained ankle which sent him to the hospital. Reporting again for service he was captured at the first battle of Gettysburg and was taken to Ft. Delaware, where he spent twenty-three months, when the war closed and he came home" (46).

Emily Harriett Watson Hull (1837–1894) was the wife of William B. Hull. She and her husband opened a hotel prior to the Civil War which she continued in her husband's absence. She was also the unofficial post mistress for the

> mail that arrived once each week. With help of a faithful negro boy and girl, Mrs. Hull carried on a farm and probably the battle against starvation was never more energetically waged. Many times provisions ran very low, but soldiers' wives had a good friend in Capt. Mizell's father, who, too old to go to war, would, upon calling at the post office, make diligent inquiry as to the supply of food, and when Mrs. Hull was out of meat, "Uncle Dave" would butcher a beef and take a quarter to her.
>
> The hotel had few guests during the war, but when court was in session, Mrs. Hull furnished dinner to every man in the county." (Blackman 46)

On the 1870 census, she was listed as thirty-three and keeping house. The Hulls' children purchased a beautiful stained-glass window for the church in honor of their parents.

B. F. Hull may be the same person as Benjamin Franklin, an uncle of William B. Hull. Benjamin lived at Lake Fairview and died in the 1890's. Other members with the Hull surname included *Ezekiel Hull, Lane Hull, Lizzie Hull,* who was probably Elizabeth Hull, daughter of William B. and Emily (see Isaac O. Barber, above), and *Mary Hull* (see Mary Self, below).

Little is known about *P. B. Jaudon, Mrs. Jaudon,* or *F. M. Jaudon. Aaron Jernigan* was a founder of Orlando. Actually, there were two or three Aaron Jernigans in Orlando. It is unclear which one was a church member, but that man and his family joined the church in 1879. One Aaron Jernigan was born on September 14, 1813. He married Mary Hogans, who was born on October 4, 1814. They produced at least nine children, one of whom was Aaron, born March 29, 1835, and another was Martha (later Martha Jernigan Tyler), who was born on February 14, 1839. This first Aaron Jernigan was called "Capt." From a newspaper piece by Mark Andrews, Jernigan was described both as "the first permanent American settler in what is now Orange County" and "a brawler and a vigilante who ruthlessly exploited and sometimes killed Seminoles" ("Early Settler"). Jernigan set up a homestead close to Fort Gatlin. Despite his tarnished reputation, he was a leader in the community and stuck out living in the area during harsh times. Another Aaron was Aaron Moses Jernigan, who was Emma Jernigan Yates' father. Reference is made to *Mrs. Jernigan*, but because no first name is given, it is hard to tell who this might be. It could be Aaron's wife; if so, her name would be Martha. *Mary Jernigan* might be Aaron and Martha's daughter; if so, her full name was Mary Jane and she was born April 2, 1846.

Joseph Johns was on the list of registered voters (Bacon I, 358). *Ellen Johns* and *Marshily Johns* were early members, as was *Anigenel Keen*. *Charles King* was listed as seventy-one and a farmer on the 1870 census. *Elizabeth King* was listed as sixty-four and keeping house on the 1870 census. *Mrs. King, Josephine Laurie, Annie Lee*, and *Ellen Lee* were listed among early members.

S. A. Luckey was thirty-three and running a sawmill, as can be read in the 1880 census; he was also a registered voter in 1876 (Bacon I, 358). Other members included *William Luckey, Elizabeth Luckey, I. J. Mahon*, and *Aaron McDuffie (Negro)*. *Prof. McQuaig* was possibly the same McQuaig listed as being elected as a delegate by Bethel Baptist to attend the Wekiwa Associational meeting in 1882. *Mrs. McQuaig* was a member as well. *E. K. Meeks* was probably Elvis Meeks who, with his family listed below, joined the Bethel church in 1872 and then with the Wofford and Russ families formed the Fairview Church in 1873. His family included *Martha E. Meeks, Eldorada E. Meeks*, and *Mary Meeks*.

A. L. Mills was on a list of 1876 registered voters (Bacon I, 359). He was a deacon at First Baptist Church in Apopka in 1885. *A. J. Mosteller, Mrs. A. J. Mosteller, Miss* (or *Mrs.*) *Price*, and *Easter Raulerson* were all members. *O. W. Prince* owned a citrus grove in the Apopka area.

E. H. (Ned) Rice, for a number of years, was the clerk for the church. George, Joe, and Ned Rice owned a furniture store on Orange Avenue in 1886. "E. H. Rice, a Georgian, opened a furniture store on South Orange Avenue under the firm name of E. H. Rice and Company. It was the first furniture store to handle exclusive merchandise" (Bacon I, 97). Little is known about *Celetie Roberts*. *Norman Robinson*, "another 1870 arrival, was a native of New York State. A noted chemist, he had studied in Europe for two years, and had a worldwide reputation in scientific circles. He filled the chair of natural science at Rollins College and was appointed by Governor Francis Fleming as state chemist, a position he held for four years" (Bacon I, 39). *Mrs. Robinson* and *Nettie Robinson* were church members, as well.

Charles Russ was possibly Charles F. Russ, who was a registered voter in 1876 (Bacon I, 360). *Martha Russ* and *Sarah A. Russ* also appeared on the list. *S. A. Russ* was a deacon at Bethel Baptist. The Wekiva Association bulletin, in 1880, announced his death: "Brother S. A. Russ, of Bethel church, after a long life of patient endurance, of well doing, has departed to his eternal reward, leaving behind him glorious testimony of the beauty and loveliness that marks the true and humble follower of Jesus. We thank God for his life, and for the hope in his death" (4). *William R. Russell, Susan Russell, G. W. Ryley*, and *E. J. Sears* were early church members.

G. T. Self was listed as twenty-two and a carpenter on the 1880 Florida census. "The Reverend George T. Self was born in a log cabin on the north shore of Lake Ivanhoe in 1857. His parents moved to South Carolina but in 1875 Self returned to his native city and became a building contractor. He assisted in the building of many of Orlando's homes, and was ordained to the ministry in 1892 by the First Baptist Church. He attended Stetson University to prepare himself for his ministerial work" (Bacon I, 66–67). *Mary Self* was twenty-one, wife of G. T. on the 1880 census. The Greenwood Cemetery census of Section A gives the following: "Mary F. Self 1858–1892." From one of Mrs. Mildred Talton's binders is a clipping about Mrs. Self. There were several entries about her life and death. The following clipped from the *DeLand Record* shows in what high esteem Mrs. Self was held in that city:

> The *Record* regrets to announce the sudden death of Mrs. Geo. Self at her late residence on New York avenue, Monday morning at 5 o'clock. Her remains were taken to her former home, Orlando, for burial Monday afternoon. On July 30th she was the mother of twin boys, one of whom died on the following Monday. Mr. Self has the sincere sympathy of our people in his sad affliction. He removed to this place from Orlando last spring and he and family have always been devoted to the Christian faith.
>
> News reached Orlando Monday from DeLand, concerning the death of Mrs. Mary F. Self, which occurred at the latter place at 6 o'clock A.M. of that day, at the age of thirty-four years.
>
> The remains, accompanied by the family, arrived in this city Monday evening, and the funeral took place at 10 A.M. Tuesday, at the Orlando cemetery, Undertaker Hand in charge, the services at the grave being conducted by Rev. N. A. Bailey, and attended by a number of sympathizing friends. The deceased was well and favorably known in Orlando, where the family resided for many years, having only removed to DeLand a few months since. Her strong Christian character and

example of purity of life, will leave a lasting influence for good upon a large circle of relatives and friends.

From the *Sentinel*: "She had many warm and admiring friends. Besides a grief-stricken husband, she leaves two small sons and a little infant but a few days old. Mrs. Self was a member of the Baptist church, a conscientious and devout Christian, a devoted wife and mother and a valuable lady in the community in which she resided. The bereaved family has the profound sympathy of their many friends in Orlando."

"It was her great desire to see these two bright boys educated at our own University [Stetson]. However, she did not live to see this consummated. God took her to her home, where she awaits her beloved" (*Florida Baptist Witness*).

N. A. Bailey wrote in the *Baptist Witness*: "Mrs. Mary F. Self was the daughter of Mr. and Mrs. W. B. Hull, of Orange county, Fla., and was born on December 8, 1858. She was married to Geo. T. Self May 23, 1877, and died August 8, 1892. She was converted in 1872 and united with the Baptist church soon after. From that time to her death she was an earnest Christian worker. She exemplified in her daily life the genuineness of her profession. Too much cannot be said in her praise as a faithful servant of her Lord, as well as a dutiful daughter, an affectionate sister, a devoted wife and fond mother.

"She leaves parents, brothers, sisters, husband and two sons to mourn her departure. They mourn their loss, they joy in her gain. They fondly expect to meet her 'beyond the smiling and the weeping,' where she now awaits their coming."

Then more tragedy struck: "Died—At Mr. Hull's near the city, yesterday, the infant son of Mr. Geo. T. Self. It survived its twin brother two weeks and its mother one week."

H. S. Self, Annie Shepherd, and *Mariah Smith* were among the early members. *Samuel Summerlin* was born into the famous and prosperous Jacob Summerlin family. He was Jacob's son and helped him in the cattle business. Supposedly Sam and his brother Bob named Lake Eola. *Isaac Tison* was a registered voter in 1876 (Bacon I, 361).

The final names on the list of early church members included *Jane Tiner* (or *Tyner*), *Clem Tyner, Mary Tyner, Theodora Tyner, John Walker, Carrie Walker, Sarah Walker, Elizabeth Whitted, Benjamin Wofford, Thomas Wofford, Annie Wofford* (or *Wooford*), *John Yates, Thomas Yates, Mary Yates, Susan Yates, John Young, G. W. Young*, and *Mary Anne Young*.

CHAPTER FOUR

Early Pastors, 1858–1912

But you, man of God, flee from all this, and pursue righteousness, godliness, faith, love, endurance and
gentleness. Fight the good fight of the faith. Take hold of
the eternal life to which you were called when you made
your good confession in the presence of many witnesses.
—*1 Timothy 6:11–12*

EMILY HULL'S DILEMMA
TRIALS OF AN EARLY SETTLER

"'But when you pray, go into your room, close the door
and pray to your Father.'"
Matthew 6:6

With eager hands Emily took the few letters James Hughey left with her and looked for one from William. She had heard nothing for four months and was quite worried. It was March 1864, and times were hard in the little community of Orlando. Devout Baptists, Emily and William Hull had been disappointed when their little home church had to disband during the war. Emily missed the monthly services which had always strengthened her faith. As the awful war continued, more and more people drifted away. Nearly all able-bodied men joined the Confederacy, most with Captain Joshua Mizell's company of "Home Guards," William one of them, and many of the women and children moved back to Georgia or other places to the north. Then the

67

terrifying toll of war dead began to grow. Her heart trembled as she recalled the names of two former Orlando sheriffs, Jonathan Stewart and Andrew Jackson Simmons, now dead and buried. How soon life could end. She feared for her beloved Will.

As she gazed over the bare shelves in the kitchen of her little boardinghouse, her prayers went up for William, now a prisoner at Fort Delaware. If the rumors were to be believed, he must be suffering greatly. His last letter had described the poor food and the cold. But he had tried to reassure her about a possible early release. She feared he was overly optimistic. He had requested a blanket, which she had sent.

Although her little hotel had been empty for several weeks, she had received notice of an election to be held in two days. That meant at least five men would need lodging and food. The beds were no problem. Yesterday, she had washed the sheets and aired the rooms. The food, however, was another story.

She moved to her prayer closet, knelt down, and asked the Lord to provide provisions for the evening meal and comfort for her husband. Confident of the Lord's intervention, she returned to the kitchen and began to make some wheat bread. In no time at all, her fingers and the heels of her hands were expertly kneading the fragrant dough. The rhythm of the movement seemed to comfort her. She set the bread to rise near the window where the sun had begun to shine; then she dusted the flour from her arms and apron and went to investigate the quiet. When children were making no noise, it usually meant trouble. This time was no exception.

As she quietly entered the nursery, her eyes met a common sight. Her daughter, six-year-old Mary, struggled with ropes that held her arms and legs to a chair. A piece of rag had been wound around her head and stuffed in her mouth, forcing her silence. Tears of frustration coursed down her cheeks. Emily ran to her, quickly untied the knotted rope, briefly hugged and kissed her child, and ran to find her miscreant sons. They were hiding and giggling in the hall closet. After a good scolding, she tried to conceal a smile behind her hand. They really weren't bad boys, just mischievous. They needed their father's strong presence as much as she.

Moments later, Hughey ducked his head back in the door. He apologized for his absentmindedness. He had remembered to give her the letters for the community—she was the unofficial postmistress—which he had received on his trip to Gainesville, but he had forgotten to leave her a parcel. As quickly as he had returned, he was gone. Emily, puzzled, opened the large package and was delighted to find enough fruit, vegetables, and canned goods to last them for two weeks. She hadn't ordered anything; she couldn't with no money in the household account. Who could have sent this gift? Remembering her prayer of a few moments ago, she received her heavenly answer. The earthly answer probably fell on one of the kind townspeople who, as circumstances permitted, left unexpected treasures on her doorstep. But that's how the people of Orlando were. They looked out for one another. Thanking God for this answer, she carefully shelved the cans and began washing the fruit and vegetables. A hot vegetable soup sounded like a good entree for supper.

The stew smelled good. Uncle Dave said so as his creaking bones settled into the kitchen chair. Father of Captain Mizell, he often was found visiting the families of his son's regiment, checking on their welfare. He had dropped by two days earlier and had noticed the decided absence of any meat in the Hull's storehouse. Today, he had brought a quarter of beef. A grateful Emily took some of the precious pieces and cut them into the soup. As the old man made his way down the street, Emily watched him. Her eyes noticed a very small cup on her stoop. It was filled with sea salt. Some neighbors had recently returned from a trip to the coast on a money-making venture to harvest salt to sell to the Confederacy. Although they probably needed every precious grain, they had freely left some for her. The Lord's goodness never failed.

Now, as she gazed at the kitchen shelf, it was no longer bare. In fact, it nearly groaned with the weight of the Lord's provision. She turned to the stove and gave the stew another stir. The bread dough was ready to be shaped into loaves. Emily happily went about her work. Five hungry men were due to arrive in two hours. Her hands flew to her task as her voice softly lifted in a hymn of praise.

As each area in Florida was discovered, settlers would band together for survival. While their physical needs were necessary and important, spiritual needs, for many, were equally desired. At first, a family might worship in its home. Later, as families settled nearby, they would often join together for services. As time progressed, the families developed the desire for a larger assemblage, and a brush arbor might be constructed.

Often one of the men would conduct services or a group of men would take turns. Later, a traveling preacher might visit the area and agree to conduct a meeting. Apparently it was into this setting that William Miller paid a visit to Orlando.

William Miller, 1858–unknown. The Reverend William Miller from Apopka (another entry says Lake Eustis Settlement) helped start a Baptist church with twelve members. He did not have ties with the Baptist church in Apopka, since it was not founded until 1860. No William Miller appears on either the 1850 or 1860 census for Orange County. A listing for William M. M. Miller is on the 1850 census for Marion County, which would lend credence to the Lake Eustis Settlement location for him. This Miller was listed as twenty-nine, a farmer, married to Caroline C., age twenty-one, with a son William, age two. Of course, all of these ages would be added by eight for the 1858 time period. Many, if not all, pastors supplemented their income with another occupation, so it would not be surprising to see him listed with the occupation of farmer rather than pastor. If this was the same William Miller, he was probably a circuit rider, periodically traveling as the Lord directed him to places requesting religious guidance. Tradition, rather than official record, has the small body of Baptist believers first meeting in the home, near Lake Fairview, of William B. and Emily Hull.

It is not known how long this group met, but some time during the Civil War, probably 1862, it was disbanded, presumably due to the absence of the men. A WPA report relates that G. C. Powell wrote a history of these early days, but such a record has not been found in the church archives. A few years after the Civil War, a group of Baptists requested the presence of Rev. G. C. Powell to help them reestablish a Baptist church.

G. C. (George Cader) Powell, 1871–1872. The Reverend G. C. Powell was born in Georgia. From Sharon P. Tate, one of Powell's descendants, are the following notes:

> George C. Powell was born in Burke County, Georgia on December 13, 1809, near the Botsford meeting house. He was immersed by Rev. John Blackston into Mount Paran Church, in Crawford County, Georgia on December 28, 1828. He married in 1830 and was licensed to preach in Talbot by the Antioch Church and ordained in Russell County, Alabama at Liberty Church in 1847, with Elders Reuben Thornton, Willis Jones, and Thomas Granberry acting as Presbytery. In 1848, he was called to the Beulah Church in Stewart County, Georgia. In 1859, he moved to Florida and settled near Bellville. He preached for Providence Church in Bradford County for at least one year. In January 1868, he moved to Lake Jessup in Orange County, Florida. He died at West Apopka, Orange County, Florida in November 1881 at 72 years of age.

He was a fervent church planter. In 1869, he helped organize a brush arbor church for Oviedo near the W. H. Luther home. He served as pastor there for several years and gave the lot for the first church built in Oviedo. He traveled on horseback and in a one-horse wagon to Tampa, Clearwater, and other distant places carrying the gospel where it was most needed.

From pages that came from the Florida State Library with the WPA report, and possibly written in 1895, we read, "In conformity to God's law a party of Christians moved by love to God and man met on the 5th of March 1871 and under the leadership of Bro. Powell organized a church which they named The Bethel Baptist Church."

G. C. Powell met with eighteen charter members to organize Bethel Baptist Church, which was the first name given to First Baptist Church of Orlando. On the 1870 census, he was listed as George C. Powell, age sixty, with his primary occupation given as blacksmith. His wife's name was listed as Patricia Powell, age fifty-eight. This first name is possibly an error. In speaking with Powell's great-granddaughter, Jewel Powell Fillmon, the name was given as Patience Carolyn. In 1881, Powell pastored at Geneva and was the moderator of the Wekiwa Association's Sunday exercises. At the time of its organization, it is presumed the church met in the courthouse approximately once a month, alternating with the Episcopalians and Methodists.

The next official record of the church described a business meeting held on February 3, 1872. That was a Saturday, and the church met in conference. "Church doors were opened; none came forward." There was a call to business. It was "moved and seconded that Brother W. J. Brack be appointed clerk—carried." W. J. Brack was listed as clerk and G. C. Powell as moderator or pastor.

On March 3, seven members were joined to the church by letter: William B. Hull, Emily Hull, Henry Meeks, Mary Meeks, Elvis [Elius?] Meeks, Martha Meeks, and Eldorada E. Meeks. It seems puzzling the Hulls were not listed as charter members since they were so prominent in the pre-Civil War church. Apparently something must have prevented them from attending the organizational meeting in 1871. W. J. Brack was again listed as clerk, and G. C. Powell as moderator.

As stated earlier, the church's first meetings were probably held in the courthouse on Central and Court Streets until the Union Free Church and School was completed in 1872. Eve Bacon wrote that "when the Free Church was completed in 1872, the southeast corner of Pine Street and Central Avenue was used as a church cemetery" (I, 85).

In early September, on the first Saturday, the church conducted a business meeting and carried a motion to have communion twice a year in October and May. "Brother Powell is requested to invite all or as many of our sister churches to commune with us as is convenient." As early as this, our church seemed to enjoy a fellowship with its sister churches of Orlando. Two delegates were chosen to attend Deep Creek Association, John Wofford and W. J. Brack, with Henry Meeks serving as alternate. Brother Henry Purvis was granted a letter of dismission. Once again, W. J. Brack was recorded as clerk with G. C. Powell as moderator.

Within a report from the Florida State Library that accompanied a WPA form concerning First Baptist Church, this comment was made about Powell: "Bro. Powell was a good preacher, a very earnest Christian whose life was saddened by the ill fate of his son, who was implicated and executed with Wilkes Booth" (2).

E. H. Gore writes in his *History of Orlando Baptists: First Baptist Church*, "Brother Powell was a good preacher and a very earnest Christian. . . . He was strict in his discipline and had some of the members turned out for nonattendance. The church became tired of his strict discipline and in October 1872 they called Rev. A. C. Tindall as pastor."

A. C. Tindall, 1872–1873. Gore writes, "During [Tindall's] ministry the church made annual calls upon the membership. His pastorate lasted only a year when the church called Elder J. A. Parker as pastor." Tindall was described as "a drinking preacher. . . . A man of good mind but weak-lived. He died below Kissimmee" (Talton notes). And from a form sent by the Florida State Library: "In Oct. 1872 the Rev. A. C. Tindall was elected pastor, the church following the custom of making annual calls. It is thought that the church was tired of the strict discipline of Bro. Powell, some being expelled for non attendance. Bro. Tindall only served one year, on a salary of $100.00. He was a man of good head and heart, but uncultured and addicted to whiskey. His delivery was very vociferous, gathering volume and inspiration as he proceeded and often ending with the injunction, 'Do as I say Brethren, not as I do'" (2–3).

During his pastorate we find the following minutes: On Saturday, October 3, 1872, at the business meeting two came forward: Ezekiel Hull and Easter Raulerson. On the Saturday before the first Lord's day in November, the church met in business meeting with the "divine service" given by "Bro. Tindall. Bro. Blitch came forward and placed himself under watch care of the church until such time as he could obtain his letter. W. J. Brack, clerk; A. Tindall, moderator."

In March 1873, divine services were given by A. C. Tindall. G. W. Hesmith was granted a letter of dismissal and was "joined to another church of the same faith and order." In August, "Sis. Hesmith excommunicated for treating the church with contempt." Brack was listed as clerk and H. L. Meeks as moderator. A. C. Tindall was no longer mentioned in the records.

J. A. Parker, 1873–1878 or 1879. Gore wrote that Rev. Parker lived out in Long Prairie. "He was very poor, very humble and talked very low in preaching. . . . Elder Parker was loved by the brethren and served the church several years."

The Florida State Library form notes that Parker "served the church six years, when he resigned. During his pastorate there was admitted into membership a negro woman named Annie McDuffie. The last three years of his pastorate we have no record" (2).

At the October 6, 1873, business meeting, Parker was listed as conducting divine services. Josephine Lourie was granted a letter of dismissal. The church then went into the call of a preacher, and Parker was unanimously called. Volunteers were called to attend the association. Brack, Blitch, William Hull, Jeptha Purvis, and Isaac Tison were commissioned. A call was given for funds for minutes and association purposes in the amount of $8.85. Two were baptized, Isaac Tison and H. S. Self. "One came forward, Annie McDufee, colored. W. J. Brack, clerk; Parker, moderator."

In February 1874, Parker gave the service. "Bro. Hull & Brack were appointed to wait on Bro. Wm. Hodges and notify him that the church would take action in his case for missing two successive meetings." Church attendance was strictly enforced. In the September meeting, the matter of Hodge was resolved. He called for his letter of dismissal "on the grounds that he lived near the Fort Christmas church." Also at the September meeting, Parker was voted as pastor for the ensuing year.

At the October 4 meeting, J. J. Davis moved that the house [church] be opened only for worship and school and that the key be delivered to E. A. Richards. It is unclear why Richards was given the key. By occupation, he was an undertaker. Perhaps he was also a teacher. Divine service was conducted by Parker and A. J. Gandy. There was a gap in the church records from this point to 1879.

L. J. Simmons, 1878 or 1879. Gore writes, "Elder Parker was succeeded by Rev. L. J. Simmons of Hillsboro County who was a good preacher and the church prospered greatly."

In August 1879, Hull was listed as clerk and "Simmon" as moderator. At that meeting, S. A. Lucky was in disorder before the church for the charges of billiard playing and "other public offenses." A "vigilant committee" was appointed, including W. B. and Emily Hull (the first mention of a woman holding an office in the church) along with W. M. Luckey. Some time during the first five or six years of the church's existence, eight to ten of its members requested their letters to form a church at Fairview. Then at the time of Simmons's pastorate, the Bethel Church increased in members as the "Fairview church having no pastor joined with the Bethel church. Fairview members at that time were Bro. S. A. Russ, Sister Eliz. Russ, Bro. A. L. Mills, Sister Sarah A. Russ, Bro. W. W. Bracken, Sister Caroline Wofford, and Sister Moriah Barber."

By September 6, 1879, the church had appointed a committee to investigate the "property case." The members were S. A. Russ, A. Bass, and W. B. Hull.

The Florida State Library report states that Simmons "was a stronger preacher than the ones before and the church prospered greatly, but he had to come over by land, a two days' journey, so he gave up the church after one year. In his pastorate the church appointed a vigilance committee to watch and report on conduct of membership" (2).

Sam F. Gove, 1879–1882. Gore states that Gove "was a good worker and an earnest Christian but a poor preacher, talked low and made little impression. He was a good organizer, however, and the church prospered. His discipline being sharp and impartial, a brother was expelled for playing billiards, another for horse racing, another for nonattendance, one for drinking and one for heresy." Apparently he pastored Apopka Church and Bethel at the same time. Later, in 1886, he was employed by the association to pastor in needy areas as a missionary.

Church records state that on November 1, 1879, "Bro. Gove was chosen to serve church as pastor." Also at that meeting, the property committee made a report. Hull was listed as clerk and S. F. Gove was listed as moderator. "In January 1880, a committee was appointed by the Bethel Baptist Church to purchase a lot for a church building" (Gore *History*). In June 1880, Gove initiated a reorganization of the Baptist church in Apopka (Florida State Library Report 2). In August 1880, Walter Davis was charged with drinking, swearing, and horse racing. In September W. B. Hull presided as moderator.

In the 1879 roll of members, Aaron Jernigan was listed. It is unclear whether he was the better-known Aaron Jernigan. Aaron Jernigan also had a son named Aaron to add to the confusion. In November 1880, Jernigan was charged for not attending. "In December 1880, Brother Blitch was appointed to receive donations for the church building" (Gore *History*).

Also in 1880, the church received twenty members by baptism and three by letter. The church lost one member by excommunication, three by letter, and two by death. The total membership for 1880 was listed as fifty-eight in the association bulletin.

Wekiva Association bulletins give valuable information concerning the Baptist denomination in general and Bethel Baptist in particular. Most churches, as they grew and prospered, felt the need to join an association. Our church was no exception. The statistical table of churches, in the associational bulletin for 1880, lists Live Oak, Apopka, Concord, Bethel, Orange Grove, Lake Harney, Pine Grove, Harmony, Indian River, New Salem, and Moss Bluff.

The Wekiva (sometimes spelled Wekiwa) Association's articles of faith give a clear indication of the Baptist faith at that time. They include twelve statements, each followed by several Scripture passages.

1. We believe in only one true and living God, the Father, the Son or Word, and the Holy Ghost.

2. We believe that the Scriptures, comprising the Old and New Testaments, are the Word of God, and the only rule of faith and practice.

3. We believe that Adam, by sin, fell from the state of purity in which he was created; that all his posterity are degenerate, and that all human nature is corrupt and depraved.

4. We believe that man is utterly unable, by his own free will and ability, to recover himself from the fallen state in which he is by nature.

5. We believe in the doctrine of election, and that God chose His people in Christ before the world began.

6. We believe in the covenant of redemption and salvation by grace, entered into by the Sacred Three, in behalf of the elect on which Grace and Glory were settled forever in Christ, their covenant head.

7. We believe that sinners are justified in the sight of God by the imputed righteousness of Christ only, and that they receive pardon and reconciliation through Him.

8. We believe that God's elect shall be called, regenerated, and sanctified by the influence and operation of the Holy Spirit.

9. We believe that saints shall be preserved in Grace and that none of them shall be lost.

10. We believe in the resurrection of the dead, and the general judgment, and that the joy of the righteous and the punishment of the wicked will be eternal.

11. We believe that baptism and the Lord's Supper are ordinances of Jesus Christ; that true believers are the only fit subjects of baptism; that immersion of the subject in water is the Apostolic mode, and that none but regularly baptized members have a right to commune at the Lord's table.

12. We believe that no minister has any right to administer the ordinances of the Gospel unless he has been regularly baptized, called, and come under the imposition of the hands of a Presbytery." ("Association Bulletin" 1880, 6–7)

On April 30, 1881, the building committee was instructed to proceed to collect a sufficient amount of money subscriptions and purchase the lumber for the church building, and the clerk was instructed to write a copy of the order and forward it to each of the members of the committee. Gove was moderator and Carter was clerk. The church's desire for a building of its own was certainly understandable. A delightful explanation for building churches was given in the Wekiva Association's minutes of 1899: "God's first temples were trees, and under these the primeval fathers bowed and worshiped. But the civilization of ages has demanded neat and sometimes elegant houses of worship, and the Almighty set His approval to this demand centuries ago by giving to David and Solomon a pattern for a temple the most elegant and costly the world had ever seen. Modern experience has shown that a church, to thrive, needs a 'local habitation.' Fully recognizing this fact, our State Board of Missions encourages the building of meeting houses, and solicits funds from the stronger churches already housed, to aid the weaker churches that are seeking to be housed" (12). At times, critics may scoff at a church raising funds for an "elegant" structure, but we should take comfort in the example cited above.

On September 3, 1881, William F. Russell was received into fellowship. Brother Mills was granted a letter of dismissal. S. F. Gove was called and accepted the pastoral care of the church for the ensuing year. On September 30, October 1, and October 2, Bethel Baptist Church of Orlando was host to the twelfth annual session of the Wekiwa Baptist Association with S. F. Gove, moderator; E. Carroll Culpepper, clerk; and J. M. Blitch [from Bethel], treasurer.

From church records, on November 5, 1881, P. B. Jaudon and his wife Fell Jaudon were received. It was resolved that the building committee of the church be vested with full power to act as attorney for the church in all matters pertaining to the building of a house of worship and the disposal of any property. J. M. Blitch was reelected as church treasurer. There was sadness in the church: "It was resolved that whereas it has pleased our divine Master to take from our midst Bro. John Young that Bethel Church has lost a consistent member but feel that our loss is the deceased brother's gain" ("Church Record Book One"). Gove was listed as moderator with Carter as clerk.

On May 6, 1882, a committee was appointed "to labor with Bro. Lee, charge not attending church." Theodasher Tyner came forward and was joined by restoration. Gove remained as moderator, with William Hull as clerk.

In August 1882, Gove, Hull, Wofford, Blitch, Jaudon, McQuaig, and Tanner were elected as delegates to the Wekiva Association. Also in 1882, Gove attended the state convention in Lake City. In November 1882, it was agreed to organize a Sunday School at the church. At some time in 1882, "G. W. Culbreth asked to be ordained but on examination he was refused and expelled" (Gore *History*).

While official church records do not indicate when the church moved into its building, the WPA reported that the meetinghouse "was completed in December 1882." Eve Bacon wrote that "The dream was accomplished in 1882 with a small building at the northwest corner of Pine Street and Garland Avenue" (I, 89). What a time of rejoicing it must have been.

On December 24, 1882, a special meeting of the church was called. J. D. Beggs was chosen as moderator. The object of the meeting was to call a pastor. The resignment of Gove as pastor was read and accepted. J. S. Mahan was called.

J. S. Mahan, 1883. Gore writes, "Rev. J. S. Mahon, a visitor from the north was chosen pastor and took charge on January 7, 1883. He came to Florida in search of health and after a few months went home to die. During his pastorate the building committee, led by Brother Jaudon, was discharged with a vote of thanks for their attention and labor in building a house of worship. Several prominent members were received into the church, among whom were Prof. Norman Robinson with his wife and daughter, Jeanette, and also E. W. Rice. It was during this pastorate that another advance was made by having preaching service two Sundays a month instead of one, as heretofore." Apparently Mahan served for only a brief time, being called on December 24, 1882, and leaving in May of 1883.

On January 6, 1883, J. D. Beggs was elected clerk, a position he held for a number of years. He was a prominent lawyer and became judge of the criminal court. On February 3, 1883, Brother Bell joined the Kissimmee Church. Church services were changed to the second and fourth Sabbaths of each month. J. D. Beggs was serving as clerk of the church with J. M. Blitch and J. B. Graves as delegates to the associational meeting. In May J. S. Mahan requested the church to release him as pastor due to ill health. A claim of Patrick Boone was paid. In September there were two business meetings as the church tried to locate a pastor. J. W. Butts of Georgia was asked to visit.

J. W. Butts, 1883–1884. J. W. Butts was elected as pastor on October 14, 1883. Gore records that "Elder J. W. Butts of Georgia . . . served until the following April in 1884, when he was succeeded by Brother A. Barrell or Barrelle, who supplied until September but declined a call to become pastor." The *Orange County Reporter* for February 1884 lists the Baptists as meeting every second and fourth Sundays both morning and night.

A. Barrelle (or *Barelle*), 1884–possibly 1885. There are no thorough notes about Barrelle. In the associational bulletin for 1884, he is listed as pastor of Bethel Church, along with clerk E. H. Rice and delegate J. M. Blitch. The 1885 bulletin lists two Bethel pastors, Barrelle and A. L. Farr. It was at this time that the church record book indicates a name change for the church from Bethel Baptist to Missionary Baptist Church. The second name was to remain until 1894. The Florida State Library report sets forth, "During the latter part of Brother Butts' pastorate and a short time by Rev. A. Barrelle, the church was greatly concerned at some of the members signing petitions to sell whiskey" (2). Presumably this means the members signed petitions to allow the sale of whiskey, not that they were selling whiskey themselves. Orlando went through a time of alternating as a "dry" and "wet" community.

Also at this time the association was publishing information in a very lyric fashion about the whiskey situation.

> Its extent reaches far beyond our land and nation: beyond Greenland's icy mountains or India's coral strand; from sea to sea; from shore to shore; from man's highest civilization to his lowest degradation. Under the broad canopy of Heaven there are but few places where its insatiable, all-conquering power is not known. Its evil no tape line can measure, no ladder scale, no plummet sound. Far beyond that of fire, flood, pestilence and famine, its blasting, blighting and consuming power reaches. It is the avowed foe of joy and hope, of comfort and happiness. Its history is the history of crime.

This great evil exists because Christian people, so-called, permit it to exist. It can be annihilated only when God's people appreciate their responsibilities and are willing to perform their duty. Therefore, be it resolved that it is expected of each church in this Association that it will not tolerate or fellowship any member who will sign a whisky petition or vote in its favor." (1893 Associational Bulletin 14)

A. L. Farr, 1884–1885, July and August of 1886. According to the Florida State Census of 1885, Farr was fifty-eight and married. His place of birth was given as New York and his given occupation was minister. Gore writes:

> The church then called Rev. A. L. Farr of DeLand to the care of the church as the first real pastor the church ever had. He was the first to preach every Sunday. From the records it seems he was the 'Moses' of the struggling band that led them on to a better footing. He received a salary of $40.00 per month. . . . Rev. Farr soon won all hearts, being a highly cultured and a very spiritual man. The church grew in unity and fellowship as never before. The membership increased and we find among the members the names of Brother and Sister J. L. Empie and Brother and Sister A. J. Mosteller. Failing health caused the resignation of Rev. Farr in August 1885, much to the regret of the church.

On December 12, 1886, A. L. Farr died. Until his death, his attendance at church was a benediction to all.

The Wekiwa Baptist Association minutes of 1887 reported on his death: "Your committee would report that since our last Associational meeting [1886], it has pleased our Father, in His all-wise providence, to remove from our midst and his earthly labors, Bro. A. L. Farr, the beloved pastor of the Orlando church; and it is with heartfelt sorrow and deep regret we miss his presence amongst us; yet, we have the consolation that he has gone across the River, and is now resting from his labors in the bosom of our Saviour, whom he loved and served so well" (11).

Rev. Bebee, 1885. Bebee, a visitor, was called as a supply but left to go north after a few months. In the association bulletin of 1885, it was reported that the Ladies Mission Society raised sixteen dollars. As the church experienced the transition of pastors, the membership seemed to decline to one of its lowest points with a total membership listed as thirty-nine in the association bulletin.

William Powell, 1885–1886. Gore wrote, "In October 1885 the church called Rev. William Powell, an English bachelor of the Pickwick type, who was filled with a desire to go as a missionary to the negroes in Africa. During his term the church was repaired and put in good condition. A number of members was received among whom were Sisters Paramore and Papot. In May 1886 Rev. Powell resigned to fulfill his long cherished desire to be a missionary." In Webb's *Orlando Directory*, William Powell is listed as pastor, John Hudson and E. H. Rice as deacons, E. H. Rice as clerk, Mrs. A. L. Farr as organist, Mr. Mosteller as sexton, and J. D. Beggs as superintendent of the Sunday School (477).

Gore writes: "Rev. Farr again came to the rescue in July 1886 and the church received him with open arms but it was apparent to all that his days were few. He preached two months when he asked the church to call someone else, so in September 1886 the church called Rev. N. A. Bailey, who took charge on January 1, 1887" (Gore *History*).

N. A. Bailey, 1887–1890. During Bailey's pastorate, the church doubled in size from a total of forty-four members in 1887 to ninety in 1890. Prior to his coming to the church, he was employed by the Florida State Board of Missions as a missionary.

In 1887, a Ladies Missionary Society was organized. They made quilts, aprons, spectacle wipers, and emery cushions to sell for money to give to missions. Later, they gave a table and funds for a new organ.

Gore wrote that Bailey's pastorate was a fruitful one with several prominent people joining the church, among whom were J. M. Rice, R. M. Bennett, Miss A. Kimbrough, and Mrs. A. T. Scruggs. "The church agreed to pay Rev. Bailey $800.00 per year but at the end of the first year found they could pay him only $600.00 per year. He introduced the envelope system of collecting money and increased the membership and strengthened the church in many ways. He was an able man, a good speaker, a zealous Christian. He preached a strong sermon on temperance to which a leading deacon, who loved his dram, took exception and scored his pastor, whereupon Rev. Bailey resigned but continued until March 1890."

Reverend Bailey was secretary of the Florida Convention 1885–1897. He preached the Convention Sermon in 1885 on Isaiah 53:11. He was the Editor of *Florida Baptist Witness* in 1886. Mrs. N. A. Bailey was executive secretary of the WMU 1881–1886 (Joiner 305–08).

C. S. Farris, 1890–1892. Gore in his *History* writes, "There is recorded, 'that experience teaches us that a change of location of our church house is necessary to the success of the Baptist cause in the city.' The trustees and deacons were ordered to purchase a site at the corner of Pine and

Main Streets and move church building as soon as possible." However, a new church was not ready until 1897.

Gore goes on to describe Farris: "He was a faithful pastor and many new members were added to the church. The church seemed to have much trouble and delay in securing a successor to him. They first called Rev. J. S. Curry, offering a salary of $1000.00 but he declined. The Rev. W. M. Wamboldt was called. He demanded a salary of $1200.00 and a collector was appointed to raise same and receive 10% for his services. Of course he failed and then a double call was made to Reverends W. D. Jolly and C. H. Nash, both declining." The 1892 Wekiva Association's twenty-third annual meeting was held at the church. The bulletin reported that "Bro. Farris in his usually happy manner said a word on behalf of John B. Stetson University" (10). The back cover of the bulletin advertised "Stetson: John B. Stetson University, DeLand, Florida. The State Institution of Florida Baptists. Second Term Opens Wed. Oct. 2, 1892." Blackman reported that Farris was a vice-president of Stetson University and held the chair of ancient languages for a number of years (156).

In 1891, E. H. Rice was church clerk and our messengers to the associational meeting in Kissimmee were A. J. Mosteller, N. A. Bailey, and E. H. Rice. The church membership was given as 101. E. H. Rice was also superintendent of Sunday School with seventy-five pupils. The pastor's salary was given as $877. The value of total church property was $4,200. The Ladies Aid Society purchased an organ for the church. Earlier, they had purchased a table. Besides overseeing the building of the church pews, they were instructed to place insect powder under this organ.

Minutes of the afternoon session of the associational meeting at the church showed: "The moderator suggested that in as much as we had one hour before the appointed time for adjournment that it would be well to spend at least a portion of that time in prayer for the success of missions. That soul-inspiring hymn 'Work for the night is coming' was sung with animation by almost the entire audience, followed by prayer."

S. M. Hughes, 1893–1894. "The church then called a young preacher, Rev. S. M. Hughes at a salary of $800.00. He took charge in January 1893 and did a splendid work in increasing the membership. In April 1893, Rev. W. D. Jolly held a meeting for Pastor Hughes and the result was a great uplift to the church and eleven were baptized in Lake Eola. In June of this year the church began the practice of union services with other denominations. Rev. Hughes resigned in February 1894" (Gore *History*). The associational bulletin listed the membership total as 137 in 1893. E. H. Rice continued as Sunday School superintendent with seventy-six members.

One month prior to Hughes's resignation, "On January 4, 1893, the church and lots were voted put on sale. If sold the congregation to have use of the building for 6 months longer" (Gore *History*).

W. J. *Bolin*, 1894–1896. In the church minutes for April 22, 1894, and following, the church's name was changed to First Baptist Church.

> On April 22, 1894, the church called Rev. W. J. Bolin as pastor for an indefinite time at a salary of $900.00 per year. A committee was appointed to secure a new lot and build a new house of worship. They reported in August 1894 that a site had been purchased and a design drawn for a $6000.00 house of worship. On December 5, 1894, the report of the building committee was adopted and the committee discharged. Then a new building committee was appointed consisting of J. W. Cain, S. S. Waterhouse and James Delaney. On October 30, 1895, this committee claimed they had not been able to accomplish anything toward building a new church and asked to be discharged. Rev. Bolin was a good pastor but also strict in discipline and some were turned out for signing petitions for saloons, not paying their debts, drunkenness and unchristian conduct. On January 26, 1896, Rev. W. J. Bolin resigned to take effect March 1, 1896." (Gore *History*)

He was called a "boy preacher" and left to move to Tampa (Talton notes).

The 1894 associational bulletin stated that A. J. Mostler was clerk, the church had 153 members, E. H. Rice was Sunday School superintendent with eighty-five attending, and the value of the church's property was three thousand dollars. Concerning the church's more recent property purchase, Eve Bacon wrote about a grisly discovery: "When workmen were excavating for this building, they found a number of old caskets that had been overlooked when the old Free Church cemetery was moved to Greenwood. Though unidentified, they were also moved to Greenwood" (I, 197).

The 1895 associational bulletin stressed the important role of Christian teachers, but said, "Let us not forget that no teacher can take the place of the parent in the home. Every home should be a nursery of virtue and a school of ethics. God holds each parent responsible for the education of his own child. For the glory of God and the good of our nation, let us see to it that our educational interests do not lag" (14). These words certainly continue to speak to us over one hundred years later.

At the 1895 associational meeting, Bolin preached the missionary sermon from Revelation 3:8: "Behold I set before thee an open door."

M. J. Hull was listed as Sunday School superintendent with 120 pupils and 11 officers and teachers. At some point a library had been established, for it was reported to have three hundred volumes. A. Crossley was WMU representative, and one mission band was reported. The church membership was listed as 155.

J. W. Gillon, 1896. Perhaps because of the debilitating freeze in the winter of 1894–1895 which wiped out most of the citrus industry and dropped Orlando's population from ten thousand to twenty-five hundred, the church postponed its new construction. Finally, however, the new church

J. C. Massee

building was begun: "December 4, 1896, it was voted to build the church auditorium at once and let the Sunday School rooms wait until some future date" (Gore *History*). In other words, the church had to trim its earlier plans.

From the associational report, it appears that the church had a lot of comings and goings with 9 received by baptism, 17 received by letter, 4 excommunicated, 14 dismissed by letter, and 3 deaths. The total membership was reported as 157.

"On February 12, 1896, the church held a prayer service and considered calling a pastor. The names of Rev. J. W. Gillon, J. G. Murray, J. C. Newman and A. S. Tatum were presented and voted upon. Rev. J. W. Gillon was called and began his work on March 1, 1896. The church grew in membership under his pastorate, but on Sunday, November 15, 1896, Rev. Gillon resigned as pastor to take effect, December 20, 1896" (Gore *History*). Gillon had come straight from seminary and went on, later, to serve several leading churches of the South. He was also pastor of First Baptist Church of Shawnee, Oklahoma. The church was without a pastor until J. C. Massee accepted in March of 1897.

J. C. Massee, 1897–1898. "On March 31, 1897, Rev. J. C. Masse [sic] was called as pastor and he entered upon his duties on May 9, 1897. During his pastorate the time for holding the Lord's Supper was changed from quarterly to the first Sunday in each month. He seems to have been pastor when the new church building on the corner of Main and Pine Streets was built and occupied. He resigned in October 1898 and a call was extended to Rev. Claude Raboteau" (Gore *History*).

A white-frame building with a steeple rose in 1897. Ladies held public dinners, ice cream socials, and quilting parties to help buy much-needed church equipment. "April 28, 1897, $1,200 insurance taken out on new church building and windows ordered. There is no record of when the house was accepted but it was probably in September 1897 when Rev. J. C. Masse [sic] was pastor. During that month a new church constitution was drawn up and on September 22, 1897, a vote of thanks was extended to all friends who aided in building the new house of worship. This was a frame building painted white" (Gore *History*). The church was dedicated in September. The associational bulletin for 1897 listed 146 members with 164 in 1898, 16 members being received by baptism, indicating a revival.

From Talton's notes about Massee: "Probably pastor when the building at Pine and Main was occupied. He also pastored at Kissimmee. Later he was pastor of several of the great churches in the Northern Baptist Convention. Then he engaged in general evangelistic work. In 1897 he was Clerk of Wekiwa Association; in 1898 he was speaker at the Pastor's Conference. He returned to hold revivals in 1931 and 1932."

Claude Raboteau, 1898–1900. Raboteau accepted the call and "said he would stay with them as an acting pastor until May 1, 1899. He remained as pastor until February 16, 1900, when he was called to his Heavenly home. He was a good pastor and a fearless preacher beloved by all who came to know him" (Gore *History*). The associational bulletin for 1899 has C. H. Nash as the interim pastor. The bulletin listed 156 members in 1899. The 1900 associational bulletin had a page in memorium for Raboteau. Deacons were W. J. Sears, S. H. Pike, W. C. Nutt, and E. H. Rice.

M. A. Clounts, 1900–1901. Gore wrote that M. A. Clounts was from Saint Petersburg and was called as the regular pastor on May 3, 1900. "He was a good pastor and many joined the church by baptism and letter and the record shows that only a very few were expelled. He resigned in July 1901 to take effect on August 1, 1901, and he moved to Key West."

In 1901, the annual association meeting was held at First Baptist. During one of the meetings, "R. C. Calhoun, principal of the Eatonville Colored Industrial School, was present and was introduced to the Association by the Moderator and made a very able and interesting address to the body on behalf of the school, at the close of which, at the suggestion of the Moderator, a rising vote of interest in his school was taken" (Bulletin 5).

From notes on microfilm concerning WMU, January 6, 1901: "Society met in the church. Devotional exercises were conducted by the President. After reading of the minutes [by the] President, the Vice Pres't. to take the chair. Then Society proceeded to the business of electing officers for coming year. Elections resulted in retaining former officers. The Pres't made very appropriate remarks asking the members to cooperate with her in the work. After a short discussion, decided to postpone the week of prayers. Mrs. Heeffield presented the Society with a beautiful side board cover. To be sold for benefit of Society." On the facing page, "Miss Kimbraugh reported several Bap. people new in the city, asking the sisters to call upon them and extend them help and sympathy where needed." Mrs. J. L. Empie was recording secretary.

A drop of over fifty in church members was recorded from total membership of 178 in 1900 to 122 in 1901. A period of decline was being experienced, or perhaps the church was merely cleaning up its records, for forty-eight were dismissed by erasure. Even so, the church's mortgage was paid off. J. A. Rogers was clerk and E. A. Heffield was Sunday School superintendent.

A. E. Crane, 1902–1905. "The pulpit committee supplied the preaching until January 8, 1902, when Rev. A. E. Crane of Camden, S. C. was called as regular pastor and he entered his duties in February. The church was in good financial condition, having paid off the mortgage during the previous year. The church reports show that during his pastorate all departments were progressing and new members added. No record of any members being expelled. On December 28, 1904, Rev. Crane tendered his resignation to take effect on February 1, 1905, at the end of his three years service as pastor" (Gore *History*).

In the 1903 associational bulletin, a loving memorial for James Delaney was recorded. "Brother James DeLaney, of Orlando, has been called from the church below to the church above" (16). Mission fields were given as Cuba, China, Japan, Africa, Italy, Mexico, and Brazil. Orlando Baptist's WMU had "raised during the year $32.00. This Society is daily growing in love and loyalty for the Master. Donations to Foreign Missions $25.00; Orphanage $2.35; Self-Denial $4.65" (19). The church membership for the years 1902 to 1905 was listed as 129, 127, and 141, respectively. In 1903, Eunice Delaney was Sunday School secretary. In 1904, the Florida Baptist Children's Home was established in Arcadia.

W. A. Nelson, 1905–1907. About W. A. Nelson's years in the pastorate, Gore writes:

> Rev. W. A. Nelson of St. Augustine, Florida, was the next pastor and he arrived on February 22, 1905, taking charge at the mid-week prayer service. He was a great spiritual leader. His sermons were taken strictly from the Bible and sent conviction to the heart of the unconverted. The membership was strengthened and edified. Soon a revival broke out which lasted for the duration of his pastorate. At almost every preaching and prayer service there were baptisms and many joined the church by letter. [The first year of Rev. Nelson's pastorate, the membership increased by forty-seven members.] Rev. Nelson was a man of faith and trusted in his Lord for all things. He would not take a stated salary but only what the church was willing to give. One Saturday night he lacked funds enough to pay his grocery bill so went to the Lord in prayer and on Sunday morning he opened the pulpit Bible and there was a $20.00 bill in it. He offered a prayer of thanksgiving to God and said the Lord had never failed him. In June he received an invitation from a friend in Alaska to come up there and help in the dedication of a newly built Baptist Church, with expenses paid. The church granted him a three months' vacation so he could go and he left on June 26.
>
> During his absence the pulpit was supplied by Rev. J. H. Richardson of Sanford, Rev. Geo. F. Self of DeLand, Rev. L. D. Geiger of Apopka, Missionary N. M. McCall of Havana, Cuba, and Rev. Howard B. Gibbons of DeLand, Florida.
>
> Rev. Nelson was back in the pulpit in October. In March 1906 he asked for a vacation on account of poor health. This was granted to take effect April 1st and lasted until October 7, 1906. Rev. E. Lee Smith filled the pulpit during his absence. May 2, 1906, it was voted to have a pastorium and a building committee authorized to build same. January 2, 1907, they reported it had been built at a cost of $2800.00. May 19, 1907, Rev. Nelson resigned on account of ill health and preached his last sermon June 2nd. He went to Pittsburgh, Pa., to reside." (*History*)

Eve Bacon writes: "Orlando suffered a three month drought in 1905. Dr. W. A. Nelson, pastor of the First Baptist Church, went to the newspapers and announced on the next Thursday morning all faiths were invited to church to pray for rain. His church was jammed to the rafters that morning, and promptly at 4:00 P.M. Orlando had a real downpour of rain. The Reverend Nelson next announced a special meeting to be held the following Thursday, to give thanks for the rain. Ironically, on that day, after plenty of sod-soaking rain, the pews of the church were only half filled" (1, 230). In the associational bulletin, the church recorded 188 members, a jump from 141 the previous year.

In the fall of 1906, the associational meetings were held at the church. The value of the church's property was reported to be $9,500 and the pastor's salary was $986.30. The church membership continued to rise to 218.

An advertisement for the church appeared in the *Daily Reporter-Star*, June 29, 1907: "Church Services— Baptist church. Sunday school at 9:30 A.M. Preaching at 11 A.M. by Rev. H. B. Gibbons from Daytona. B.Y.P.U. at 6:30 P.M. Evening services at 7:30. Public cordially invited to attend."

W. A. Nelson—Courtesy Greater Orlando Baptist Association

During the interim between Nelson and Callaway, the pulpit was filled by the pulpit committee, with Reverend Geiger of Apopka and Reverend Gibbons of Daytona being mentioned. In 1905, J. W. Prentis was both church clerk and Sunday School superintendent. In 1906, D. O. Kinney was clerk and F. M. Baldwin was Sunday School superintendent.

T. F. Callaway, 1907–1911. Gore writes:

> Rev. T. F. Callaway preached on July 7, 1907, and was asked to supply the pulpit for three months. On September 1, 1907, he accepted a call to become the regular pastor. He was a fine Christian young man and soon won the love and esteem of the members of the church. He was the first pastor to occupy the new pastorium. His first work was to hold a revival service assisted by Rev. Earl D. Sims and the result was that eighteen were baptized and several joined by letter. [The membership increased by seventy-one during his first year and by fifty-one the second.] He made regular calls upon the membership and was always ready to go to the help

of any in distress or sickness. He took an active part in the religious activities in Orlando and won the love and esteem of all who came to know him. He resigned on April 16, 1911, to accept a call to the Second Baptist Church of Macon, Ga.

In January 1907, the pastorium east of the church was completed at a cost of $2,800 for lot and building Rev. T. F. Callaway was the first pastor to occupy the pastorium." (*History*)

T. F. Callaway

The associational bulletin for 1907 mentioned Columbia College at Lake City as another fine place for Baptist students to attend. Our church membership was 289.

Henry S. Symonds wrote:

I came to Orlando December 9th, 1908. Our city then had a population of 3500. I was in my teens and was brought up a Methodist. At this time my brother-in-law Rev. F. M. Ross was holding a revival meeting at this church [First Baptist]. Rev. T. F. Callaway was then pastor. The church building then was constructed of wood and stood on the corner of Pine and Main streets. The membership then was about 300. My brother-in-law urged us to attend these meetings which we did and being singers we were invited to sing in the choir, my brother John and wife and myself. The people of the church were so friendly and we liked it so well that we decided to join the church which we very soon did. This was probably late in December 1908 or early in the year of 1909. We were baptized in the baptistery, which was under the floor behind the pulpit, by Rev. Callaway. At this time my brother John was employed as janitor of the church and during our church services on Sunday he pumped the organ by a lever on the organ. Mrs. Stevenson was organist.

For a time, the church again had to depend on the pulpit committee supplying the pulpit services. Some of those in attendance were ministers Cloar of Jacksonville, Geiger of Apopka, S. G. Mullens of Leesburg, and Frank W. Cramer of Cordele, Georgia.

In 1908, the church membership was 340, with 353 in 1909. Also in 1909, a picture in memory of W. A. Nelson appeared in the associational bulletin. The church clerk was S. A. Newell, with W. T. Haizlip holding the Sunday School leadership role. The pastor's salary was $840.

Frank W. Cramer, 1911–1912. "On July 30, 1911, a call was extended to Rev. Frank W. Cramer to become pastor. He accepted and took charge on September 3, 1911. The membership at that time was given as 409. On November 1, 1911, a new covenant and articles of faith were adopted. Rev. Cramer was a good preacher and a fine Christian man but seemed to have come to the church in troublesome times. Two factions sprung up in the church and the pastor was unable to bring them together so on November 24, 1912 he resigned and this was accepted at a business meeting held on December 8, 1912" (Gore *History*).

The Wekiva Baptist Association held its meeting at First Baptist in 1911 with S. A. Newell as clerk. He was also clerk in 1912, with F. N. Boardman as Sunday School superintendent.

Henry S. Symonds wrote, "I well remember driving our horse and wagon through the rain during the rainy season the three miles we lived

Orange Avenue, 1912—Courtesy OCHM

from the church. It took us a good thirty minutes to drive in. One Sunday evening after driving through a very hard rain we were the only ones present except the minister . . . Dr. Cramer. . . . He read from the Bible and gave us a short talk."

The transition between Cramer and Poulson was a turbulent one. Some members thought young men were needed to join the current, and older, deacon members. Others disagreed. Reverend Cramer and his family left for Indianapolis. Supplies were called to preach in the interim. Some of them were Kerr Boyce Tupper, J. B. Jones, C. T. Douglass, and H. B. Fitch.

Tensions were so great that on "February 23, 1913, several members asked for their letters to organize a new church. This was laid on the table and a church council was called on March 4, 1913. This consisted of ten members from the churches of Kissimmee, Sanford, and DeLand. The result was that the minority was given the right to form another church and the First Church was requested to grant their letters in good standing. At a business meeting held on March 5 [the church's forty-second anniversary], the letters were granted and a new church was organized on March 6, 1913, known as the Emanuel Baptist Church with Rev. A. Preston Boyd as pastor." Then on

> April 2, 1913, several members who lived in or near Winter Park, Florida, asked for their letters to organize a Baptist Church in Winter Park. Their request and letters granted on April 9, 1913. At this same meeting Rev. E. T. Poulson of Bluffton, Ind., was requested to hold a series of revival meetings in the church. He arrived on April 27, 1913, and held his first service that evening. He soon won the hearts of the membership and on May 5, was called as their pastor. He accepted to take effect on July 13, 1913. Rev. C. T. Douglass supplied the pulpit until the new pastor arrived upon the field.

> On June 8, 1913, the church voted to do away with the old reed organ and purchase a pipe organ. This was done and on September 10, 1913, the old organ was given to the newly organized Baptist Church in Winter Park. (Gore *History*)

The time of discord and interim pastors and supplies was over. E. T. Poulson would become the First Baptist Church's first pastor to remain for an extended period of time.

CHAPTER FIVE

E. T. Poulson, 1913–1918

"Again, I tell you that if two of you on earth agree about anything you ask for, it will be done for you by my Father in heaven. For where two or three come together in my name, there am I with them."

—*Matthew 18:19–20*

FEAR

AN EPIDEMIC SCARE

"The angel of the Lord encamps around those who fear him, and he delivers them."
Psalm 34:7

W hen Eunice "Miss Nune" Delaney opened the envelope, an announcement from Principal J. W. Simmons fell out. The instructions authorized her to post the notice on her classroom door at Orlando High School banning anyone from entering for a week. Should no outbreaks occur during that time, the school might be allowed to reopen. The year was 1918; the month was October. The town's newspaper, the *Orlando Morning Sentinel*, had faithfully reported the world's death toll each week. The devastating effects of the "Spanish flu" epidemic cut across all social and political boundaries. Added to the misery of their combat during the Great War, some returning military men came home to empty houses, finding their families wiped out from the illness. In addition, military camps in Europe reported hundreds of deaths.

Amazingly, Orlando had suffered no such tragedies. No one could explain the town's exemption, so far, but all were delighted. In contrast, Tampa and Jacksonville reported great losses. Just to be on the safe side, however, Health Officer S. McElroy issued an order closing all schools, churches, theaters, and places where people congregated. They were advised to remain in their homes and not visit other families. Children were asked to remain inside and not play in the streets with their friends.

Miss Nune picked up the newspaper and read the following: "The symptoms in the present pandemic have an acute onset, often very sudden, with bodily weakness and pains in the head, eyes, back and elsewhere in the body" (*Orlando Morning Sentinel*, October 8, 1918). Other signs to watch for were vomiting, dizziness, chills, temperature of 100–104, sweating, loss of appetite, prostration, constipation, and drowsiness. Just reading them made her grip her chair.

As she glanced around her classroom, her eyes fell on the collection bags of peach pits, nut shells, and seeds. Like industrious squirrels, her students had enthusiastically gathered these items to help in the war effort. They were told a mere two hundred peach pits or seven pounds of nut shells would be enough to make carbon for one soldier's gas mask. Now that effort would have to be stopped until the quarantine was lifted.

Stepping outside for a breath of fresh air, she noticed Mayor Giles hurrying down the street. His shoulders seemed weighed down with the many burdens of his various responsibilities. She bowed her head in prayer for his guidance and peace of mind.

Back in the classroom, she took out her roll book to make a few last-minute entries before going home for the forced vacation. She smiled when she saw Elizabeth Yowell's name. As senior class president, Elizabeth was indeed proving an able leader. Guylynn Evans and Mildred Dovell, the other class officers, were also leaders in their class. In the yearbook, Bob Duckworth was described as a "pot boiler." Ruth Hanchett was labeled an "innocent child"—not a bad nickname in Miss Nune's way of thinking. Paul Brewer was named the best sport. His athletic ability did seem to be God-given. Flipping back a few pages, she glanced at the instructors. Coach R. E. Hawes ably led his team of boys, and Bessie Quigg's portrait conveyed her beaming pride in her athletes. She must have been thinking about the past victories of her girls' basketball team. The domestic science class picture and the photograph of the orchestra also brought a smile to Miss Nune. As she closed the book, she realized once again just how much the Lord had blessed her by placing her in this worthy area to spend her life and devote her energies.

While the world would continue to experience plagues and wars, her little town gave her great comfort. On the far wall, the needlepoint of the Lord's Prayer caught her eye as she gently shut her classroom door. She hoped it wouldn't be too long before the ban was lifted and she could continue her ministry of training up young minds to face, unafraid, this world and the one to come.

Ever since its beginning, First Baptist Church had frequently changed pastors. During the early years, it was the custom in most Baptist churches to have an annual call for a pastor. Sometimes the same man would serve for a second or third year, but it was rare for him to remain an extended time. The transient nature of the state's citizens accounted for some of the changes, also. However, when E. T. Poulson became pastor of First Baptist Church in 1913, the tide had turned, and pastors of the church were to remain for a longer period. Beginning with Poulson, First Baptist Church has only had five pastors in the ensuing eighty-three years to 1996.

In Gore's *History* we may read about Poulson:

E. T. Poulson

> Dr. Poulson was a Virginian by birth, a southern gentleman of the old school. He was a splendid Christian and a strong preacher. He had belonged to both southern and northern conventions and understood how to lead his people. He came to Orlando about the time the tourists were beginning to come here and soon filled the little church to overflowing. He decided that the old church had served its purpose and in order to keep up with his fast increasing congregations and the growing city the Baptists needed a new church. He

wanted to unite all the Baptists in Orlando into one body, so invited the pastor and deacons of the Emanuel Church to meet with him and his deacons. The result was that on Sunday morning of October 13, 1913, the members of the Emanuel Church headed by their pastor returned to the fold of the First Church. Rev. Boyd was associate pastor for a few weeks but resigned to enter the government as chaplain of the leper colony at Carville, La.

The church on November 23, 1913, agreed to call a "New Church Rally Meeting" to be held on Wednesday evening, November 26, 1913, to raise money for the new church building. A large and enthusiastic audience was present. Mr. M. O. Overstreet was present and offered to save the church about $10,000 if they would allow him to purchase the material for them. He was made chairman of the building committee although he was not a member of the church. The members of his family were and his heart was in the work and he wanted the Baptists to have a building that was up-to-date and in keeping with the other modern buildings of the city. Subscriptions were requested and $12,205 was pledged for the new church to cost about $40,000. Mr. S. A. Newell was elected Secretary of the Building Committee and Mr. M. O. Overstreet as Bond Trustee of the Church Building Fund. [J. E. Green of Birmingham, Alabama, was the architect and L. C. Townsend of Orlando was the superintendent of construction.] Articles of Incorporation were drawn up and bonds not to exceed $25,000 were ordered issued. The cornerstone of the new church was laid on Wednesday afternoon, October 14, 1914. The names of the pastor, E. T. Poulson and M. O. Overstreet and the date "1914" were placed thereon. The dedication of the new church took place on Sunday, May 30, 1915, with the Rev. B. D. Gray, D. D., L. L. D., of the Home Mission Board of Atlanta, Ga., preaching the dedication sermon. This was an all day service and the church which was built to seat 1200 was filled to its capacity and chairs were brought in so that it was estimated that 1400 people attended the evening service, when the Presbyterian, Methodist and other neighboring Baptist churches united in one great service. Following the dedication service a two weeks revival service was held, the pastor being assisted by Rev. John A. Wray of Miami, Fla. There were many additions to the church from these meetings. The church grew and prospered.

Poulson wrote the following for the church's newsletter, "The Baptist Young People," in the September, 1914 issue:

Christ Enthroned. Some few years ago I heard Dr. A. C. Dixon, now pastor of Spurgeon's Church in London, tell of a young Japanese in New York City, who attended one of the Gospel Missions and was converted to Christianity. He was the son of a wealthy man in Japan, while he himself was a clerk in New York, getting only twenty dollars per month. He wrote home and told his father about his conversion to the Christian faith. The father, pagan like, thought he had brought reproach upon his whole ancestry. He sent the son a special message, telling him that if he would give up that Christian religion and return to the faith of his fathers he would give him fifty thousand dollars with which to begin business for himself. Immediately the son wrote back, saying: 'Father, your message just received, and I thank you; but, Sir, I cannot accept your offer—Jesus Christ is worth more to me than any fifty thousand dollars!' A temptation? It didn't take him three minutes to decide the matter. He had enthroned Christ in his life, and there was no money or power sufficient to take His place.

The *Morning Star* reported in 1914 that Poulson was educated at Richmond College, a southern Baptist school. A doctorate of divinity was conferred on him by Franklin College, Indiana. He was "an eloquent preacher and sermons noted for creativity, unity, simplicity within the grasp of a child. They had accuracy and much thought. He is loved by all his people and held in high esteem by the entire community."

Poulson was invited back in 1925 to help burn the mortgage note. He had left in 1915 and in 1916 was pastoring Pine Castle twice a month.

In 1914, Poulson wrote a one-page entry for the church cornerstone. From the *Evening Reporter Star* on Wednesday, October 14, 1914:

LARGE ASSEMBLAGE WITNESSES EVENT WHICH MARKS EPOCH IN HISTORY OF ORLANDO BAPTISTS. The cornerstone of the First Baptist Church, which is being erected at Pine and Main streets, will be laid at 3:45 this afternoon. . . . The ceremonies will be opened with music by the City Orchestra, followed by invocation by Dr. John W. Stagg, of the Presbyterian church; Scripture reading by Dr. J. E. Wary, pastor of the Methodist church; remarks by Chairman M. O. Overstreet; laying of the stone, following which the address of the occasion will be delivered by Senator Charles A. Carson, of Kissimmee, President of the Florida Baptist State Convention. The benediction will be pronounced by Dr. C. T. Douglas, of Winter Park. Dr. Edward T. Poulson, pastor of the church, will preside over the services, and read the following church history, which will be among the documents sealed within the stone: 'The church was first organized in 1858, A. D., but went down during the Civil War. It was reorganized in 1871, and built a church house on Pine Street, west of the railroad. In 1901 the church built a house on the present lot. On July 27, 1914 the workman began tearing away the old building to make way for this new building, the corner stone of which we lay today, Wednesday, October 14, 1914, with the Masonic Order placing the stone.

Henry S. Symonds wrote, "In 1914 Dr. Poulson was our pastor and we built a new church building which was erected on the same spot as the old wooden church. This was the year Mrs. Symonds and I were married and I was so proud to bring my bride to such a beautiful church. She was a Presbyterian at the time but later became a Baptist and joined with us."

From the *Orange County Citizen* on April 15, 1914: "The Baptist propose to build a fine new church. Their present building, though only a few years old, will be torn down within a few weeks and the new building, represented above, will be erected as speedily as possible. The cost will be about thirty thousand dollars. Dr. Poulson, the pastor in charge, has been very active in getting his people prepared for this great church enterprise." J. E. Green was the architect.

Some names found on "The Cradle Roll of the Orlando Baptist Sabbath School," begun in 1913 and ending in 1920, included Frederick W. Brokaw (b. 1/3/1914), Henry D. Symonds (b. 1/14/1919), Albert Giles (b. 2/5/1913), Dorothy Meadows (b. 2/2/1918), and twins Alton W. Walker and Allene R. Walker (b. 4/1/1914). The 1913 associational bulletin listed R. J. Stevenson as clerk and C. M. Tichenor as Sunday School superintendent, with 275 in Sunday School.

From the 1914 bulletin: "We feel that Sabbath School is the right arm of the church and any Minister of the Gospel will tell you that a good wide awake Sabbath School is half of the work done in his charge." The bulletin continued by discussing the pastors' financial condition:

> Ministers receive less remuneration for their services than do men of any other profession. In a certain Florida town, a fair sample of all others, 5 resident ministers, 5 physicians, and 6 lawyers—equal mental ability and education advantages, except that ministers as a whole received better education advantages. The physician received $4,000 a year salary, the lawyer—$3,800 and the pastor—$850. This is a fair sample of

them all. Yet, the minister is in more demand than the others. He must dress better, his family make a better appearance, his children better behaved, entertain more, give more to charity, attend more functions, visit sick, attend more funerals—and for all he receives nothing. The physicians, undertakers, and grave diggers all present bills.

When he reaches retirement age, he has no place to retire to, and nothing to retire on.

The pastors were then urged to join the association. The WMU president was Mrs. F. W. Topliff. The BYPU president was Eugene Reid. The Ladies Aid president was Mrs. W. M. Davis.

In 1915, the new church building was occupied. It was a Greek-style, cream-colored building with columns at the corner of Pine and Main (now Magnolia). The associational bulletin reported forty-six baptisms and fifty letters, increasing the membership of the church to a significant 494. There was preaching every Sunday and the pastor received a salary of $2000. The value of the pastorium was $6000 and the value of the total church property was placed at $65,000. A church charter was in place.

In 1917, the Florida Baptist Convention was held in the church on January 9–12. From a 1916 church bulletin, the following were listed on the roster: William S. Branch Jr.—organist, Prof. H. S. Pope—choir director, M. E. Weeks—chairman of the deacons, A. B. Johnson—chairman of the trustees, E. H. Allen—superintendent of Sunday School, Eunice Delaney—teacher of Burke Class, Claudia Delaney—teacher of Filth Class, Mrs. George A. Folding—president of the Ladies' Aid Society, Mrs. E. Lee Smith—president of WMS, Alfred Link—president of Senior B. Y. P. U., and Mrs. E. Lee Smith—leader of Junior B. Y. P. U. From Gore: "In December 1917, Dr. Poulson resigned to go to the First Church in St. Petersburg, Florida. He left in January 1918."

For over a year and a half the church was without a full-time pastor. Gore's *History* describes this transition period between Poulson and Adcock: "Rev. Kerr Boyce Tupper, a winter visitor supplied the pulpit during the winter months and was called to supply from October 1, 1918 to June 1, 1919. [At the beginning of his time with the church, the church was ordered closed by the city as a flu epidemic raged in Florida. Rev. Tupper was] a graduate of Mercer University, native of Georgia and at one time pastor of the First Baptist Church in Philadelphia, Pa. He was a brilliant preacher and the new church could not hold the crowds that came to hear him. Dr. Tupper was a teacher of theology and public

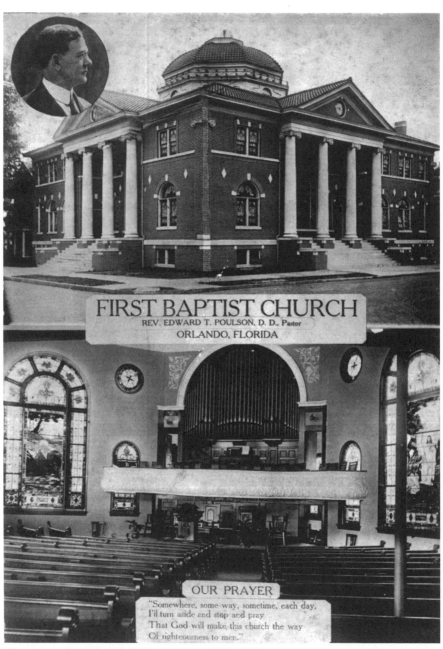

FIRST BAPTIST CHURCH
REV. EDWARD T. POULSON, D. D., Pastor
ORLANDO, FLORIDA

OUR PRAYER

"Somewhere, some way, sometime, each day,
I'll turn aside and stop and pray
That God will make this church the way
Of righteousness to men."

Exterior and interior of third sanctuary, 1915–1961

Men's Bible Class, George W. Fox, teacher

speaking and returned to his college work in June 1919."

In 1918, the church membership was 546; the pastor's salary was $1945.24; and the amount given to state missions was $180.22, home missions $22.52, foreign missions $39.52, and the poor $60. Alfred Link was Sunday School superintendent.

Gore continues: "During his [Tupper's] absence in the summer of 1918, a young Canadian preacher, Rev. Ernest J. Bingham supplied the pulpit and was so well liked that he was called as pastor on September 29, 1918, to begin his duties on June 1, 1919, at the end of the time the church had called Dr. Tupper as supply. Rev. Bingham went to Bradenton to preach during the winter months of 1919 and was taken ill and passed to his Heavenly home."

During Bingham's pastorate, the church held a special patriotic service on July 7, 1918. The following were listed on the military honor roll: Captain Preston Ayres, Frank Boardman, Paul Brewer, Maxie Bennett, Archie Braddock, Palmer Carris, Robert Carter, Harvey Connell, Sinclair Delaney, Roy Ford, J. C. Harrison, Forest Kilgore, Alva Kilgore, Hazel Kilgore, Louis Kilgore, John R. Link, Evans Lucius, Arthur Meadows, Hugh Murphy, James Platt, Charles Rogers, Walter Tucker, Claude White, Sesler Walker, and Roland Weeks. The following verse was also given:

Women's Bible Class, Mrs. F. N. Watkins, teacher

"Pray for these brave men while in this house of prayer, pray for these and brave men everywhere who go forth to fight for Freedom and for Right, Trusting only in their God and in His Holy might."

"Then supplies filled the pulpit again. Rev. J. Dean Adcock of Tallahassee occupied the pulpit one Sunday and he had preached at both services on March 23, 1913, so was not a stranger to the membership. On July 20, 1919, he was extended a call as pastor and accepted to take effect October 1, 1919" (Gore).

Delegates to the association were the J. Dean Adcocks, E. Lee Smith, E. P. Eagerton, R. T. Peel, S. A. Newell, W. H. Brokaw, the O. S. Langs, J. L. Dillard, Mrs. M. E. Limerich, Alfred Link, C. M. Tichenor, the Charles Phillipses, H. S. Symonds, the Topliffs, Mrs. M. O. Overstreet, the Bryans, and Mrs. Wilson. The membership was 461. With the coming of Adcock, once again First Baptist was to have a full-time pastor for an extended period of time.

CHAPTER SIX

J. Dean Adcock, 1919–1937

Shout for joy to the Lord, all the earth. Worship the Lord
with gladness; come before him with joyful songs.
—*Psalm 100:1–2*

FORT GATLIN
MARKER UNVEILED

"He will bring down your high fortified walls and lay them low."
Isaiah 25:12

On Thursday, March 27, 1924, at noon, a light wind blew. Mrs. Charles Tidwell reached for her hat to keep it from flying away. Nearly to the back of the crowd of four hundred, she strained to hear Mrs. F. X. Schuller, founder of the Orlando chapter of the Daughters of the American Revolution, as she introduced Captain B. M. Robinson. Clerk of the circuit court and secretary of the Board of County Commissioners, he was to accept the marker on behalf of Orange County.

The wind continued to blow and lifted the corners of the flag that draped over the granite tablet. She bowed her head as the Reverend C. Stanley Long, dean of St. Luke's Cathedral, pronounced the invocation.

She shifted her position to better see Martha Jernigan Tyler. At eighty-five, the elderly woman looked quite feeble. On this very site where they stood, an invincible fort had once served the area. Mrs. Tyler, in 1849, was the ten-year-old daughter of Orlando pioneer Aaron Jernigan when she lived for a year within the stockade of the fort. Indians had been troubling the area families, so her father had invited others to join him and his family within the fort's protection. The army had vacated the fort in November of that year.

Lifting her voice, Tidwell joined the other four hundred as they sang two verses of "America." The sound filled her heart with pride for this great country and this beautiful spot she called home. She imagined the blood from both white and red men which must have soaked into this very ground. Thankful for more peaceful times, she placed her hand over her heart as a group of Boy Scouts saluted the flag. Next, her little Calvin lifted his instrument for the bugle call. His clear notes thrilled the crowd and made his mother proud.

After several speeches, prayers, and presentations, the two small children, Elinor Estes and Calvin Tidwell, moved to the stage and gently lifted the corners of the Stars and Stripes from the imposing pile of granite. The inscription was read for the benefit of those who were much too far away to see it:

Daughters of American Revolution: Dedication of Fort Gatlin Marker—Courtesy OCHM

Erected By The
Orlando Chapter
D.A.R.
March 27, 1924
Marking the Site of
Fort Gatlin, 1838
Military Outpost

As the crowd dispersed, Tidwell thought about all the changes being made in her growing community. While the marker was all that remained to remind them of a once important fort, construction was going on all around her. The new fire station and public library recently had been built. Evidence of other changes was everywhere. City hall was almost finished and workmen continued to renovate the San Juan Hotel adding on an expansion of 250 rooms to the already imposing structure. As more tourists flocked to central Florida to enjoy the beauty and climate, the little town grew.

She hurried home with young Calvin to prepare dinner for her family. While a look at the past was always interesting and a look at the future was exciting, she had a family to feed in the present. She thanked God for the blessing of allowing her to be alive and living in Orlando.

J. Dean Adcock became pastor in 1919. He was described as a pastor, preacher, singer, evangelist, church builder, and denominational leader. He was also thought to have an "understanding of the Signs of the Times." One of his greatest passions was mission building, and he wanted to be involved in this effort in all parts of Orlando.

Once again, we turn to Gore's *History* for a synopsis of the Adcock years:

J. Dean Adcock

He began at once on a campaign to raise money to pay the church mortgage and in 1920 the mortgage was paid and a special service was held at
which time [former First Baptist Pastor] Rev. E. T. Poulson [currently] of
St. Petersburg came and helped in the mortgage burning service. This was
the second time the church had been out of debt. Rev. Adcock was not
only a good preacher but a splendid singer and often stopped in the
middle of his sermon to sing some song appropriate to his text. He was a
good organizer and the Sunday School grew so large that they wanted to
move the pastor out of the pastorium and use it for Sunday School purposes. $12,000 was borrowed for this purpose. A lot was secured on East
Livingston Avenue and a new pastorium built. $30,000 was ordered bor-
rowed from The Missouri State Life on July 5, 1922, and the large three
story brick Sunday School annex was built on the east side of the church.
Dr. Adcock was missionary minded and wanted to organize missions in
all parts of the city. April 19, 1922, it was voted to establish a mission in the
northeast part of the city. On May 10, 1922, lots at the corner of Mills Street
and Woodward Avenue were ordered purchased. On May 18 workmen
gathered and erected a building in one day. The ladies came and served
them dinner on the grounds. This was known as the North Park Mission
and on September 6 was organized into the North Park Baptist Church
with thirty-four charter members and Rev. M. J. Schultz the first pastor.

Deacon W. P. Miller died on May 10, 1922, and in his will left a building
site for a mission on the Winter Garden Highway. This was exchanged
for a lot in the 2000 block on West Central Avenue and a church known
as the Miller Memorial was built in 1927, with Rev. Walter B. Knight as
its first pastor. Rev. Knight had served for some time as extension
worker for the First Church. In 1923 Dr. Adcock asked the Workers'
Council of the church to appoint a committee for the purpose of orga-
nizing missions in different parts of the city. Messrs. O. S. Lang, W. C.
Appling, S. A. Newell, W. D. Napier and E. H. Gore were appointed.
They began at once to plan the work and on November 4, 1923, organized two missions. The Myrtle Heights Mission on Muriel Avenue in a
tent with Mr. E. C. Turk as Superintendent. The Yancey Mission in a
garage, corner of Hughey and America Streets with Mr. Ernest
Ammerman as Superintendent. The Myrtle Heights tent began to leak
and the mission was moved to a building on Kuhl Avenue. In 1895,
Deacon John Link had given two lots on the corner of Esther and
Osceola streets to the church and a mission building was erected
thereon. The Myrtle Heights Mission was moved into this building and
the name changed to the Link Mission. Later Mr. Link gave two lots on

the corner of Delaney and Esther streets and this mission building was moved to that site. It was remodeled and organized on September 14, 1928, into the Delaney Street Baptist Church with thirty-six charter members and Rev. T. E. Waldrup as pastor. The Yancey Mission was later moved to a building on Atlanta Avenue and then to the corner of Division and Raleigh streets where in 1925 it was organized into the Lucerne Park Baptist Church with Rev. J. Bookhardt as pastor.

Three other missions were organized later. The Palmer Street Mission in a tent corner of Palmer and Mills streets with Mr. Cramer Van Duzor as Superintendent was given up when the tent became weather beaten. The Concord Park Mission was organized in a building on the corner of West Amelia and Revere Streets with Mr. W. C. Appling as Superintendent. This was moved to Edgewater Drive and Yale Avenue and the name changed to College Park Mission with Mr. Paul Anderson as Superintendent. It was organized into the College Park Baptist Church in 1928 with Rev. M. M. Bales as pastor. The Mission known as the Fuller Mission was organized on the Cheney Highway but was later given up.

The Southern Baptists put on a $75,000,000 campaign and the quota for the First Church was set at $16,000 but the church voted to make it $20,000. When the campaign was over the church had exceeded its goal and paid over $25,000.

On December 13, 1933, the property at 130 E. Central was given to the church by Mrs. Louise Williams and was fixed over for the fast growing Sunday School. During the boom of 1925 the church was offered $50,000 for the new parsonage at 63 East Livingston Avenue but refused the offer.

The church had a debt of $42,000 but in March 1934, through the efforts of Dr. Adcock this was reduced to $20,000 and part of this was paid during his pastorate. The church made rapid strides during the pastorate of Dr. Adcock.

The associational bulletin for 1920 records that the association's yearly meeting was held at Orlando Baptist Church. The pastor's salary was cited as $2,875. In 1921, it had increased to $3,575 and the membership had increased to 678. This number went to 934 in 1923. In 1923, First Baptist Church was recognized as having the largest Sunday School in the state.

Henry S. Symonds writes the following:

About 1923 our church was without a choir. I was much troubled about it and went to Dr. Adcock and obtained his permission to start a choir, and after this was announced many of our people who could sing responded and it wasn't long before the choir loft was entirely too small to hold our singers. After several years I felt that something should be done, so I made a proposition to the church that we would move the choir loft to the main floor of the church and I would assume one half of the cost for the entire operation. This proposition was accepted by the church and it was done. Mr. B. J. Lord and I did the planning, and he did all the supervising. This arrangement gave us much more room for our choir and proved to be a good arrangement.

From minutes of the Ladies Aid Society of August 5, 1919: "The Ladies Aid Society of the First Baptist Church held its regular monthly meeting Tuesday August 5, 1919 with 17 members present." The president was Mrs. J. P. Holbrook. Hymn No. 179, "God Will Take Care of You," was sung. Prayer by Mrs. J. Goodwill was offered. Mrs. J. T. Johnson was secretary. Mrs. Irving and Mrs. Coppage were appointed to decorate the church through the month of August, and a committee was to meet with the trustees about getting the pastor's home cleaned and fixed up for Adcock, the new pastor. Several members reported visits to new and sick members. An offering was then taken, which totaled $11.30. Members of this society would quilt and hold rummage sales in order to raise money to finish off the church kitchen. At other times the women discussed book reviews. Another fund-raising helped buy a piano. In records for May 3, 1921, Mrs. Adcock told of a poor family on West Central and asked that the ladies call and see if help could be extended them. On June 6, 1921, the WMU and the Ladies Aid Society met in an all-day session at the church to quilt for the hospital in China. On another date they made children's clothes to help out a busy mother. Still other times, clothing was sent to Europe. Their members also served suppers to YMCA boys.

In 1931, the deacon meeting minutes record some sort of problem with Hugh Wallace, a "former pastor of Miller Memorial causing dissension and leaving town with unpaid debts." A letter about this incident was sent to the Executive Board of the Florida Baptist Convention in Jacksonville.

When Adcock came to Orlando, there was only one Baptist church. First Baptist had a membership of 461. Membership rose to 1,619 by 1934.

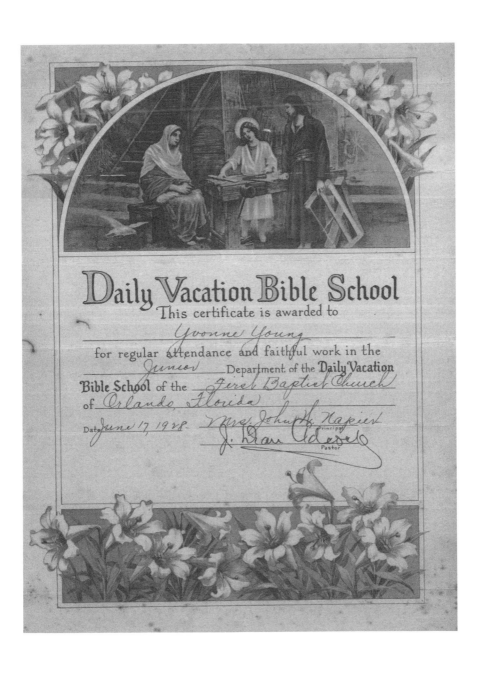

Daily Vacation Bible School
This certificate is awarded to

Yvonne Young

for regular attendance and faithful work in the
Junior Department of the **Daily Vacation**
Bible School of the *First Baptist Church*
of *Orlando, Florida*

Date *June 17, 1928*   *Mrs. John H. Napier*
Principal

J. Dean Adcock
Pastor

Notes by Mildred Talton summarize Adcock and his ministry: "Came from Tallahassee. Was pastor for eighteen years. Quite a singer. A good organizer. Very mission minded. Founded five churches while here as well as supplying at Pine Castle. Attended all sixteen annual assemblies—only man in State to do so. President of Florida Baptist Convention in 1935 and 1937. Paid off mortgage on new sanctuary in 1925. Church in best financial condition of any church in state despite the Depression. Left in 1937 for Fifth Avenue Baptist Church in St. Petersburg. Built new pastorium on E. Livingston for $12,000. Also added a Sunday School Annex in 1922 to take care of the crowds."

Adcock moved into the new pastorium on Livingston. A full orchestra performed from 9:30 to 9:45 each morning under the direction of F. N. Boardman. There was a motto in the church at that time speaking of the good attendance: "Come early if you want a back seat. Better be on time if you want any seat." Visitors during the year included Dr. Prince Burroughs of the Sunday School Board, Dr. B. D. Gray from the Home Mission Board, Dr. Garwood of Stetson University, and Howard Williams, a Christian pilot and editor.

In 1923, a Sunday School training school was given with several prominent names leading: Dr. Sutton of Kissimmee; Rev. William, the state secretary; Tom Gurney; and Dr. Sampey as the Bible lecturer. A missionary pageant was given by the children in March. All were urged to attend Baptist night at the McConnell Tabernacle on April 20th. Adcock went to Kansas City for the Southern Baptist Convention. The state convention was in DeLand in December. The "every member canvas" was held. The Wekiwa Association held its annual meeting in Winter Garden at the new $150,000 church. Adcock reported that our church was well represented with one-third of the membership, one-third of the money given, and one-third of the baptisms of the whole association. Myrtle Heights held a tent meeting in which Adcock shared the pulpit with Pastor Sutton of North Park and E. A. Milton. An annual union Thanksgiving service was held at the Christian Church. Our membership was given as 934.

In 1924, seventy-five men participated in the "every member canvas." Charles Butler, a singer and storyteller, was in the church. Sunday School attendance averaged eight hundred. Over one thousand were enrolled, including Cradle Roll. Six from the church attended the Baptist Organized Bible Class Conference in Atlanta. The Men's Bible Class had 115 of their 175 members attending a banquet at the Angebilt Hotel in February. H. C. Smith from the Baptist Institute in New Orleans spoke at the church, with forty states and two foreign countries represented to hear him.

In March, Sunday School training school was led by Mr. Barnes, Dr. Watts, and Rev. William as teachers, and Dr. Sampey as lecturer. On March 9, it was reported that our Sunday School, with 975 members, was the largest school in the state. Prior to the March 16–April 6 revival given by Len G. Broughton of Jacksonville, the church observed a week of prayer with cottage prayer meetings. During the year, the Seventy-Five Million Campaign was in progress. Adcock went to New Orleans to direct the Baptist Bible Institute. The church secretary gave the following report: Membership last year—934; members received—148; members dismissed—49; membership now—1,031; sermons and addresses—220; conventions and councils—34; calls, sick and pastoral—1,040; funerals—22; marriages—35; financial report balance begins—$754.27; general receipts—15,062.93, general disbursements—14,626.63; building receipts—14,206.85, building disbursements—14,461.03; mission receipts—4,544.16, mission disbursements 4,397.74; benevolent receipts—497.70, benevolent disbursements—494.41; S.W. missions receipts—1,091.83, S. W. missions disbursements—1,080.83; total receipts—$35,403.47, total disbursements—$35,060.64; balance—$1,097.10. One-seventh of the budget went to missions. A junior board was established. The associational bulletin listed J. A. Stinson as church clerk and J. T. Gurney as Sunday School superintendent, with 808 enrolled.

In 1925, the Cooperative Program was begun by the Southern Baptist Convention. The church adopted a new charter. An enlargement campaign was held in April. The Southern Baptist Convention was held in Memphis, Tennessee. On June 11, the annual Sunday School picnic took place at Lakeside Park. Because of poor health, S. A. Newell resigned as church treasurer and went to California for a while. Jewell Davis replaced him. In August, former pastor E. T. Poulson returned to preach, filling both services. The note on the church sanctuary was burned. The WMU gave money for the boys' sleeping porch at the Arcadia Orphanage. They were also busy making surgical dressings for the hospital at Yang Chow, China. J. E. Dillard from Southside Baptist in Birmingham spoke at both services on August 23. A new church constitution was adopted. It was reported that Orlando had three Baptist churches with a total of fourteen hundred members. Mrs. Guy Stapp, the oldest member, died. There was a homecoming revival with evangelist George R. Stain preaching. The associational meeting was held at our church. Adcock had charge of the song service. His salary was $4,500 with church membership of 1,180.

W. D. Napier was Sunday School superintendent with 1,134 enrolled. J. A. Davis was treasurer. Our church hosted the union Thanksgiving service, with Rev. Jenkins of the Methodist church preaching. The choir sang Christmas carols at Eola Park twice during the holidays.

In 1926, our men met at the Presbyterian church to take a religious census of the entire city. Church women served lunch. On April 11, 1926, the following was written: "The fields are white to harvest in Orlando. We have two lots already deeded to this church, the Long and Miller lots, situated on the extreme west and in the northwest of the city. Men's Bible Class has assumed responsibility and raised fully the amount necessary to erect a modest chapel on the Miller lot. Some of the deacons have already indicated their desire to start a fund, if we will rise up immediately, to build a house of worship on the Long lot." One Wednesday evening, our church enthusiastically accepted the generous gift of two lots in Fleming Heights, donated by the Franklin Investment and Realty Company.

In 1927, our WMU organized a similar organization at Miller Memorial. W. D. Napier, Sunday School superintendent, moved to Lake City to assume the duty of the general extension workers of First Baptist there. The WMU held a reception for Napiers. The Men's Bible Class was working toward a goal of two hundred members with Milton Bales as teacher. The men did room-to-room visitation in the hospital and conducted services at the county jail. E. H. Gore was superintendent of juniors, with 158 enrolled. Their motto for the year was "Every member a Christian, every Christian a worker, every worker, trained." Jacob Gartenhaus, our Hebrew evangelist, held a mass meeting. The church's Jewish friends were invited. Our sixteenth annual assembly was held July 12–21. The WMU hired a nurse to work in the nursery on Sunday and Monday afternoons. In October, our Woman's Bible Class attained the Standard—awarded the Certificate of the Organized Class Department of the South, our first Standard Class. In December, we took an offering for the Children's Home in Arcadia.

In 1928, a group from our church canvassed the College Park section of the city with a view of opening Baptist work out there. A Sunday School was being organized with Milton Bales assigned to preach for them. Bobby O'Rork won a prize for being the first to pass the Royal Ambassador (R.A.) test. He received ten days at Ridgecrest at the R.A. Camp. He was the seventh boy in Florida to pass. The Glee Club of Florida State University gave special music one evening for a revival meeting. Lee MacDonald was Sunday School superintendent with 1,294 enrolled.

In 1929, the Men's Bible Class sent $115 to the Baptist orphanage at Arcadia. In February, the church honored the Adcocks' twenty-fifth wedding anniversary with a reception. Their vows were renewed with C. M. Brittain. A reception and shower were given for Inez Crane, who was going as a missionary to Burma, India. She had been baptized in the church in 1914. After attending high school and Stetson, she returned home, where she taught the Fidelis Class for two years. Responding to the call, she volunteered for mission service and left for Louisville to seek training. She sailed for Henzada, Burma, India on August 15. First Baptist hosted the associational meeting. C. M. Tichenor was our church's clerk and G. W. Broyles was Sunday School superintendent. Perhaps in an effort to clear up our records, our church erased 281 former members. The total membership was given as 1,435.

In 1930, the church gave a Graham-Paige car to the Adcocks. The WMU had a speaker from Mount Zion Church who spoke on "How to Help the Negro." On March 10, Pussyfoot Johnson, a famous Prohibition speaker, attended our church. On December 8, Bob Jones gave his famous lecture, "Where We Are Headed," in our auditorium.

On May 3, 1931, one church service each Sunday began to be broadcast over WDBO, paid for by voluntary contributions. Fifty young people of our church finished the BYPU study course. This union had a goal of recruiting two hundred new members. Princess Rahme Haidar of Damascus spoke one evening. The Easter offering went to the purchase of the new hymnals. Adcock attended the Southern Baptist Convention in Birmingham. The Adcocks' daughter was married on June 7.

G. W. Broyles wrote a tribute to Adcock on his pastor's twelfth anniversary, which was printed in a church bulletin dated October 4, 1931: "When I came to Orlando as a winter guest more than eleven years ago I was deeply impressed with the religious zeal of Dr. J. Dean Adcock, but it was not until six years later when I moved my citizenship here and became a member of the First Baptist Church that I learned of the richness of his devotion to the Master. Through these years I have grown fonder of Dr. Adcock, and especially in the last two years through my superintendency of the Bible School have I enjoyed and greatly appreciated his fellowship. He is sound in the Faith and his sermons grow better all the time."

The same bulletin lists the following statistics for 1931: Church membership—1,531; Value Pastorium—$25,000; Church property—$210,000; Bible School Enrollment—2,275. The church had achieved the following mission outgrowth in the previous twelve years: North Park Church,

organized in 1922; Lucerne Park Church, organized in 1925; Miller
Memorial Church, organized in 1927; College Park Church, organized in
1928; and Delaney Street Church, organized in 1928. It supported six ministers in the homeland and five missionaries on the foreign fields: Inez
Crane in India, the W. F. Sharps in Cuba, and the D. F. Stampses in China.
The church clerk was John Bethea and the Sunday School superintendent
was W. R. Smith, with a Sunday School enrollment of 1,136.

The First Baptist Church bulletin from Sunday, January 17, 1932,
included the following information:

> First Baptist Church. Corner Main and Pine Street, East, Orlando,
> Florida. J. Dean Adcock, D. D., Pastor. Residence 63 E. Livingston—
> Telephone 7295. Office hours 10:30 to 12 A.M. Every Day Except
> Thursday. Miss Marg G. Dudley, Church Secretary and Financial
> Secretary . . . We preach Christ crucified, buried, risen, ascended inter-
> ceding and the imminence of His return as our blessed hope. "To all who
> mourn and need comfort, to all who are tired and need rest, to all who
> are friendless and want friendship, to all who are lonely and want com-
> panionship, to all who are homeless and want sheltering love, to all who
> pray and to all who do not but ought, to all who have sinned and need
> a Savior, and to WHOSOEVER WILL come, this church opens wide her
> doors, and in the name of our blessed Lord, whom she seeks to worship
> and exalt says: WELCOME. Church Officiary. G. W. Broyles Bible
> School Superintendent, C. M. Tichenor Church Clerk-Treasurer, Mrs.
> F. F. Bronner as W. M. S. President, William G. Rose B. Y. P. U. Director,
> Miss Mildred Adair Organist, Henry Symonds Choir Director, S. A.
> Newell Chairman of Advisory Board, B. J. Lord Chairman of Board of
> Deacons, G. A. Barker Chairman of Board of Trustees, W. C. Lanier
> Chairman of Board of Ushers, M. C. Weimer House Committee."

Page two of the bulletin announces former First Baptist Church pastor
J. C. Massee, "a Bible Expositor and Pastor Evangelist of Boston," coming
to preach during a revival meeting. Some of his sermon titles were "God
Introduces Himself," "What Would I Do if I Were the Devil," "Why Does
God Let Us Suffer," "The Assault on the American Home," "Is God
Dead?" and "Paint, Lipsticks and Perfume." He had been pastor of First
Baptist Orlando in 1897 and 1898. It must have been wonderful to have
him return here.

In 1932, the church again hosted the association. Adcock gave an
inspiring sermon titled "Go ye therefore," and Mildred Adair gave an

organ recital with the choir singing special music. Massee came back for another revival.

The statistics for 1933 showed the pastor's salary as $3,120, the church clerk as John Bethea, the church membership as 1,560, and Robert Hodges as Sunday School superintendent, with 1,094 enrolled. Our church's property was valued at $210,000, plus a pastorium valued at $25,000. Our total debt was $34,500.

In 1934, the Florida Baptist Convention was held in DeLand and Adcock was elected president. Also that year our adult choir presented the cantata, "The Greatest Gift." A young people's choir was begun by Mrs. Shearouse.

The 1935 associational bulletin reported that Adcock gave an inspirational address at their meeting. Speaking, he drew many lessons from the book of Philippians apropos to the current day of loose thinking and loose living. First Baptist gave the largest amount to the association. The Business Men's Class was paying the salary of Brother Chao in China. The Fidelis Class was helping to support a missionary from Jerusalem. Adcock attended the Southern Baptist Convention in Memphis. Our adult choir presented a cantata called "The Star of Bethlehem."

On February 28, 1936, the deacon meeting minutes record a letter sent to "Sister E. H. Westover for her long and faithful service in preparing and furnishing bread for use of the Church in observing the ordinance of the Lord's supper." Later in that same year, at the July 31 deacons' meeting, they discussed the purchasing of electrical fans for the church. And in September, the deacons recommended giving aid to Sister W. H. Adams for expenses she recently incurred in the illness and death of her husband. The matter was referred to the benevolent committee.

In 1936, the association bulletin had comments on liquor and gambling: "One of the biggest problems in the state is liquor. Liquor is sold in hardware stores, groceries, restaurants, drug stores, where women and children are. Truly the liquor business brings with it an avalanche of suffering, sorrow, regrets, sin, ruined lives, homes and death! Parallel is the gambling craze." It also reported that unemployment was high. William King, missionary to the Seminole Indians, spoke to the WMS. Inez Crane spoke to the Business Women's Circle. Brotherhood had twenty-five members with E. N. Upshaw as president.

In 1937, Adcock attended the Florida State Convention in January in Ocala as its president. Attendance on Easter Sunday was 731. On August 4, 1937, Adcock resigned as pastor, to take effect on October 1, 1937. "He served the church as pastor eighteen years, the longest period of service by any pastor Orlando ever had. He left here to accept the pastorate of the Fifth Avenue Baptist Church in St. Petersburg, Florida" (Gore *History*).

Among his achievements during his pastorate, Mildred Talton, in her "Pertinent Facts About Pastors," lists the following:

> J. Dean Adcock 1919–1937. Full orchestra which played each Sunday morning 9:30–9:45. Established a Jr. Board of Deacons 1925–27. New Constitution adopted. Largest delegation in state to DeLand Assembly 1928. Only man in state to attend all assemblies. R. A.'s re-organized. In 1928, Juniors led in honors at Sunday School Convention in Sanford. Services broadcast 1931. Five Mission Churches begun: North Park 1922, Lucerne Park 1925–1966, Miller Memorial 1927, Delaney Street 1928, College Park 1928. Buildings: S. S. Annex in 1922 where pastorium had been. New pastorium on Livingston. Missionaries: Inez Crane to Burma India, Dr. and Mrs. Stamps to China, and Mrs. W. F. Sharp to Cuba. Other Work: Reduced indebtedness to $13,000. Despite Depression, church was second in state in Mission giving. In the best financial condition of any church in the state. 1919 pastored at Pine Castle. Personal Facts: Educated at Union University and Southern Seminary. Married Frances Rives of Mansfield, La. Was pastor at Mansfield, Burkie, and Leesburg, La., Tallahassee, Orlando, and Fifth Avenue, St. Pete. While singing third stanza of a song in First Baptist Leesville, La. he collapsed and died. Buried in Mansfield, La. Outside Responsibilities: Director of Baptist Bible Institute. President Florida Baptist Convention 1934, 1936. On Cooperative Program Committee SBC 1927. Moderator of Wekiwa Association 1934.

Barbara Kelsey remembers Adcock having thick, wavy hair and a very winsome way with children. Virginia Taylor also remembers admiring his hair, thinking it looked like silk. She recalled that he made many trips to Orange Memorial Hospital. Some pastors would ask for the names of those ill in their denomination. Adcock didn't do that. He asked for the names of anyone who might need a pastor's help or prayers. As she said, "He was always there for you" (interview).

From the *Florida Baptist Witness*, June 1, 1944, as a tribute after Adcock's death, an article was given listing his achievements and then the words: "A Prince in Israel has fallen."

On October 2, 1944, four members of the WMU—Lorena Willox, Jami Appling, Mildred Golden, and Mary Horne—signed a letter of

First Baptist Church Orchestra, 1920, Frank Boardman Sr., director. Back row (l/r): F. A. Asenkamp, C. E. Limpus, unknown, Mrs. McNeil, Ruth Jump, Master McNeil, and George Jump. Middle row (l/r): W. S. Ranch Jr., Gladys Kelly, unknown, and unknown. Front row (l/r): S. E. Limpus, Dr. Frank Boardman, Frank Boardman Sr., and E. H. Westover—Courtesy OCHM

condolence to the Board of Deacons about Adcock: "Gentlemen: The passing of Dr. Adcock left a mark of sorrow on the hearts of all who knew him. He was deeply loved and esteemed by every member of his flock while our pastor. The members of the WMU feel that they would like to have a part in placing some token of love as a memorial to Dr. Adcock in our church building. A committee was appointed to bring this suggestion to the other departments of the church life. After discussing the matter, this committee felt that the movement to place such a memorial in the building should start with the deacons. So the undersigned respectively submit to you this idea. Cordially yours."

Also in 1937, the services of Miss Dudley were recognized. Although our country had been going through a severe depression, our finances were in good order: "During these eight years we have passed through the most painful depression of all, but our church has never failed to pay—nor have we made a new debt. Today we are in the best financial condition of any church in the state." An offering was given to the orphanage on March 28 in the amount of $112.52. Our church was second in the state for gifts to missions—$5,539.78. E. G. Rich was Sunday School superintendent.

For three months T. V. Crawford was the supply pastor from October 3, 1937, to January 5, 1938. The church didn't have to wait long for its next full-time pastor. "On November 10, 1937, the church held a prayer and business meeting and extended a call to Dr. J. Powell Tucker, D. D., of Raleigh, N. C., to become the regular pastor. He accepted and preached his first sermon on January 9, 1938" (Gore *History*).

In 1944, Adcock was honored. The church held Adcock Day. A plaque was presented which reads:

> In loving memory of J. Dean Adcock
> Pastor this church 1919–1937
> A good minister of Jesus Christ who
> illustrated precept by example
> and illuminated truth with life.

CHAPTER SEVEN

J. Powell Tucker, 1938–1956

"I have been crucified with Christ and I no longer live, but Christ lives in me. The life I live in the body, I live by faith in the Son of God, who loved me and gave himself for me."
—*Galatians 2:20*

TUCKER

MAN OF GOD AND FISHERMAN

"As Jesus walked beside the Sea of Galilee, he saw Simon and his brother Andrew casting a net into the lake, for they were fishermen. 'Come, follow me,' Jesus said, 'and I will make you fishers of men.' At once they left their nets and followed him."
Mark 1:16–18

The alarm clock buzzed loudly as George struggled to find it and turn it off. It was one minute past midnight, so technically it was Monday morning, not Sunday. His father never wanted to be "tagged" for fishing on a Sunday. George fumbled in the dark searching for his clothes so as not to wake his younger brother Richard. He met his brother James in the hallway, and they walked to the kitchen where their father awaited them. His mother had fixed a pot of coffee but had returned to bed, not sharing her husband's enthusiasm for fishing. However, occasionally she had been known to accompany the others. She would concentrate on her knitting, but casually wet a line, and in the process catch more than the dedicated fishermen.

Looking out the window, George saw the peach tree from which his mother used to get switches to keep her boys in line. His father preferred a belt. Both of his parents were strong believers in the admonition of not sparing the rod. Now that George was getting older, however, the punishments were more verbal than physical.

"Hurry up, boys," his father said. "Rusty and Miss Gennie [E. G. and Gennivee Rich] just drove up." With that, J. Powell Tucker and his two teenage sons joined the Rich family for the long drive to the east coast. As lights from an occasional car shone into the back seat, young George studied his father's profile. The hair was turning gray, the ears stuck out a little, his body was pencil thin, but his strong character was revealed in his upright bearing. George also noticed his father's ready smile as their eyes met. It was often hard being a "preacher's kid," but he wouldn't want anyone else for a dad. He was proud of his father's many talents, not the least of which was his ability to take time out for his family and enjoy an occasional fishing trip. And oh, how he loved to fish—both kinds—men and trout!

After a short nap, George awoke to the sounds of the Rich's car parking near the shore and the smell of the sharp salt air. Pulling rods, tackle, bait, and lanterns from the car trunk, the group made its way to the bridge, climbed the stairs, and set up the equipment. The bridge was called Mathers Bridge, located where the Indian and Banana rivers came together. On the bridge was the restaurant where they often went for breakfast after a night of fishing. George's stomach rumbled when he saw it, but he knew it wouldn't open for several hours. Light from the lanterns placed on the bridge's wooden handrail pierced the clear water and directed their lines to the vulnerable fish. It didn't take long for Miss Gennie to get a backlash. Tucker actually enjoyed when her line got fouled. He reached for her rod and reel, sat down, and patiently untangled the mess. His laughter broke the silence. Whatever he did, he did it with patience, enthusiasm, and a concentration superior to most other men.

Sometimes they parked at the inlet and waded waist deep in the Indian River. The fish would bump against their legs, but they cast out further for the "really big ones." They caught "whatever was biting" until their buckets were full and the sun was just starting to rise. Then it was time for the next ritual—a trip to the restaurant for a hearty fishermen's breakfast. The aroma drew them to their seats as the waitress almost immediately brought them plates brimming with bacon, eggs, toast, and grits and filled their cups with coffee. George admired the large rattlesnake skins which decorated the walls. Then, happy, sleepy, but somehow refreshed, George walked to the car with the others for the return trip home. His happy home, where his mother and brother waited to hear the fish stories and share the bounty inside the buckets. He could see his father already shifting gears as he removed his fishing hat. The carefree time of fishing for trout was over. It was time to cast a different line. It was time to return to his higher calling as a fisher of men.

Gore declared that J. Powell Tucker preached nothing but the gospel of Jesus. He said Tucker's sermons had no modernistic ring in them but presented the Scripture teaching in a strong and forceful manner. Christians were edified and sinners converted by his preaching. Mildred Talton wrote that "he became known throughout the whole Southern Baptist Convention for his marvelous power with words. Certainly he was a golden-tongued orator who presented the Scriptures in a strong and forceful manner" (notes). Others remembered him as one of the greatest

J. Powell Tucker

pulpiteers, an eloquent preacher, who gave abundant support to world missions. Still others remember him as the consummate fisherman. How he loved to fish. Not wanting to be tagged for fishing on Sunday, he would wait until one minute passed midnight, at 12:01 A.M. Monday, to go on his trips with his sons and friends. His wife didn't share his enthusiasm, but she was described as kind, gracious, warm, and cheerful. She was an example for all wives. The Tuckers had four sons: John Powell Tucker Jr., James Tucker, George Tucker, and Richard Tucker. Susan Tucker is quoted as saying, "I look after our boys, and 'Tuck' looks after everyone else."

Virginia Taylor remembers Tucker's unique way with words. "He could paint a picture with words so that everyone could see" (interview).

The following letter, dated December 4, 1937, from the board of deacons was sent to Tucker prior to his coming as pastor:

> My dear brother,
> In our monthly meeting last night, the Board of Deacons discussed with pleasure the nearness of your coming. We are fondly anticipating your entrance into our midst and our future fellowship. Naturally the question arose as to whether there might not be some special instruction you desire us to have prior to your arrival, or some pre-arrangement you wish us to make. We are anxious to enter into the work freely with you to the end that Christ may be exalted and God glorified. We invite you to be perfectly free to name any request which seems to you for the best interest of the occasion. With personal regards, and praying God's continued blessings upon you and yours, I am, Very sincerely, G. W. Broyles, Secretary, Board of Deacons.

In 1938, the associational bulletin gave Tucker high praise: "Dr. Tucker presented the sermon 'Jesus Christ and Him Crucified.' He swept the audience by mastery of his subject, the obvious sincerity of his soul, the earnestness of his expression, the vehemence of his words, and the perfect equanimity of his bearing [which] have won for him first place among great living preachers of America. In him seem combined the orthodoxy of Spurgeon, the eloquence of Joseph Parker, the simplicity of Dwight L. Moody, and the courage of John the Baptist." At the arrival of Tucker, changes were made in the church's constitution and by-laws. The charter was redrafted with provisions for a board of trustees. It was discovered that the charter which had been adopted in 1925 had not been recorded, so the church was still under the 1915 version. A committee was set up to guard monies on their way to the bank. Missionary activities of the Men's

Class were brought to the attention of the church. Permission was given to the Federal Historical Society to examine the record of our church for information worthy of a place in a church history published by the United States government and furnished to libraries throughout the nation.

Jo Kesler was Tucker's secretary and remembers him as a "great orator," who, during the war, lost one of his sons and "his preaching was never quite the same." She remembers Mrs. Tucker as a pretty woman, active in the WMU, who felt homemaking was her calling. George Shearouse said that Tucker led him to the Lord at age twelve. Jean King related a funny story about Tucker. She and her husband were active in the church before becoming members. The Sunday they came forward to join the church, Tucker became flustered and forgot to have the congregation vote on accepting them (interview).

Tucker had a gift with words, both written and spoken. One of his books was titled *Eternal Involvement*. It was printed by E. J. Daniels, who also wrote the introduction.

From a newspaper article, George Eidson Jr. remembers Tucker as a "slight man with rimless glasses and the fiery delivery of an Old Testament prophet. Dr. Tucker was a marvelous preacher who painted a picture of hell so vivid and terrifying that it kept a whole generation of boys from the wages of sin— not entirely, perhaps, but far enough. Every Sunday, those of us in Mrs. Hart's Junior Department sat with our families in church, and every Sunday Dr. Tucker scared the daylights out of us" (*Sentinel* August 7, 1994). He remembered Tucker as quite a fisherman.

Virginia Taylor, the next-door neighbor to the Tuckers, remembers the family well and especially admired her pastor. When she first lived in Florida, Taylor kept to her family's ritual of being well dressed, never going outside without a hat and gloves. But the longer she lived in Florida, and the hotter the summers seemed to become, the more she longed to go without her shoes. And soon, she did so. Whenever Tucker would come to the door, she would shout, "Wait a minute. Let me find my shoes." He would jokingly respond, "Why bother, I've never seen you with them on unless in church" (interview).

In 1938, J. B. Walker was elected chairman of the deacons. The salaries of the music department were recorded as thirty dollars a month for the church organist and forty dollars a month for the choir director. In 1939, the church clerk was Alex Young and the Sunday School superintendent was E. G. Rich. Director of the BTU was Nelson Axton. Martha Shearouse was choir director, with Pauline Tiller as organist. Betty Shirley was president of the WMU. Membership of the church was given as 1819, Sunday

School membership was recorded as 1,331, and the pastor's salary was $4,200.

During the Sunday worship services of November 19, pledge cards were given. From that bulletin "A Word from the Pastor": "Into your hand today will be placed a blank card, which you are privileged to fill-in for just One Person and for one purpose; for Jesus Christ and to sustain His Word. There is no appeal so heart-searching as this; there is no consideration so intimate and precious and holy as the consideration of what I should do 'For Jesus' Sake.'

"Whether you are able to pledge much or little, may it be done as unto the Lord, and when you depart from this Service today, may you have in your heart the joyful abiding consciousness that you have done your best for Christ."

From the associational bulletin, E. J. Daniels reported on Baptist literature: "rotten literature is flooding the land" and cautioned, lest we forget, that people "do what they read," saying not only is the country flooded with bad secular literature but also with false religious literature, which is "about as free as water and extremely damaging." Churches in the Wekiwa Association "baptized only 360 persons during the year. We need a revival. We seldom have over half our membership in Sunday School, very few come to prayer meeting, about one third of our members do absolutely nothing for the churches! We need a revival of zeal for the lost! We need a revival of love and respect for God's way and God's House. We need a revival of spirit and practice of prayer."

In 1940, E. G. Rich resigned as Sunday School superintendent because of ill health. He was replaced by Alex Young. The church clerk was P. L. Woodward, and BTU director was Nelson Axton. The church voted to install a six-point record system in Sunday School. Doug Aldrich won first place in a Better Speaker's contest. He would represent Florida at Ridgecrest. First Baptist Church participated with other churches in a Christmas parade.

In 1941, First Baptist endorsed the Boy Scout movement and established a troop. The mortgage was paid off in October, and the church was free of indebtedness. Phyllis Sokel, a converted Jew from Austria, spoke at a special service for Jews in Orlando. The church clerk was Roger Barber; Mrs. George Swain was WMU president; and S. A. Newell was chairman of the deacons.

In 1942, the church appointed S. A. Newell, E. H. Gore, and Eunice Delaney to gather a history of the church. This was finished in 1945 and was available to the church body. Also in 1942, Inez Crane came home on furlough because of danger in Burma. Soldiers were presented with New Testaments. There were radio broadcasts of two services a month at a cost of thirty-five dollars each. A communion service was given to Conway. There were twenty-nine registered Boy Scouts in the church. The June 8 deacons' meeting minutes recorded, "A plan for forming transportation groups in various sections of the city for the purpose of assisting people in getting to church because of gas and tire restrictions was offered by Dr. Tucker." Summer camps for R.A.s, G.A.s, and YWAs were enjoyed at Camp Wewa. The Delaney Sunday School Class celebrated its twenty-second anniversary. Because of gas and tire rationing, the Wekiwa Association meeting was reduced to one day; it was held at North Park Baptist. The Sunday School superintendent was J. B. Walker; the church clerk was Sprugeon Gage; the BTU leader was A. G. Graham; and the WMU president was Mrs. George Swain. Church membership had grown to 2,145.

During the first six years of Tucker's pastorate, the membership of the church grew to over twenty-two hundred with many improvements being made. For the third time in its history the church was out of debt. The Sunday School grew so quickly, with a membership of over twelve hundred, that it outgrew its building and some classes had to move to the Williams property.

On March 3, 1943, the church voted to purchase the property east of the Sunday School building for eighteen thousand dollars. This added eighty feet of frontage on Pine Street to the church property; a large three-story building known as Duke Hall Annex was acquired. The church membership was numbered at 2,230, and the pastor's salary was listed as $4,800. Our church gave Miller Memorial fifty dollars to enable them to retire their outstanding indebtedness.

In 1944, our church gave Holden Heights a communion tray. Also in 1944, the board of deacons included E. G. Rich, chairman; Spurgeon Gage, vice-chairman; Paul Anderson; W. C. Appling; A. L. Batts; D. H. Darnold; D. E. Denson; John W. Elliott; A. G. Graham; J. C. Haley; Claude G. Hunter; Eugene W. Kelsey; J. G. Manuel; N. B. McGuffey; S. A. Newell; J. D. Peck; W. D. Shupe; J. A. Stinson; Henry S. Symonds; Judson B. Walker; Alex E. Young; and G. R. Swift, deacon emeritus.

The Board of Trustees included George A. Barker, chairman; S. A. Newell; J. C. Haley; W. M. Davis; M. C. Weimer; and W. K. Price Sr. For the first time, the church had the position of church hostess with Leona Swain filling that role.

For the Bible School, Judson B. Walker was the general superintendent; J. B. Bookhardt was the assistant general superintendent; Myron Guymon was the general secretary; T. D. McGraw was the treasurer; and L. R. Pigford was the assistant treasurer. A. G. Graham was the director of the Training Union, with N. B. McGuffey as assistant director, and Roy T. Kesler as general secretary. Mrs. R. M. Martin was president of the WMS, with Mrs. J. S. Lipthrott secretary and Mrs. T. D. McGraw as chairman of the Business Women's Circle. Inez Crane was the church's missionary to Toungoo, Burma, India. On October 1, Mrs. Shearouse resigned as choir director, and Henry Symonds, a former director, was chosen to direct the music.

During World War II, over 150 of the church's young men, three of them Tucker's own sons, left to fight. His son John Powell Junior (called "Powell") died in the war. Perhaps prompted by this loss, Tucker took a special interest in young people and held an open forum every Sunday evening after church services when servicemen and young people of the church met together and discussed religious questions. This was led by a young person of the church, with Tucker standing by to help them understand the truth as taught by the Scriptures (Gore *History*). George Tucker, the pastor's son, recalled that his brother was killed at the Battle of the Bulge. He was a Thunderbolt pilot of a P47. George spoke about his father with much pride and admiration. He remembered his father suffered from poor health, having had polio as a child and also scarlet fever, but that didn't stop him from running rings around most other men when it came to yard work or preaching. Later in life he shook with Parkinson's, but his voice remained strong and vibrant (interview).

In 1944, former pastor J. Dean Adcock returned to the church for a ceremony called "Adcock Day." In the Sunday bulletin for that day, February 27, 1944, Tucker wrote the following:

> It is a matter of great personal joy to me to have Dr. Adcock with us today. From the very beginning of my work here as Pastor, he has never failed to manifest every possible interest in me and in my ministry. He has blessed me time and again with gracious words of encouragement and our hearts have been united in strong bonds of personal friendship and love.
>
> In a ministry that was distinguished for splendid achievements—in his proclamation of the Gospel, in his unfailing allegiance to the truth and authority of the Word of God, in his unselfish devotion to the cause of our Lord in this church and community—Dr. Adcock laid a firm foundation for his successors to build upon. We are profoundly grateful for

the abiding inspiration of his noble influence, his personal consecration and his successful leadership.

With sincere personal admiration and affection I welcome him to this service, and find unlimited joy in assuring him that this "Adcock Day" is intended to convey to him the highest and most loving expression of our united honor and esteem.

From that same bulletin, the WMU had an item about their program the next day with Alice Price speaking: "A treat is in store for all who attend. Miss Alice Price, Associational Young People's Leader, and an outstanding personality in our church, will be the principal speaker." March birthdays for servicemen were listed: Albert Carroll, Aubine Batts Jr., Howard Thomas, Allen Haley Jr., C. L. Bruce, Robert Ivey, Maurice Linton, and Eddy Ekdahl.

Also during 1944, the baptistry and choir loft were rebuilt. A canvas designed by Rose Cox became a backdrop for the baptistry. In a church bulletin was the following anonymous poem:

We can only see a little of the ocean,
Just a few miles distant from the rocky shore,
But out there—far beyond our eyes' horizon,
There's more—immeasurably more.

We can only see a little of God's love
A few rich treasures from His mighty store;
But out there—far beyond our eyes' horizon,
There's more—immeasurably more.

In 1945, the history of our church was published. The church library was begun. Henry Symonds was elected choir director for the rest of the year. In May a "Temple Builder's Club" was begun to raise money for the new educational building. From deacon meeting minutes of May 7 is the following: "Dr. Tucker mentioned that a member of the church was operating a beer and liquor place. In discussion it was brought out that it was understood the place was formerly operated by her husband who had died and the lady continued to operate the place. Discussion. Moved by Manuel, seconded by Walker, and carried that the Chairman appoint a committee of two to call on the lady prayerfully and see what could be done." Our church gave fifteen thousand dollars to the Cooperative

McGuffeys and Kelseys

Program and missions. In December there was a fire in the Junior Department of the Sunday School. The adult choir presented "The Story of Christmas." The president of the WMU was Mrs. R. M. Martin.

The mid-1940s was a time of much church activity. Josephine Kesler wrote a letter to the pastor detailing the many monthly scheduled dinners, luncheons, and suppers, citing WMU covered-dish luncheon, church night supper, Young Matron's Circle luncheon, Business Women's covered-dish supper, Young Business Women's covered-dish supper, Delaney Class covered-dish luncheon, Women's Bible Class covered-dish luncheon, Alathean Class luncheon and party, BTU covered-dish supper, YWA meeting and refreshments, and Young Adult Department meeting and refreshments. This confirms the belief that Baptists like to eat together. June Dobson remembered that when she and Howard returned to Orlando they joined the first mixed class, called the Golden Circle. Mrs. Swaidmark was their teacher. Barbara Kelsey's father, Ben McGuffey, was the Sunday School superintendent.

In 1946, our church donated one hundred dollars to the Florida Industrial College. We also gave twenty thousand dollars to missions for the year. A permanent Visual Aids Committee was set up. A Building Committee was appointed for the educational building. It included J. B. Walker, W. D. Shupe, E. G. Rich, J. C. Haley, and A. G. Graham. The WMU report in the Book of Reports for October 1, 1945, to September 30, 1946, gave the following information: Mrs. E. G. Rich was president. Exactly $1,416.98 was given to the Cooperative Program through church envelopes and circles. Gifts to special projects, such as charity, relief and rehabilitation, special offerings, Stetson University, Arcadia, Training School, Emergency Home, BSU, Margaret Fund Student—$2,253.05. Special mission gifts (Lottie Moon, Annie Armstrong)—$993.86. Contacts through flowers, trays, visits, cards, phone calls, letters, magazines, and tracts—2,750. Other services: community mission work, garments to the needy (485), Red Cross work, jail services (7), visits to T. B. Sanitarium (18), visits to County Home (9), day nursery, Indians, clothing sent to Europe (8 boxes). The number of members who were enrolled was 184. Number of tithers was 86.

M. G. Manuel headed a committee which kept up with the service personnel and in 1946 presented to the church *A Roll Book of Honor*, which was beautifully inscribed by Nancy New. The roll contained the names of all the men and women who were engaged in the war. During the war, the church flew a service flag, which was lowered on May 25, 1947. A memorial plaque for the seven who gave their lives for their country was presented by the Gold Star mothers and fathers at this service. This plaque states: "1941—World War II—1945 Doyle H. Darnold, Jr.; Marion Clark Phillips; Conoly Guice Anderson; John Powell Tucker, Jr.; William C. Mashburn; Robert Paul Harrell; Thomas Stansel Griffin. Dying for the cause of liberty, light, and truth, they did not die! They live forever in the sacred esteem and the grateful memory of their countrymen. To them this tablet is affectionately dedicated by their parents. 'Greater love hath no man than this.'"

In 1947, the church sent the Tuckers to Copenhagen, Denmark, for the Baptist World Alliance in July and August. Also in 1947, a fund to help members of the church dedicated to full-time Christian service was begun. The initial gift was one thousand dollars given by the E. R. Gertners. From the 1946–1947 Book of Reports: "This year, through the generosity of Mr. and Mrs. E. R. Gertner, an Education Foundation was started whereby young people in our Church who are planning to enter full time religious work can secure aid if needed for their education. This is indeed a worthy project and one that bears the support of every member of our church." Other contributions were added through the years.

In 1947, First Baptist Orlando was second in the state in gifts to missions. The church voted to pay for the salary of missionary nurse

Mary Evelyn Fredenburg for the first three years. She went to Nigeria. Also our church loaned Holden Heights five thousand dollars to help with their building. Sunday School superintendent was D. E. Denson with an enrollment of 1635. The building committee for the educational building added some new members: D. E. Denson, James Keith, W. K. Price Sr., E. W. Kelsey II, Mrs. Mabel Cloud, D. H. Darnold, Charles W. Maywald, and E. R. Gertner.

On February 25, 1947, Marshall C. Dendy, pastor of the First Presbyterian Church in Orlando, sent the following letter to Tucker:

> My dear Dr. Tucker, I believe I am correct in saying the First Baptist Church has made an appropriation for the teaching of the Bible in the public schools for the year 1946–47. We are coming to the close of our year and we are in need of the funds that were anticipated for this work.
>
> We would be so glad for the treasurer of your church to forward whatever amount your church wishes to give to Mr. Paul Kuhns, treasurer. Let me assure you that the support of your people is greatly appreciated.
>
> We have been pleased to have more than 1500 boys and girls in our elementary and high school studying the Bible under consecrated and competent teachers. Sincerely your friend and fellow-pastor. (Deacons' minutes)

On March 3, 1947, the deacons minutes, in part, have the following: "Bro. George Barker was present and in behalf of the Board of Trustees, reported he had contacted Miss O'Neal regarding the prospective purchase of Duke Hall, adjacent on the east to our property, and was assured by her that when she was ready to sell she would give our church the refusal of same. Bro. Barker said he was under the impression we could probably purchase the property for about the same price and same terms the Duke Hall Annex was purchased."

At the end of the deacons minutes for May 5, 1947, the following entry: "The meeting adjourned at 9:25 with prayer led by Bro. Kelsey, remembering those on beds of affliction and special intercessory prayers were uttered for the recovery of Miss Roberta Haley, who is the daughter of Mr. and Mrs. R. U. Haley."

At the beginning of the deacons minutes for July 7, 1947: "Brother Arthur Newell presented two matters to the board for consideration. First, the Gideons requested an opportunity to present their story to the church, either some Sunday evening or Wednesday prayer meeting. Second, the Christian Business Men's Committee requested the use of the church for two weeks, during a six weeks conference of the Moody Bible Institute, the last two weeks of February from the 15th through the 29th, 1948."

In the days before air-conditioning, paper fans were often distributed to the church. "Moved by Coram, seconded by Gertner that we accept the fans from Carey Hand Funeral Home, which will contain a picture of the church on the front side. Motion carried" (deacons minutes July 7, 1947). And later at the same meeting: "Regarding the presence of mosquitoes in the auditorium, Bro. Coram will contact Mr. Culpepper of the USDA to obtain an effective spray for their extermination."

Virginia Taylor related a funny story about Tucker and those fans: "Oh, the old sanctuary could get hot,

Virginia Taylor

especially on Sunday night services. One night some of the women seated up front were really sweating and fanning furiously. Dr. Tucker interrupted his sermon to say, 'Now, ladies I'm going to have to stop my preaching if you don't stop using those fans. All that motion is making me dizzy.' The ladies quickly stopped" (interview).

During the Tucker years, two men were made deacons emeritus: J. C. Haley and S. A. Newell. Several men were also ordained into the ministry: Herbert Kirk and John M. Tubbs in 1945, Maurice Taylor in 1946, James Rankin in 1948, George Stephens in 1953, and Paul Wrenn Jr. in 1955. Two young ladies went out as missionaries: Mary Evelyn Fredenburg as a nurse to Iwo, Nigeria, in 1947, and Alice Price Gaventa went with her husband to Nigeria in 1949.

In 1948, the clerk was R. G. Summers. Our church's membership was twenty-five hundred with 1806 in Sunday School. From deacons minutes for January 14: "The meeting opened in prayer by Brother Walker. Bro. Durrance brought a recommendation from the committee appointed to recommend an assistant pastor, that Rev. C. C. Kiser Jr. present pastor of the Baptist Church in Palmetto, Fla. be employed as assistant pastor at a salary of $4,500 per year. It was mentioned that at present he is getting a salary of $3,600 and the use of the pastorium. Dr. Tucker expressed himself favorable to calling Bro. Kiser. Considerable discussion ensued and the matter was deferred temporarily until a report was received from the Trustees, regarding the Duke Hall property."

From minutes of the March 8, 1948 deacons' meeting: "Bro. Denson reported that the Boy Scouts have 24 enrolled and Scoutmaster Eugene Kelsey III is doing a good job. The windows of the scout cabin have been shuttered to prevent further breakage [vandals had broken them]. An acknowledgement of a package received from CARE was read from Mrs. Maddment in England." Deacons minutes for April 5, 1948: "Dr. Tucker also spoke of the immoral situation in this county and again stressed careful weighing of candidates for office in order to put Christian men in these offices. The prayers and support of all Christian people are needed."

For some time, the church hired musicians to perform in the church. The May 3, 1948, deacons minutes record: "Bro. Henry Symonds, Musical Director, presented to the Board the need of an additional $400 to maintain the musical program for the balance of the church year. This amount is needed to pay the special talent and will enable the church to hold them intact during the summer." Also in the same minutes: "Bro. Walker mentioned that considerable dissension has arisen regarding teaching the Bible in the schools, since the recent Supreme Court decision, and that the teaching of the Bible in the schools will end with the present school term." That was certainly a sad day for America.

The Sunday, October 10, 1948, bulletin gave the following suggestion for silence upon entering the sanctuary: "Keep silence, friend, for some have come—To cast their care on God today; And some to praise from thankful hearts—And some 'Thy Kingdom come' to pray. Keep Silence; let Him speak anew—To every heart—perhaps to you."

W. A. Criswell, pastor of First Baptist Church, Dallas, Texas wrote the following letter to Tucker on July 26, 1949:

Dear Dr. Tucker: You cannot know with what eagerness I would look forward to being with you in a revival meeting. I simply fell in love with the wonderful people who represented you and your glorious church at

Ridgecrest. One marvelous thing about them is that they love you so much and are so proud of the work you are doing in the church and what the church is doing for the Kingdom of Christ.

It may be a long time before I could come and be with you in a revival meeting. There is a possibility, however, that I might be able to come in February of next year. If I have a cancellation concerning that date, I shall write you of it immediately. If you are, then, able to place it in your calendar fine, if not, we shall seek a place in the years that lie ahead.

God bless you ever in the wonderful work you are doing. Prayerfully yours.

On April 28, 1949, Child Evangelism Fellowship sent a letter to the church commending it on its contribution to their cause and saying in part:

You will be glad to know that in the first year of operation, using only volunteer workers, we have maintained eleven weekly Good News Clubs, in which over 600 different children have heard the stories from God's Word. Over 100 of those boys and girls have made the decision to accept Christ as Savior, for which we praise God.

It would be of great help in this work if the funds set aside for it in your budget could be mailed to our treasurer, Mrs. E. J. Pace, at this time. We are undertaking to give each child a suitable award at the close of the school term, and are also planning Vacation Bible Schools for areas where no churches are able to carry them on. . . . Yours in His service, Vivian E. Pain, Director.

Winston Smith was Sunday School superintendent in 1949, and Gene Kelsey III was church clerk. BTU leader was R. G. Summers. The Sunday, October 16, 1949, bulletin gave the following proposed budget for the fiscal year 1949–1950: salaries and wages—$21,250, operating expenses of buildings, equipment, and grounds—$4,945, general supplies and expenses—$6,955, special activities—$4,725, and other items—$1,775. Total anticipated general fund expense—$39,650. Building and expansion reserve fund—$16,005. Missions and Cooperative Program—$19,825. Grand total—$75,480. At Christmastime, First Baptist Church held the first churchwide pageant at the Coliseum.

On January 27, 1950, a grisly discovery was made: "S. B. Collier points to the metal casket unearthed in excavation work behind the Baptist Church yesterday while workmen were preparing foundations for the $165,000 addition to the church. Crowds started gathering soon after the casket was discovered. Orlando old-timers recalled the site was once a cemetery before Greenwood Cemetery was established. It had been thought that all of the bodies had been removed. The casket was believed to have occupied an unmarked, unrecorded grave" (*Morning Sentinel*, January 28, 1950). Over forty years later, another casket was discovered when Downtown Baptist did work on an elevator. The first educational building was completed at a cost of $165,000 and dedicated on September 24. Our church gave one thousand dollars to Lake Hill Baptist Church at Orlo Vista to help with their building program. The salary of our pastor was raised to six thousand dollars.

In 1951, a house on East Amelia was purchased for the assistant pastor C. Cleveland Kiser Jr. Later this home was occupied by the Hansens and then the Ireys. The association was provided office space in our church. A new and improved telephone system was installed. Six thousand dollars from the sale of two lots was used to reduce the mortgage indebtedness of the church. The church gave $1000 to Forest Park, $500 to New England Heights, and $231 to Fairview Shores. Our Training Union was led by R. G. Summers, and the church clerk was R. L. Marrero. The church bulletins, for the first time, had covers in color.

The church celebrated Christian Home Week in May 1951. The April 22 bulletin commented on this special time.

> God is concerned that every home be a Christian home. His command is recorded in the sixth chapter of Deuteronomy, wherein He shows a pattern for a home. A part of the responsibility for building and strengthening Christian home has been placed upon the church. Read carefully the command of Jesus as recorded in Matthew 28:19, 20. Notice particularly these words, "Teaching them to observe all things whatsoever I have commanded you." Does "all things whatsoever I have commanded you" include teaching parents to do diligently and regularly what is commanded in the sixth chapter of Deuteronomy?
>
> The observance of Christian Home Week is a brief step, not more than a step, toward the desired goal, "A Christian home for every child." Our church is taking the opportunity of placing special emphasis on Christian

homes, their relationship to the Church, the dedications of homes, family devotions, and the enlistment of entire families in all the services of the Church, during the week of May 6–13. Prayerful preparation is being made for Christian Home Week. We urge that you place it on your prayer calendar asking for God's leadership and guidance that many homes may be brought into proper relationship with Him and His church.

From deacons minutes on June 1, 1951: "Bro. Jack Ramsey appeared in behalf of the softball team of the church. He reported on the activities of the group, including the spiritual work of the team members. He requested that the church procure uniforms for fifteen team members and requested $200 for that purpose." And within the same minutes: "Bro. McGuffey brought up the subject of the noise in the streets during worship services and suggested that 'Quiet' signs be placed on the streets during the hours of services. It was moved by Perry, duly seconded and carried, that Bro. McGuffey, as chairman of the committee, contact the other churches affected and see if the cooperation of the City can be obtained to abate the street noises during the hours of worship. Bro. McGuffey asked that the pastor and chairman of the Board of Deacons work with him on this matter."

Also in 1951 during the associational meeting, V. N. Maggard, from the Resolutions Committee, made the following report for the association's bulletin: "Inasmuch as the Baptist churches of this association are [having] a very aggravated problem of infiltration and influence of a nondenominational character, that has brought conflicting teachings, and which creates division and weakens our Baptist program . . . therefore be it resolved . . . [that we] put on a vigorous program of teaching."

At the December 1951 deacons' meeting:

Bro. Bond reported that our janitor, Bro. Witsil, who has served the church faithfully, is now suffering from a double hernia and in great need of surgical repair of this disability, and financial assistance to accomplish the same. It was moved by Bro. Elliott, duly seconded and carried, that the cost of such operation and hospitalization be paid by the church from the Avera Fund; that Bro. Witsil be given a leave of absence with pay of one month for that purpose; and that a committee be appointed to take care of the matter. Thereupon the chairman appointed Bros. E. R. Gertner and Gordon Talton and Dr. Tucker to work with the House Committee in taking care of this situation.

Also, at the same meeting: "Bro. Anderson presented the suggestion of Mrs. Elmer Jones of the local Welfare Board concerning a family of fourteen who are now living in a one room lean-to. It was further reported that the father of this family is trying to build a block house, but is without sufficient funds. Bro. Anderson volunteered to personally investigate the matter and thereupon moved that subject to his investigation the sum of $100 be allocated from the benevolent fund of the church to assist this family. The motion was duly seconded and carried."

In 1952, Southern Baptist seminaries had the following enrollments: Southern—1,039, Southwestern—2,074, New Orleans—730, Golden Gate—238, and Southeastern—102. Sixteen hundred dollars was given by our church to reduce Killarney's indebtedness. The church league had a championship softball team. The associational Resolutions Committee asked that we recognize Wekiva Youth Camp at Rock Springs under the direction of WMS's Mrs. W. J. Garnett. Our Sunday School superintendent was C. A. West with 1961 enrolled. Our WMS was led by Mrs. W. Martin. Our church's pastorium was sold and a new one was built at 1609 South Summerlin.

The February 4, 1952, deacons minutes reported the church's insurance adjuster's offering the church $548.52 in settlement of the burglarized church safe. A new safe was ordered to be purchased. At the August 4, 1952, deacons' meeting: "Bro. Chiles brought a report on progress of the work at Fairvilla Trailer Park with special reference to the equipment furnished by this church on loan, namely, 50 chairs and a number of children's pews. It was moved by E. W. Kelsey, Jr., seconded by Earl Clay, and carried, that this equipment be sold to the Fairvilla congregation for $1.00."

In 1953, another mission was begun. A committee was charged to raise ten thousand dollars by personal subscription for the construction of a building at Pine Hills. A lot at Alhambra and Deauville Drive was given, and the chapel was completed by 1954. V. N. Maggard was called as the pastor for Pine Hills in 1955. One hundred nine members were transferred from our church. Our church's enrollment was 3,205. Tucker's salary was given as $6,600. There were 2,123 enrolled in Sunday School. Dorothy Aly won the Better Speaker's Tournament. W. A. Criswell of Dallas held a revival meeting. The April 12 bulletin announced Youth Week with scores of young people taking part. Jerry Denson was indicated as serving as youth pastor, and his picture was on the cover of the bulletin along with Ken Baskin, Eleanor Clark, Marie Williams, Frances Denson, Bill Jones, Shirley Drake, Dave Frech, Evelyn Brown, Brent Arterburn, and Sylvia Britt.

The youth held a retreat at Camp Joy. Gaines S. Dobbins and E. J. Daniels spoke in church. There was a mothers/daughters banquet in May. The first G. A. Coronation service was held with Travis Plummer as the Queen. Our church clerk was Russell Dobson.

In 1954 at the associational meeting, Tucker gave a sermon and the bulletin stated that "he was at his best." Mrs. Garnett reported on the youth camp, and it was at this time it was first called "Camp Joy" (Bob Hodges was legal council for the church and helped in getting this camp). One thousand dollars was pledged for improvements to the camp. Joe Slade placed first in Better Speaker's contest. There was a ground-breaking for Pine Hills on June 6. A drama, "A Letter to Mother," written by Tucker was put on during Mother's Day. Tucker was very gifted in writing as well as speaking. Our church membership was 3,201.

Also in 1954, a committee began raising funds for the construction of a second educational unit. Unfortunately, there was also trouble within the church. Growing pains were being experienced in other areas. The program of the church enlarged until the pastor could not carry it along with part-time and voluntary help. The need of a full-time church hostess was felt. The advantages of a comprehensive music program were seen. The demands of the youth were increasing. From 1944 on, various combinations of help were tried: pastor's assistant, promotional director, music director, and youth director—but the church did not progress as it should. As early as 1948, an adverse wind of dissension began to blow. Two factions sprang up: those who wished to hold to the traditional patterns and those who felt the need to expand to meet the enlarged needs of the community. Because of this unrest, there was a rapid turnover of church staff. The need for a new pastor was keenly felt by some. Personalities became involved as the differences grew until the chairman of the Board of Deacons was formally unseated in a business meeting. A deacon brought suit against the church. Virginia Taylor remembers, "The case went to the Supreme Court in Tallahassee. Bob Hodges represented the church. Chief Justice B. K. Roberts said, 'Gentlemen, I have studied your brief. The only real democratic body left is a Baptist church. They can fire, they can hire, and they can throw out members, and we want to keep it that way!' With that he banged his gavel and said, 'Case dismissed!'"

From notes by Talton:

In reality, very few members were actually involved. The disagreement was in the methods used rather than the ends desired; however, the repercussions made it impossible to fully harness the great energy and talent of the church. It was a distressing time.

Despite our human frailties, the Lord continued to bless us. Crowds were so large that Youth Church was begun in Duke Hall under the direction of Reverend Cleveland Kiser, Assistant Pastor, in 1949.

The church served as host to the State Convention in November, 1947; the Statewide Clinic in 1950; the State Woman's Missionary Union Convention in March, 1953; and the State G. A. Houseparty in October, 1954.

The church apparently had a problem with burglary during 1954. From the December 5 bulletin:

> A Word of Precaution. We have been working with our Insurance Agency and the Police Department in order that we may best protect our property and prevent the many break-ins which we have been having. One of our Janitors MUST now be on hand to open and close the church for ALL activities and for individuals coming and going. May we ask that small groups wanting the use of the church facilities contact the office and consult the church calendar and as far as possible arrange their meetings at the same time that other activities are going on, so that the janitors will not be called out unduly. . . . Thanking you for your help and suggestions. Your House Committee.

In 1955, dual morning worship services were conducted in the winter months. The early service was led by Kenneth Hansen, who had replaced Kiser. The regular service was conducted by Tucker.

On November 27, 1955, Tucker resigned to become effective on March 1, 1956. During his pastorate, the church membership increased from 1,796 in 1937 to 3,217 at the end. Other noteworthy events not mentioned above included his establishment of Sunday night worship services, his introduction of the six-point record system, and the revival of the church library.

At the December 5, 1955, deacons' meeting, "Mr. Gertner introduced Mrs. Tiller with the explanation that she has been asked to explain the music department's needs and desires. Mrs. Tiller said that the choir has grown from a membership of 19 on June 1, 1953 to the present membership of 257, comprised of 67 in the Senior Choir, 60 men in the New Male

Dr. and Mrs. J. Powell Tucker

Chorus, Senior High 35, Junior High 47, Carol 36 and Primary 34, with rehearsal each week. There are now available 69 robes for the Senior Choir, 28 for Carol Choir, 40 for Primary Choir, none for Jr. or Sr. High School Choirs. A pianist and organist will also be needed for the 8:30 Sunday morning service, and robes for the choir also." A motion was made and carried to sell the old robes and buy new ones and hire the musicians on a temporary basis.

In 1956, a Sunday School structure was built at a cost of two hundred thousand dollars. On February 26, 1956, the church celebrated Dr. Tucker Day. He was made pastor emeritus. One statement that Tucker continued to make during his life was, "God made the world for one purpose—to glorify His Son Jesus Christ."

For a time after Tucker's retirement, Kenneth Hansen and Polly Tiller, who was music director, filled in. Also W. R. Clark, a member of the church, served as interim pastor and was a contributing factor to the uniting of the fellowship. The pulpit committee began diligently to seek God's man as pastor. On July 22, 1956, they recommended that Henry Allen Parker become the pastor.

CHAPTER EIGHT

Henry Allen Parker, 1956–1977

But the man who looks intently into the perfect law that gives freedom, and continues to do this, not forgetting what he has heard, but doing it—he will be blessed in what he does.

—James 1:25

PASTOR IN THE MAKING

YOUNG PARKER

"Timothy, my son, I give you this instruction in keeping
with the prophecies once made about you, so that by
following them you may fight the good fight, holding
on to faith and a good conscience."
1 Timothy 1:18–19

Henry Allen Parker's humble beginnings did not foreshadow his life as a distinguished man of the cloth. He was born in Windom, Texas, while his father was on an evangelistic trip. As an adult writing about his childhood, he wrote, "I am grateful that God permitted me to live in the country when I was a boy and I feel that I gained a kind of education there that simply cannot be obtained any other place."

Young Henry left the one-room schoolhouse in a thoughtful mood. His feelings were hurt. Some of the bigger boys had called him names during recess, and their words echoed in his memory. He decided to turn his mind to more pleasant thoughts: the fresh-baked apple pie cooling on the farmhouse sill, the collard greens cooking on the back of the stove, his mother's voice softly singing "When the Roll is Called up Yonder," his grandmother joining in with her alto strains, his grandfather working the fields hoping his grandchildren would hurry home to lend a hand.

Taking a detour away from his siblings and friends, he broke off a small tree branch and fashioned a fishing line from items in his pocket. Surely his mother wouldn't mind his adding catfish to the dinner menu. Scrambling down the bank of the creek, he dropped his line into the water and waited for the first bite. This was heaven! Going fishing could cure almost any trouble of the heart.

Trouble. Hurt. Heartache. He had experienced them all in his short life. The pain of his father's death continued to stab. Fishing and sleep helped for a while. He thought of heaven. He knew his father was there, but what was he doing? Was he fishing? Was heaven just one big afternoon of uninterrupted casting a line? Surely not. The family Bible didn't ever mention fishing in connection to heaven, but it did talk about streets of gold. Was his father walking on them right now? It comforted him to think that might be the case.

Later, with chores done and the fish dinner eaten, Henry joined his brothers and sisters outside for a game. His sisters, as usual, wanted to play school and began to assemble some books and chalk, but Henry tried to convince them to play church. Before they could protest, he jumped on an old pine stump, gathered the others to sit on the grass, and began delivering a message of fire and brimstone. "Sister, do you know you're saved? Farmer Ike, are you ready to meet your maker?" His voice rose in volume as he warmed to his sermon, strangely like the one they had all heard last Sunday in the little country church in southwestern Alabama.

His siblings were used to his preaching, and they were used to preachers. Their father had been one until his untimely death at twenty-eight in the 1918 flu epidemic. In fact, their father, grandfather, and great-grandfather had all been Alabama preachers. God's word was in their blood, as well as in their hearts.

As Henry's message came to a close with the sunset, his mother wearily walked out to the porch, drying her hands on a dish cloth. Too old to be able to sit on her lap, but too young to suffer all of life's burdens without her, Henry joined his mother on the porch swing and laid his head on her shoulder. As he did so, she saw the light from the rising moon rest on his forehead. It certainly wasn't like a halo; he was too much a boy for that. It was more like a blessing, a confirmation, a sign of peace. Like Jesus' mother, Henry's mother pondered these things in her heart and was comforted. She picked up the Bible on the table at her side and began to read to her son and to herself about heaven. "And the twelve gates were twelve pearls; every several gate was of one pearl: and the street of the city was pure gold, as it were transparent glass. And I saw no temple therein: for the Lord God Almighty and the Lamb are the temple of it. And the city had no need of the sun, neither of the moon to shine in it: for the glory of God did lighten it, and the Lamb is the light thereof."

<hr />

Henry Allen Parker's "Autobiography" recounts that he was born in Windom, Texas, in 1913 while his father was on an evangelistic trip. He grew up in Malcolm, Alabama, thirty-five miles straight north of Mobile. "Our world consisted of a wonderful family life, a one-room school, a depot—post office—store combined, and neighbors both good and bad." One game he played at age eight or nine was "church." "It usually fell my lot to be the preacher and some of the most earth-shaking sermons you could imagine were delivered, from that old pine stump, to my brothers and sisters." His father, Douglas Raymond Parker, was a preacher. "I have the high honor and distinction of being the fourth straight generation of Parker preachers born and reared in southwest Alabama." His mother became a widow when his father died at age twenty-eight in 1918 of the flu epidemic. Young Henry Parker worked on his grandfather's farm. Fishing and hunting were a vital part of his childhood and remained so through his adult years. Later he worked in a sawmill when he was not in school.

Henry Parker was converted when he was nine years of age. "I began to wonder if perhaps God wanted to raise me up to carry on the work my father had so nobly begun." He was also attracted to drama and law. But he made the decision to enter the ministry. "And I love my calling. I have a glowing delight in its services. I am conscious of no distractions in the shape of competitors calling for my strength and allegiance. A friend made this remark to me some time ago, 'What a waste! What a brilliant lawyer you would have made.' This is not the way I feel. I know God placed His hand on my shoulder for a special work. I was obedient to this call and He has led me and blessed me all the way."

In school he loved sports—running, boxing, football—and school leadership, dramatics, debating. He was president of the student body while a senior in high school. He was given a full four-year scholarship from the *Birmingham News* to Howard College in Birmingham, Alabama. While there, he was elected president of the student body and he was also president of the State Baptist Student Union. He was called as pastor half-time to two churches while still a student. He met his future wife, Virginia Reaves, on a blind date while he was a senior in college. She graduated from Baylor University with a major in English.

After graduation from college, he enrolled in Southern Baptist Theological Seminary in Louisville, Kentucky, entering in the fall of 1936. At the end of that year, he and Virginia were married on June 1, 1937, in Birmingham, Alabama. These were busy years—carrying a full load of studies, holding down a janitorial job, pastoring two churches half-time, and then another church full-time. Virginia also worked full-time in the records office of the seminary, earning her PHT (putting husband through) degree. Parker earned his Th.M. degree in three years and his Th.D. degree in two more years. While at the seminary, he was selected as a fellow, or teaching assistant, under Professor Weatherspoon.

After graduation, he was called to the First Baptist Church of Quincy, Florida, beginning in 1941 for three years. Next he began serving at Allapattah Baptist Church in Miami in 1944 for one and one-half years, First Baptist Church of Dothan, Alabama, in 1945 for seven years, First Baptist Church of Montgomery, Alabama, in 1952 for four years, coming to First Baptist Church of Orlando in 1956 where he remained for twenty-one years. He and Mrs. Parker were blessed with three children: Walter Allen, Sara Margaret, and John David. When Parker came, the church had a very small staff and only a few tithers. Always missions minded, he traveled on several mission trips: Hawaiian Baptist Convention in November 1962, the Air Force Religious Mission Far East in 1964, Alaska in September 1965, the East Africa Evangelistic Crusade in November 1970, the Baptist Mission of Zambia in April 1972, the South Africa Evangelistic Crusade in September 1975, Belgium and Germany in October 1978, and South Africa in October 1981.

George Shearouse remembered a time when Parker was hunting that he climbed a large tree and somehow fell out of it, injuring himself rather severely. Jo Kesler remembers Parker as being very different from Tucker. Parker was a rejuvenator, a younger man, had a wonderful knowledge of the Bible, and was down-to-earth. She remembers Mrs. Parker as being very intelligent.

Howard Dobson remembered that a few weeks after Parker's arrival as pastor, he announced that he was planning a revival for a certain week, giving the date. Howard, realizing the new pastor was unaware that the Central Florida Fair was annually scheduled for that same time and also knowing that the new pastor would not understand the importance of the fair to this rather sleepy town, advised Parker of this conflict. The revival date was changed since many of the church members would be attending the fair and witnessing there.

On July 22, 1956, Henry Allen Parker, formerly of the First Baptist Church of Montgomery, Alabama, became pastor of First Baptist Church Orlando. Mildred Talton wrote that from "the first, he proved to be a man of action. Almost immediately, he led the church in adopting the unified budget which went into effect January 1957, and a committee was appointed to study the charter and by-laws. Within the first few months, he assembled a very fine staff to aid him in developing the church program. These were: minister of education—Louie Wilkinson; ministers of music—Edwin and Alberta Irey; youth director—Donnette Dunaway; and mission pastor—V. N. Maggard" (notes). Maggard was very mission minded and was instrumental in the establishment of four missions which became churches: Walnut Street, Tangelo Park, Maitland, and Southview.

Soon after the Parkers arrived, they began a ministry for the senior adults of the church. Mrs. Parker remembered:

> The senior adults seemed to be on the sidelines when we first came to the church. Henry and I decided to start a Senior Adult Ministry. We saw this age group having a marvelous potential, especially for prayer and choir work. First, we selected a committee of senior adults and talked to them about their interests and needs. The senior adults elected officers for their committee, and I was placed as program chairman. We started BXYZ (Baptist Extra Years of Zest) which held regular monthly meetings, sometimes doing crafts, eating a luncheon, having a program, and going on short trips around Florida. Later these trips were extended to other places, and buses were chartered to go to such sites as Ridgecrest for "Chautauqua." One time they even went to Hawaii. One time, the senior adults planned an old-fashioned worship service with old costumes and on old pump organ. Adele Carlson was one of the heads of senior adult activities in Nashville and we worked together on this ministry. My husband wrote a book, *Spring in the Heart*, especially for and about senior adults. (Interview)

The associational bulletin in 1956 reported that Parker received seventy-five hundred dollars in salary and there were 3,294 members in the church. During this time the Southern Baptist seminaries continued to grow in enrollment: Southern—1,765, Southwestern—2,414, New Orleans—972, Golden Gate—331, and Southeastern—459. The church began publishing the promotional paper *Beacon*. Parker felt that it tied the

The Parker family

church family together. He also felt it necessary to increase the church property as the membership enlarged, and during his pastorate four purchases of real estate were made.

The September 4, 1956, deacons' meeting recorded the following: "Bro. Alex Young reported on the poor condition of our baptistery, and stated that we had barely missed serious accidents during the last two baptisms. Mr. Young stated we should look into the matter with view of possibly repairing or rebuilding the baptistery. After considerable discussion, it was moved by Graham, properly seconded and carried, that a committee of three be appointed to go into the matter with view of ascertaining just what needed to be done in the way of improvement."

In 1957, Parker gave a sermon at the associational meeting held at College Park. In the bulletin, his salary was given as ten thousand dollars and the church membership was 3,402 and showing a steady rise. The church gave $29,525 to the Cooperative Program. On April 21, the second educational unit, which cost two hundred thousand dollars was dedicated. Also in that year, the Lake Como Mission was established.

In 1958, a new Baptist seminary, Midwestern, was announced in the associational bulletin. Our church gave forty thousand dollars through the Cooperative Program. The senior boys were city champions in basketball. The choir presented "Elijah." The need for a larger sanctuary was becoming more apparent. On August 27, the church voted to purchase the Cox property on the corner of Rosalind and Pine for eighty-five thousand dollars as the site for the new sanctuary and educational space. A New Members Department was begun on September 7. The leaders were the Millard Smiths.

In 1959, Robert New became business administrator. When Louis Wilkinson resigned to assume duties with the Sunday School Board in Nashville, Mitchell Maddox replaced him. When Donnette Dunaway went to seminary in Louisville in 1959, Ken Hofmeister became the next full-time youth director. He served two years before returning to seminary and was followed by Paul Thomas. The Harmony Bay summer encampment winners were Marcia Carow, Nancy Christopher, Valerie Murdock, Lorene Taylor, Frances Taylor, and J. G. Avent. Paul Smith Construction Company began work on the sanctuary on September 20 at a cost of $1,022,000. There was a groundbreaking for the Como Chapel on September 27. This chapel was later organized into Walnut Street Baptist Church. The WMU president was Mrs. J. B. Shearouse. First Baptist Church was recognized as having the first Standard Sunday School in Florida.

During the 1960s, Parker emphasized the following: missions, support for Baptist colleges, the evils of alcohol, youth programs, and associations—

Planning an African mission trip (l/r): Jake Dominey, Ralph Edfeldt, Dr. Parker, Loren Mallory, and Jim Wilson

especially the state Baptist associations. Many of the guest speakers were associated with the Southern Baptist Convention, the Sunday School Board, and Baptist seminaries and colleges.

In 1960, Parker began "Words to Live By" on WDBO. He conducted this radio program for twelve years. It was a fifteen-minute inspirational program sponsored by one of the Orlando banks. These talks were eventually put into books published by Parker, called *Words to Live By* and *More Words to Live By*. Other books published were *Special Day Sermons*, *Peace in a Turbulent World*, *Living at Peace in a Turbulent World*, and *Spring in the Heart*. He once wrote his life's philosophy: "1. Have a faith to live by. This includes faith in God, yourself, other people. 2. Have a self to live with. This includes a clear mind, pure heart, clean body. 3. Have a hope to live for. This includes life is still good, still adventurous. Keep on living as long as you live. Be useful as long as you are able."

There was a Standard Sunday School 1959–1960 for the first time in the history of the church, and First Orlando was the first Baptist church in Florida to have this distinction. The church led Florida Baptists in mission gifts. On September 10, the church service was called off due to Hurricane Donna. The Florida Association discussed the possibility of starting a Baptist hospital and a retirement center in Orlando. Parker's salary was twelve thousand dollars. There were 2,993 members. Ralph Clark led Training Union, the WMU president was Juanita Wilkinson, and the church clerk was Myron Guymon. Howard Dobson remembered the very beginnings of the church's media department. They met in a closet and had only two pieces of equipment: a 16-millimeter projector and a slide projector. Some of those early media people included Basil Hull, Louie Wilkinson, and E. R. Gertner. Gertner was instrumental in getting congregational approval of our church being televised. Some had felt that television, along with movies, was sinful and the church should not venture into that enterprise, but Parker saw the need for the church's involvement in television.

On January 21 and 22, 1961, a Billy Graham Rally was held at the Tangerine Bowl. During the construction of the church's new sanctuary, at least one deacon a day met with the construction crew for prayer. When the steeple was raised, nearly the whole town came out to witness the event. As the steeple, through very careful and dangerous maneuvering, was settled into place, a cheer went out from the crowd. On May 14, 1961, the church dedicated its two-thousand-seat sanctuary and other facilities. On May 14–17, the church held dedication services. Ramsey Pollard, president of the Southern Baptist Convention, Duke K. McCall, president of the Southern Baptist Theological Seminary, and John McGuire, executive secretary-treasurer of the Florida Baptist Convention were key speakers. Our church's former pastor, T. F. Callaway, was present at the dedication and said: "Its present attainment—numerically, financially, and spiritually—is almost a modern miracle."

From the "We Dedicate" program:

> The design of the new First Baptist Church building is Greek Revival. It is a style of architecture which is native to the South and more appropriate for a church building because of its simplicity and dignity. Fluted Greek Doric columns support the entrance portico and the same Doric design is dominant in the steeple which is approximately 160 feet high. . . . The new building is completely air conditioned and contains approximately 37,500 square feet of floor space. . . . Included in the new building are the following areas: a sanctuary, seating 2,000 persons; a chapel, seating 150; a large social room; two assembly areas with adjoining classrooms for educational purposes; a conference room, equipped with conference tables

and chairs, accommodating 25 persons; two brides' rooms, one adjoining the sanctuary and one adjacent to the chapel; an office for the pastor; choir rehearsal room; five choir robing rooms; an office for the minister of music; an office for the music secretary; a music library; a small kitchen; and the baptistery with complete dressing-room facilities.

The sanctuary contained a new four-manual Pels organ built in Alkamaar, Holland, by the Pels Organ Company, and shipped to the United States where it was assembled by the Pels Organ Company's Grand Rapids, Michigan, plant. This organ, given by the Henry Symonds family, was played in concert on June 14 by Virgil Fox, organist of the Riverside Church of New York City. The E. B. Moses family gave funds to build the chapel. The Harmony Bay winners were Camille Cox, Joy Edfeldt, Terry Foley, Kenneth Thigpen, and Richard Denson. Our church led the state in gifts to world missions through the Cooperative Program. Camp Joy was included for the first time in the association's budget. Our church started its first kindergarten class.

In the 1962 associational bulletin, the Christian Coalition made the following report:

> Florida today has twice as many bars as churches of all faiths. Its people spend over 5 times as much on liquor, gambling, and obscenity as on all religious activities combined. Florida has twice as many suicides as the national rate, ranks above average in venereal disease, overwhelming number of broken homes and emotionally disturbed people. What can we do?
>   1. SPEAK UP
>   a. remove all beer, wine and whiskey sales from grocery stores, etc.
>   b. reduce the flood of TV, radio, and billboard advertising promotions of alcoholic products.
>   c. eliminate advertising promoting gambling.
>   d. take whatever action required to remove indecent literature from newsstands.
>   2. VOTE.
>   3. USE YOUR INFLUENCE IN YOUR OWN CHURCH.

Also in 1962, Marcia Carow was the sword drill runner-up in the association. The church celebrated its third year of a Standard Sunday School. On April 29, the church had its first television telecast of the worship service on Channel 9, WLOF-TV. The deacons and staff gave a reception for

Sanctuary, 1961

the Parkers' twenty-fifth wedding anniversary. Parker preached at the Southern Baptist Convention in San Francisco, and later that year he preached at the Hawaii Baptist Convention. Our church's pantomime group, led by Alberta Irey, went to Ridgecrest. First Baptist Church continued to lead the state in gifts to the Cooperative Program. When Parker expressed a desire to own his own home, the church sold the pastorium on Summerlin for twenty-five thousand dollars. Parker was elected president of the Florida Baptist Convention and served 1962–1963.

In 1963, the church's resident members totaled 2,947 and the pastor's salary was $11,400. The former worship center began to be used as a recreation center. Marcia Carow was an alternate in the Better Speaker's tournament. Terry Foley placed first in the sword drill. Sheila Clarke was named Miss Appalachian by Carson-Newman College. Sharon Smith was a summer missionary to Chicago. Lorene Taylor served as a summer missionary in the Baptist Goodwill Center in Dallas. The church's drama department was organized as well as a Young People Away department. Our church set a record—first time in the history of Florida that any church had given more than fifty thousand dollars through the Cooperative Program.

Mitchell Maddox arrived as minister of education. The Sunday School superintendent was Ralph Edfeldt and enrollment was 2,862. The value of the church's property was $2,400,000 with a debt of $1,050,000.

In 1964, the local Florida association discussed the need for a home for older persons. Angebilt Manor was the place suggested at the time. It was announced that Parker was one of seven Protestant ministers invited to go to the Far East Religious Preaching Mission (U. S. Air Force Protestant Religious Mission). The church recorded 2,909 resident members, the pastor's salary was $12,000, Sunday School had 2,689 enrolled with 1,517 the average attendance, the value of the church property was $2,400,000, and the debt was $981,980. A new mission was begun in Maitland on January 1. Mr. Symonds presented a book of hymns that he had written. The sword drill winner was George Reed, and the Better Speaker winner was Marcia Carow. Our Concord Choir was invited to sing at Ridgecrest. The pantomime group went to Atlantic City for the Southern Baptist Convention. On August 16, five separate fires were discovered in the rooms on the third floor of the educational building, which the fire chief determined to be deliberately set. The church's custodian, George Pulley, discovered the blazes and extinguished the fires prior to the fire department's arrival.

In 1965, McCoy was accepted as a mission. Our enrollment was 3,576, Dr. Pipkin led Training Union, and Mrs. Ken Snelling was WMU president.

J. Thomas Gurney served as chairman of the Board of Trustees for the New Orleans Seminary. Dr. Wellborn spoke at a Bible study. In February the church had Baptist College Day and Baptist World Alliance Day. In March there were neighborhood prayer meetings. James Sullivan preached at the spring revival. The Lottie Moon offering set a record as the largest amount ever given by the church. William Smith was added to the staff as assistant pastor. At the Evangelistic Conference, W. A. Criswell was one of the speakers. There were several youth activities in the summer.

In January 1966, First Baptist Church was the host of the Florida Baptist Evangelistic Conference. G. T. Wiley was the speaker for Baptist Men's Day. The assistant pastor offered a theology course for the congregation. Also in January the Stewardship Program was begun. In February laymen continued tithing testimonies for the Stewardship Program. Henry Symonds published his first gospel book, *Glorious Hymns for His Glory*. Some of his songs were honored by being sung by the choir. The church was invited to a reception for the Tuckers' fiftieth wedding anniversary on March 8 in the social hall. In March there was a dedication of a new building, the McCoy Road Chapel. Revival services were held with Dr. Eddleman, president of New Orleans Seminary, speaking. In May the church celebrated Christian Home Week and a Family Worship Clinic. There was a G. A. Focus week and a coronation. A new ministry was offered, Juvenile Rehabilitation, in conjunction with the Wekiwa Association. Charles Millican, Florida Technical University president, spoke in the pulpit for Parker. Vacation Bible School was held in June. There was a Brotherhood Fish Fry at the Moses' lake house on Lake Conway. First Baptist Church children were encouraged to attend Ridgecrest Student Week in June. Also in June Parker led a tour to the Holy Land and Europe.

July 3–10 was Youth Week. Sunday School Leadership Training was given in August. Bob Smith, pastor of First Baptist Houston, led a revival called "Sermons in Color." September 15, Parker celebrated his tenth anniversary as pastor of the church. In October the church voted to enlarge the Deacon Body Prayer Chain. November 13–16 was Special Missions Emphasis. Baptist Young Men was begun. At Christmas the Brotherhood held a prayer breakfast. In the 1966 associational bulletin, First Baptist announced the purchase of land for future expansion. Also in that year, the church held Vision Week, a mission emphasis which changed the lives of many in the congregation. Howard and June Dobson recalled that it was a revival and a week called a "Season of Prayer," in which a group of approximately twenty-five laymen came from out of town and gave a series of testimonies in the chapel. The Holy Spirit moved in a great way, culminating in several couples volunteering for foreign mission service, namely Ed and Missy Moses, Richard and Frankee Hellinger, and Graham and Jeanne Walker. According to Mildred Talton, "We established a full weekday ministry program. And three more families joined those who had given themselves to full mission service. Quite a few of our young people volunteered as journeymen and gave two years of service on the mission field."

The church started a blood bank. Martha Snipes was WMU president. Parker's "Words to Live By," a five-minute program carried on radio station WDBO, was featured in an *Orlando Sentinel* article by Jean Reiman. The messages were called "down-to-earth" and "inspirational." "Offering practical strength rather than the preaching which might cause some listeners to defensively dial the program out, it has had a tremendous response since it was introduced six years ago." The messages were begun by Parker and John F. Anderson Jr., pastor of First Presbyterian Church. When Anderson left Orlando, M. C. Cleveland of First Methodist Church began broadcasts with Parker. Their audience was projected to be men and women on their way to work or in the home, needing "a bit of support for the day's inevitable challenges and problems."

In January 1967, the Florida Baptist Evangelistic Conference was held at the church January 10–12. The church celebrated Baptist Men's Day. Mission church support was given to McCoy Road Baptist Chapel and DeNeff Migrant Village. The death of Mrs. E. T. Poulson was reported. The church held its Annual Bible Conference February 5–8. The Ireys were honored for ten years of service. The first annual Senior Adult Week was held February 19–22. In March, the Moody Chorale sang, and missionaries Paul Bellington and Mrs. William Lewis spoke. April 11–12, our church hosted the State WMU Convention. The G.A.s held their annual Focus Week and Coronation. Grady Nutt was the Recreation Round-up speaker in May. In June Loyalty Day was observed (Stewardship Catch-up Day). Vacation Bible School was held June 5–9. The church was seeking a missionary residence. The Good News Club was a mission outreach of the church to children at Reeves Terrace. Youth Week was held July 30 to August 6. In August the pastor made a trip to the Holy Land. Findley Edge was guest speaker at the Leadership Preparation Week in September. The church was investigating the possibility of building a Baptist retirement center. There was a churchwide picnic in September. Howard Ball, speaker from Campus Crusade, spoke at the Layman's Institute for Evangelism in October. In 1967, Bob Marrero reported that the Maitland property would cost thirty-five thousand dollars. It was recommended that the church purchase it.

McCoy Chapel had a gift of an organ from two families. The 1967 associational bulletin announced the start of a mission in Maitland with Paul
Thomas as pastor. The next year a chapel was built in Maitland for this mission. In December the church produced a Christmas musical, held a week
of prayer for foreign missions, and gave to the Lottie Moon offering.

In February 1968, the church began a new literacy class for non-
English-speaking people. BXYZ (Baptist Extra Years of Zest) was
honored, also in February. The choirs made a recording in March to help
finance a trip. Richard Hellinger and his wife Frankee were appointed
missionaries to India. Sheila Clarke went to Nigeria as a two-year jour-
neyman missionary. May 12–19 was revival week. In June, nine young
college people began a Mission Outreach. In August, the ladies held their
first Ladies Prayer Retreat at Camp Joy. In September, there was a Bond
Retirement Campaign. Baptist Terrace groundbreaking was held on
September 22. Henry S. Symonds published a second book of hymns
titled *Gospel Hymns for His Glory Book 2*. In October there was a Literacy
Workshop and a Squad Day (football). In November the church held a
churchwide Mission Study. There was a Christmas cantata in December.

In 1969, our church's resident members totaled 2,690, the pastor's
salary was $13,500, Sunday School enrollment was 2,813 with an average
attendance of 1,413, the property was valued at $3,086,791, the debt
reduced to $732,117, and the total mission expenditures were $119,171.
The church began full weekday ministries programs under the direction
of Rafael de Armas. The Good Thief Coffee House was begun jointly with
College Park. John Carow became the director for this work. This ministry met a real need. Hundreds of people of all ages passed through its
doors. They were witnessed to and helped. Bob Ford was led to the Lord
through this ministry and is now a Southern Baptist missionary in Prague
with his wife and sons. A day care center called Children's World
was also started. Ed and Missy Moses left as missionaries to Africa.
T. J. DuBose was called to McCoy Chapel, and Charles Horsley was made
administrator of the soon-to-be opened Baptist Terrace.

In 1970, the local Florida association celebrated its centennial at Wekiwa
(meaning "spring of waters," an appropriate name for this great gathering). The recreation center, at the church, held an open house. Graham
and Jeanne Walker left as missionaries to Singapore. Paul Thomas left to be
the minister at Maitland. T. J. DuBose served at Southview. Our Sunday
School was listed among the top forty-five in the nation in attendance. The
church, under the leadership of Al Amos and Bill Haynes, began a tape
ministry. Baptist Terrace, a medium-income residential retirement center,

Seated: Eva Maude Foley, Henry Symonds, and Lucy Symonds. Standing center: Gerry Leonard

opened with Charles Horsley as the first administrator. Joe Pipkin and his wife Katherine, their son David, and a friend, Tim Vickers, went to Mbeya, Tanzania. Dan and Harriet Maffett went as short-term missionaries to India. Weekday ministries included counseling at Reeves Terrace, Children's World, the Good Thief, tutoring, a new program called "Mom's Day Out," weekday Bible class, English and citizenship classes, and human welfare. Bo Mitchell became Sunday School superintendent. From November 1 to 15, Parker went on an evangelistic crusade to Uganda, East Africa, at the invitation of the Foreign Mission Board of the Southern Baptist Convention. During his absence, Assistant Pastor Jim Wilson preached, and the deacons presided over the worship services.

The year 1971 marked the one hundredth anniversary of the church. Oldest members included Mrs. M. O. Overstreet, Wilson Brooks, and Henry Symonds. In March the church celebrated with several dramas, banquets, an old-fashioned hymn sing, and exhibits. Harriet Maffett reported: "During these last hundred years the name of our church has changed, our location has changed, our buildings, our methods, our pastors have changed. But through it all we know there is one constant—one person who never changes—Jesus Christ—the same yesterday, today and forever." Parker's fifteenth anniversary as pastor was also observed. There were 2,872 resident members, and the church property was valued at $3,112,791 with a debt of $623,134. The Roy Mannings led the Half Way House ministry. John Carow was made director of the coffee house. Later, this Good Thief Coffee House was closed and a new site was sought. Sunday School superintendent was Mac McCully.

In 1972, First Baptist took over care of the the Palmetto Mission (Parkway). Maitland Chapel was constituted as First Baptist Church of Maitland on January 9. The Long Range Planning Committee was formed, including R. N. Turnbow, Paul Shuler, Mac McCully, Gene Kelsey III, Trevor Hawk, Robert Robinette, Betty Lassister, Katherine Pipkin, George Shilling, Robert Talton, Ralph Edfeldt, and Wayne Johnson. J. H. Cox became interim recreation director. Clyde T. Francisco, teacher from Southern Seminary, led a Bible study January 9–12. In April the Parkers led a preaching mission for the Foreign Mission Board to Zambia. Parker led a trip to the Holy Land which included some of the church's youth. On July 16, Tom Lester, a Hollywood actor who appeared as "Eb" in "Green Acres," spoke at the evening service. In September Bill Curl became associate pastor and minister of outreach and evangelism. Also in September the church voted to buy property on Rosalind and Church Streets. Jim Wilson resigned his position at the church to enter full-time evangelism. In December, Carl Langford, mayor of Orlando, signed a proclamation recognizing the Youth Choir of First Baptist Church, Orlando on their trip to Israel—December 18–26.

In 1973, William Hendricks from Southwestern Seminary came to lead the January Bible Study. David Cunningham became minister of education. Others before him had been Mitchell Maddox and Louie Wilkinson and with Grace Johnson as education director. In March Dennis Baw was called as minister of youth. An Easter musical, "Celebrate Life," was presented. There was a revival May 6–13 with Sam Cathey preaching. On July 22 at the 11:00 morning service, Mark Hatfield, senator from Oregon, spoke. In July the church began an 8:15 morning service targeting the youth and students. In August "New Wind," the church's folk music group comprised of youth, gave their premiere performance. Also in August Bill Gunter, former First Baptist Church member and then United States congressman, spoke at a Sunday evening service. In September Wayne Ward from Southern Seminary led a revival. In October Wayne Johnson began serving as preschool/children director. The total members numbered 4,071 and the property was valued at $4,884,000 with the debt at $486,000. The church gave $99,971 to the Cooperative Program.

In 1974, Owen Cooper, Southern Baptist Convention president, spoke at the 11:00 morning service on February 17. On February 28, Virginia Parker became president of the Florida Baptist Convention. She was the first woman to serve the state convention in that role. Mrs. Parker's election was the first time in the history of Florida Baptists that two individuals from the same family had served as president. This was also the first occasion when a husband and wife had held this honor in the history of the Southern Baptist Convention. The church held a revival the last few days in March with Vince Cervera speaking. On April 26–28, John Drakeford of Southwestern Seminary led our Family Life Enrichment Conference. At the May 19 evening service the Sanctuary Choir presented "Elijah." On October 6, the church voted to build a Christian Life Center at Pine and Magnolia Streets. Gerry Leonard became director of evangelism training under Bill Curl's leadership. David Cunningham began the first singles' Sunday School classes with Frank Brasington as the teacher. This class was organized for singles just out of college. After a couple of years, the John Licktaigs became department directors for the younger group. Teaching was done by singles in the small groups. Mrs. Gerry Leonard was teacher and director for the divorced singles (Driggers's notes).

In 1975, the old brick sanctuary was demolished to make way for the Christian Life Center. The "Together We Build" program was launched to finance the new center. William E. Hull of Southern Seminary was our guest teacher for the January Bible Study. Ed and Betty Stalnecker led a revival in March. On March 19, Paul James, executive director of the New York Baptist Convention, was our speaker. The state's WMU Convention was held at our church. In August "New Wind" youth choir led in a crusade in Jamaica. On October 3, Edwin and Alberta Irey announced their plans to retire in 1976.

On January 16, 1976, the *Orlando Sentinel* had an article written by Andy Williams about the Florida Baptist Convention's three-way conference. Anita Bryant gave a tearful testimony about the Lord's strength she felt during a difficult delivery of twins. W. A. Criswell, pastor of First Baptist Church of Dallas, Texas, followed, preaching to the crowd of six thousand. A small twelve-year-old boy led others onto the field to be saved. During the service, two women signed for the fifty or so deaf people. A five-hundred-member choir sang. The first day had begun with heavy rain, but the rest of the convention experienced only some rain and cold weather. Loren Mallory came on staff as business administrator, where he served for eight years. Also in 1976, the Ireys retired. They had led the choir for over

Edwin and Alberta Irey

nineteen years. They were given a handmade quilt depicting various events in their ministry. They were also given a portfolio containing messages from choir members. The membership of the church totaled 3,968 with the property valued at $4,687,000 and the debt at $725,995. There were 2,690 enrolled in Sunday School, and $107,023 was given to the Cooperative Program. The WMU president was Jane McKinney.

On January 16, 1977, Parker gave a message titled "Our Church: Past, Present, Future," in which he discussed the accomplishments of First Baptist. At the end of his sermon, he announced his retirement plans for May of that year, a year earlier than originally planned. He listed the various missions the church had begun, including the six during his pastorate: Walnut Street, Tangelo Park, Maitland, Southview, Parkway, and *Primera Iglesia Bautista*. He also outlined his vision for the church in its future. He said, "First Baptist Church has been a mountain peak church for over one hundred years and it will continue to be so." On April 10, the Christian Life Center was dedicated and the public was

Henry and Virginia Parker

invited. Its cost was $2.2 million, and it had seventy-six thousand square feet with seven floors. The two major focal points of the complex were a recreational area and a fellowship hall.

A recognition banquet and churchwide reception were held on May 15 for the Parkers. At this dinner, Carl Bates and Harold Bennett were speakers. In addition, a generous amount of money was raised to give to the Parkers. They were also given a stained-glass window from the original sanctuary, paid salary and benefits for one year, and a cookbook with recipes from the ladies of the church. A church family presented them with a car.

Some pertinent facts about the church during Parker's ministry: the membership more than doubled, the budget mushroomed from about $143,000 to more than $1 million, the staff grew from five to sixty-five, four buildings were built, four properties were purchased, six new churches were started, and the church led the Florida Baptist Convention in all its mission causes for fifteen of the twenty years and placed second in the other years.

Bill Curl became interim pastor. "New Wind" went on a summer tour. There was a musical tribute to Henry Symonds, writer of six hundred hymns. Jim Henry had a trial sermon on August 21 and began his ministry on September 18—an important day for the church's future.

CHAPTER NINE

James Bascom Henry, 1977–Present

Humble yourselves, therefore, under God's mighty hand,
that he may lift you up in due time. Cast all your anxiety on
him because he cares for you.

—1 Peter 5:6–7

AN EASTER MESSAGE
CHOIR MEMBER CAROL AT "THE LIGHT"

"'Look, the Lamb of God, who takes away the sin of the world!'"
John 1:29

Although Ragan had asked the choir to arrive at least an hour early, Carol was unable to comply. Her boss had needed her to stop by the post office on her way to the performance. As the rehearsal recording played in her tape deck, she began singing the first song, but I-4 traffic continued to distract, then frustrate, her. She remembered Martha's warning that the devil would do everything he could to thwart the activities of God's saints. She knew he certainly wanted to hinder all those taking part in the Easter presentation.

As she waited for the cars to move again, she noticed other motorists looking at her in a strange way. Hadn't they ever seen a Hebrew costume before? She pulled the headdress down around her shoulders so she wouldn't be as conspicuous. Buses from as far away as Atlanta edged to the right lane in preparation to exit at John Young Parkway. Carol counted at least thirty buses when she glanced in her rearview mirror. She felt like Moses (better make that Miriam) leading the Israelites through the desert to the Promised Land.

After parking her car in the "secret" lot an experienced choir member had whispered to her the night before, Carol ran to the back door of the rehearsal room, her sandals flying behind her. She sat in her assigned seat, took a deep breath, and listened to Ralph give some final instructions. She glanced at the prayer board and chose a name to pray for, "Louise." She wondered if Louise would feel a stirring in her spirit as many people began to lift up her name to the Lord. Carol reached out and grasped the hands of the women seated to her left and right, new friends Emily and Murl, and bowed her head.

After another twenty minutes of prayer and instructions, Carol quietly made her way to the hall. She mustn't let Murl get too far ahead of her or she might lose her way to the sanctuary. The catacomb of halls and doors still continued to confuse her since she was a relatively new member of the church.

Her heart quickened as she pulled the blackout curtain aside and made her entrance. The audience of nearly six thousand quieted as Ken played the opening strains of the music. His deft fingers flew over the keys of the organ, and Carol once again admired his skill. Adjusting the basket of bread on her arm, she began her walk, with four hundred other choir members and drama characters, through the streets of Jerusalem. A few days earlier, many Sunday School classes had moved pews and painted sets, transforming the auditorium into the scene before her.

After she found her seat, the song "I Am" began. As stanza built on stanza, her spirit thrilled to the message. Perhaps her boss had been able to come. She had timidly given him four tickets one week earlier. She breathed a prayer of anticipation. If only he would come to know the Lord as she had. That's what made this enactment different from a secular play. The words Wayne had written, the music composed by Terry and David, the confident direction of Ragan, the powerful yet gentle words of Pastor Jim, and the months of practice by the choir and orchestra all contributed to an anointed presentation. She thought of the scores of others: parking lot personnel, audiovisual people, makeup artists, ticket-booth workers, ushers, and many more. Over one thousand people had touched the drama in some way. In a matter of minutes she saw portrayed the earthly life of Jesus. A light descended from the

Jesus on Cross

ceiling to point all eyes to the stable and the baby. A few moments later, a child of five ran, tripped, fell, and got up giggling, the representation of Christ as a youngster. Later, as a twelve-year-old boy, Jesus caused his parents distress when he stayed behind to counsel the Jewish intellectuals. Then as a young man, Jesus, strong and happy, showed

Joseph his newest carpentry creation.

About one hour into the drama, the triumphant Messiah entered Jerusalem to the shouts of the crowd and swaying palm branches. Moments later, after the betrayal by Judas, Christ stumbled up some stairs, his back covered in blood and his shoulders balancing a cross-piece. Carol braced herself for the piercing sound of the hammer pounding in the awful nails. Although she was supposed to keep her eyes forward, Carol couldn't resist peeking to the upper left as the cross was raised and Christ's battered form became visible. A mixture of feelings swirled in her mind: the awesomeness of his pain, the depth of his love, and the blackness of her sin which made such a sacrifice necessary.

"Behold the Lamb," her favorite song, moved her to tears. As she glanced around, she saw she was not alone. The woman who played Mary wept as she ascended the hill, ultimately to cradle her son's head in her lap. Thankfully, the story didn't end at that point. Soon, the tomb's stone rolled away and, in a matter of minutes, a host of glittering angels with flowing white gowns took their places while Carol's voice joined hundreds of others in the strong notes of the "Hallelujah Chorus."

Later, as she moved through the crowds, Carol felt tired but blessed. She waved at her friends Jimmy and Loren directing traffic. As she wearily sank down into her car's leather upholstery, she pressed the electronic button to lower her windows. It felt strange to move two thousand years forward to the bustling sounds of Orlando's nightlife. As she drove north to her home, the lights of Church Street Station glowed on her right. She remembered reading that nearly 125 years ago her church, comprised of only eighteen people, had first met only a few blocks away. What would the founding members have thought if they could have attended tonight's performance? She pushed in the rehearsal tape and began to practice. Before she knew it, tomorrow night would come, and another presentation of "The Light" would proclaim the joyous message of Jesus Christ, the Lamb of God!

On the cover of *Heartwarmers*, Pastor Jim Henry is described as youthful in appearance, humorous in a fresh and clean way, and wise like a sage. Another characteristic could be added: humble like a servant. One of his favorite passages from the Bible is Psalm 37:5–7 which reads, "Commit your way to the Lord; trust in him and he will do this: He will make your righteousness shine like the dawn, the justice of your cause like the noonday sun. Be still before the Lord and wait patiently for him."

He is also a positive encourager. He tends to respond with "Why not?" or "Let's do it!" rather than "No!" or "It's impossible." Usually he wears a smile on his face and has a twinkle of humor in his eyes. Children hold a special place in his heart, and he loves to hug them. After nearly every service, there is a long line of people wanting to meet with him. He has the gift of remembering names and really listening to others when they talk. His sermons begin with reading a passage from the Bible and invoking the Lord's blessing in prayer, ending with, "Let the words of my mouth, and the meditation of my heart, be acceptable in thy sight, O Lord, my strength, and my redeemer" (Ps. 19:14 KJV). Next, he usually tells an appropriate anecdote or word picture, followed by a study of the Scripture passage with practical applications. His messages include humor and practical advice, spoken in a Tennessee vernacular and southern charm. Young and old leave the service with something to take home and apply.

James B. Henry was born on October 1, 1937, in Nashville, Tennessee. The young family lived in Allentown, Pennsylvania, then near Springfield, Tennessee, then at the country home of grandparents Hazel

and Marshall Fisher, before settling in Nashville, where "Brother Jim" (as he prefers being called) finished elementary school and then seventh grade. Finally, the family then moved across town where they lived until Brother Jim finished high school. His father was James William Henry ("Daddy Jim") who was born in 1916 and died in 1994. A native of Springfield, Tennessee, James Sr. worked for the Tennessee State Highway Department and the Nashville Metro Government. He made a decision for Christ as a teenager, but in 1974 he drove down the stake of assurance and committed his life to Christ as Savior and Lord. Brother Jim's mother is Kathryn Fisher Henry, affectionately called "Mimi." She and Daddy Jim were high school sweethearts who

James B. Henry

were married on May 28, 1936. Brother Jim's only sibling is a younger brother, Joseph Shaw Henry.

It is apparent Brother Jim believes the Bible's admonition to be loving and loyal to his parents. He writes lovingly and candidly about both: "My dad worked in an aircraft assembly plant during World War II. I saw him work faithfully in a critical job. My dad had a love for the little guy, a sense of humor, and, as he grew older, a growing faith in Jesus Christ. Although he made some wrong choices in his earlier life, he overcame adversity and was an encouragement to me and my brother to be willing to tackle mountains, stand your own ground, and be loyal to family and friends."

And about his mother: "My mother was a homemaker who loved to teach and educate, creating stability and a place of nurturing in her home. She has strong Christian commitments, a love for the church, faith, endurance in testing, an outgoing love for people, and is a diligent worker with strong convictions. She is an exhorter and exemplifier. Mother often sat down at Grandmother's piano and played 'The Old Rugged Cross.' This was the first Scripture song I remember and, therefore, it has always been special to me." For a time, Brother Jim's mother worked part-time as a secretary at First Baptist Church in Nashville, beginning when he was in the sixth grade.

About both parents, he writes: "They had a wide circle of friends at all levels of education, race, religion, culture, and economic circumstances. They were participants in the political process and were respected as good neighbors. They didn't make big waves. They were just plain people who moved from a rural to a suburban setting, and successfully made the transition while growing in their love for Christ, family, church, and friends."

About his roots:

> Orlinda, Tennessee, is certainly not a byword on most people's lips . . . but this small hamlet, snuggled thirty miles north of Nashville near the Kentucky state line, has a special meaning for me. It's the home turf of the Henry family. Family ties extending to great-great grandparents can be traced to this lovely setting of rolling hills and lush pasture land. One of my great granddaddies was known for wearing a white suit, riding a white horse, sporting a flowing white beard, and carrying his rifle across his saddle as he rode around the borders of his farm. The first bridge in Robertson County was built by my great grandfather. Henry roots run deep in her fertile soil.

As a boy, I often spent weekends and evenings at the family farm. The old house has a porch that ran its length and had a big swing that was a summer night's delight. It sat on a rise overlooking a long field, usually filled with corn or cows, and ended at the Red River. There, my dad and his three brothers fished, swam, and hunted. Something I repeated on a smaller scale when I came along. Warm feelings still surface as I recall Christmas holidays and the table groaning with homemade coconut, caramel, and jam cakes, not to mention boiled custard, country ham, and all the trimmings. Cold wintry nights were spent in rocking chairs watching the fire create its own dance before our fascinated eyes; then we were tucked into our feather mattress beds, nearly smothered under hand stitched quilts and blankets with hot irons heated in the fire and wrapped in towels placed at the foot of the bed to keep our feet warm. Summers were highlighted by looking for Indian arrowheads at the fresh water spring behind the house that continues to gurgle cool, clear water to this day; and falling asleep at night to the serenade of crickets and the occasional sound of a hoot owl or the plaintive howl of a dog echoing across the hills on a still evening. Near the house is the old family cemetery. Prowling around its silent markers, you can grasp something of our family history whispering through the iron fence that encircles it; a Civil War veteran, a baby, a teenage boy, a family servant, aged aunts and uncles; and in your mind's eye you can grasp something of the litany of life and death that transpired as the black horses pulling their burden on a wagon led the cortege of mourners to a final salute to cherished loved ones.

In later years, Pap and Mama Ruth Henry moved up the road a couple of miles from the farm to live in Orlinda. They kept the farm, and family and hired hands continued to till its productive earth. We continued our visits to see them in Orlinda and experience small town life: the corner drug store; tractors and horse and wagons stopping by for refreshment and the latest gossip; and everybody seeing everybody as we made the rounds from store to bank, to post office, to barber shop.

Two doors from our grandparent's home stood lovely Orlinda Baptist Church. Built in Gothic style, it is a beautiful, well-kept building, servicing the town and community for many years. My dad and his brothers attended church there. . . . Dad was baptized there. I played on the church grounds with my brother, cousins, and friends and, occasionally, slipped inside to explore its rooms and stand in awe at its pulpit looking out upon the silent rows where my family and others had been nurtured in the faith in her gentle arms. Family and lifelong friends continue to serve Jesus through that lovely church that has stood so quietly strong like the huge trees that surround her manicured grounds.

Orlinda Baptist Church isn't large by some standards, about 160 or so study God's Word there every Lord's Day, and others come to join in the hour of worship, but it's very big in that community and in the Henry heart. ("Beacon," February 25, 1988)

Commenting about his conversion: "I 'crossed the river' at its narrow end as an eight-year-old boy in 1945 at the Hopewell Baptist Church in Springfield, Tennessee, on a Sunday morning. Later I was baptized at First Baptist Church of Nashville because my mother wanted my baptism to be where she had dedicated me to Christ before I was born. The preacher who was preaching was Rev. Oscar Lumpkin; the pastor who baptized me was Dr. W. F. Powell. I remember the lifting of what seemed like a load off my inner soul and great joy as I told my family what Jesus did for me. I gladly followed Him in baptism on a cold February night!"

Brother Jim has always had a tender spot for librarians. While a young boy at First Baptist Church in Nashville, he remembers,

The librarian was Florida Waite. The library was located in a hallway en route to the sanctuary from my Sunday School class. She would wait outside the door and catch me and say, "Jimmy, I've got some new books I think you would be interested in." She opened my eyes to a world far beyond my neighborhood. Later, the chairman of the pulpit committee that called me to Two Rivers was on staff at the Baptist Sunday School Board in the Church Library Division. His boss, Wayne Todd, preached my ordination sermon. My first opportunity to speak to Southern Baptists was at Ridgecrest and Glorietta to Church Librarians during their training conference.

Brother Jim attended Eakin Elementary School, Bailey Junior High, and Litton Senior High School. Commenting about how we are led to sin, he related the following story:

After basketball practice during my junior high days, we stopped at the local "drug" store (word not good to use today!) for cokes and candy. I didn't have any money, but wanted to join in the socializing. While no one was looking, I stole one of my favorite candy bars—a Butterfinger—and joined the group. I ate it, but my guilty conscience nearly made me choke on it! Every time I heard a siren, I thought the police were coming after me. Finally, I saved my money, worked up the courage, went back to the store, called the pharmacist, "Doc" Morgan, aside, confessed my sin, and offered the money and whatever punishment be deemed necessary. He placed his hands on my shoulders and through the glasses, I saw his clear blue eyes sparkle and he said, "You're forgiven—don't do it any more—keep your money." That's what Jesus does when we come to Him for salvation. We confess, He forgives, and we can't pay for what He gives.

While in high school, he was president of the student body. At one time when he was in high school, he hitchhiked a ride with the governor of Tennessee, Frank G. Clement, to the church where Jim had been converted, Hopewell Baptist Church, to attend an anniversary celebration. Earlier, while a junior in high school, he was serving on staff at Ridgecrest Conference Center when he needed an appendectomy. Feeling lonely and afraid, he asked an orderly for a Bible. He then asked the Lord to give him some verses of comfort. He was given Romans 8:28 and 8:31 as he opened God's word. Suddenly a great peace filled his soul.

Later, he graduated from Georgetown College in Kentucky and briefly taught school in Panama City, Florida. He writes this about his call to the ministry:

> It really began with my mother's prayers. She had given me to the Lord's service while she was pregnant, praying in a circle of women gathered for Bible study. She never mentioned it until I made public my call. I sensed from an early age the thought of pastoring or preaching, though I never mentioned it till my teen years. People would ask me if I was going to be a preacher. I kept it in the back of my mind through college and, while teaching school in October, 1959, I sensed the call so strongly, I got on my knees in my rented apartment in Panama City, Florida, and told the Lord I would answer, but I didn't want to do anything to bring shame on His name as a pastor. I made it public at First Baptist Church Panama City the next Sunday morning.

From the *Orlando* magazine: "As a junior at Georgetown College, in Kentucky, he met Jeanette Sturgeon. She first saw 'all 120 pounds of him,' she recalls fondly, wearing a red crewneck sweater and black-and-white saddle shoes. Their first date was to go to church. Jeanette told her roommate that night that she had met the man she would marry" (Meehan 51). After graduating in 1959 with a B. A. degree from Georgetown College, he and Jeanette Sturgeon were married on December 27, 1959, at Salem Baptist Church in Cave City, Kentucky. Next, he attended New Orleans Baptist Theological Seminary. While in school in New Orleans, he worked part-time in a department store and was president of the student body. He received a B. D. degree in 1963 and a M. Div. degree in 1975. After graduation, he served in rural areas in Alabama and Mississippi.

Prior to his ministry at First Baptist Church, Orlando, he was a student pastor at Mount Pisgah near Melvin, Alabama, from 1960 to 1963. There were about thirty-five in Sunday School in the rural sawmill and logging community. People were baptized in the river. As in most churches, there were some wonderful people and some difficult people. One man tried to get Brother Jim fired, but the people rallied around their pastor. Next, he served at Hollywood Baptist of Sledge, Mississippi, from 1963 to 1965. Rural in setting, the area's major crops were cotton, rice, and soybeans. The church was located five miles from town and paid their pastor sixty dollars a week and furnished his family with a house. Later the salary was increased to seventy-five dollars. The church grew from over one hundred to over two hundred. The area had racial tension because of the "Freedom Riders," but the church men met with Brother Jim and "we decided anyone could worship God with us, if they didn't disturb the service." Then, he was pastor at Two Rivers Baptist Church in Nashville, Tennessee, from 1965 to 1977. When he began there, the church was only two years old and in a suburban setting. There were lots of young families. "We grew in faith and family together from one hundred in Sunday School to fourteen hundred . . . there were a progressive people, very flexible. We probably had what would be described as the first 'drive-in' church service in Tennessee which I preached from the balcony of our new worship center. Some of the happiest, most memorable years were spent there." There he saw faith, prayer, and fasting as critical for personal growth and seeing Christ's vision.

Jim has taken a number of missionary trips. One time he, along with about twenty-five others, visited Paraguay. It was a mission trip and one of his duties was to preach to Southern Baptist Convention (SBC) missionaries at a retreat. His group stopped in Rio de Janeiro to sightsee and visit a doctor and his wife whose son was a member of the church. "On Sunday night, we decided to worship at the beach near our hotel. While we were singing, I noticed a group of young men approaching our group. I got up to preach, heard firecracker sounds, saw some activity to one side, but kept on with the service. Afterwards, we were told by some Brazilian friends that one of the young men had pointed a pistol at me, but someone deflected his arm, the bullets missed, and the boys fled." From that time, the presence of angels became an even more vivid reality.

About his call to First Baptist Orlando, he writes:

> In 1972 while on a speaking trip near Orlando, a man pointed out FBC-Orlando as we drove down the Interstate. I said, "I'll be pastor there someday" in a joking way—but it stuck in my mind. I had prayed diligently about another church that had contacted me in 1976–77. I turned them down repeatedly. In prayer, the Holy Spirit said, "You're going to Florida." That day I received a news article that Dr. Parker, pastor of FBC Orlando, was retiring early. Four months later, the committee called. I turned them down after visiting the church, but the Lord wouldn't turn me loose. I relented and asked the Lord to confirm by having someone from FBC/O call. As soon as I finished my prayer, the phone rang—it was a member of FBC/O saying he was disappointed I wasn't coming, just wanted us to know of their love. Within the next couple of hours, two more phone calls came, all unknown to each other. I knew God wanted me to go. Our call was confirmed after our submission—PTL!

Prior to his coming to First Baptist, Henry received several distinctions: vice-president of the Nashville Baptist Pastor's Conference in 1968, president of the Nashville Baptist Pastor's Conference in 1969, trustee of Belmont College in Nashville in 1970–1977, trustee of Baptist Sunday School Board in 1969–1975, and trustee of Tennessee Baptist Convention in 1969–1974. Then in 1977, he was called to First Baptist Church. September 18 marked the church's welcome to him. The sanctuary opened at 8:15 for prayer. There was one morning worship service at 11:00 with dinner on the grounds after the service. Finally at 7:15 P.M. the inaugural service was celebrated. A Western Union telegram from Paul Kujawski, deacon of Two Rivers Baptist Church, read in part: "The Lord Jesus always requires and will take only the best we have. We were privileged to share Brother Jim Henry for 12 years as God's best for us. Now following the Lord he is on your way. Pray with Jim, sup with him, walk with him, cry with him, laugh with him, and see Christ shine in him. Brother Jim is our best. The best we have and if it's the Lord's will and if it's for His glory, Brother Jim and his family are our best offering to your church. Please transmit to Jim and tell him we are praying for him and your church. In Christ Jesus we send our love."

Henry family—Back row (l/r): Danny de Armas, Betsy (Henry) de Armas, Stan Campbell, Kitty (Henry) Campbell, Jeanette Henry, Jim Henry, Kathryn Henry, Jimmy Henry, and Tammy Henry. Front row (l/r): Caleb, Seth, and Asa de Armas—Courtesy Henry family

F. Ray Dorman, chairman of the Pulpit Committee in 1977, wrote the following about Jim Henry: "The Lord gave us a new leader, Bro. Jim Henry. He brought with him a sincerity and a feeling of true Christian love that words cannot describe. That love and affection for his people has generated the momentum to make things happen."

Personally, Brother Jim enjoys a healthy lifestyle both physically and spiritually. He tries to jog three times a week, walks in between, and does other exercises. He spends a quiet time every morning with Bible reading, praise, and prayer. When he gets up from his knees, he raises his face to heaven and says, "I'm reporting for duty, Lord." He schedules family time on his calendar, spending quality and quantity time with his wife, their children, and their grandchildren. His children are Kitty Campbell, Betsy de Armas, and Jim Henry II. At the time of publication, there were five grandchildren: Caleb, Seth, and Asa de Armas, and James (Trey) Henry III and William (Will) Louis Henry. Two other interests he has are reading and travel. He and his wife have made several trips to the Holy Land with members of the church and others in attendance.

Other noteworthy events for 1977 include the dedication of a new fellowship hall. On October 18, our local Baptist association had a new name: Greater Orlando Baptist Association. Ken McNutt became the activities minister. Brother Jim's first book, *Heartwarmers: Reading that Makes God Real,* was published. The Ralph Cottrells were the first couple to be married by Brother Jim in our church.

The 1978 associational session was "dedicated, lovingly, to the faithful ministry of pastor emeritus of First Baptist Church, Orlando, J. Powell Tucker, who ministered from 1938 to 1956" (bulletin). Ragan Vandegriff joined the staff as minister of music. The Sunday School enrollment was three thousand. A program called "500 Praying for 10" was begun. Jane McKinney was chosen as food services director. Our church was listed as second in the state for the number of baptisms. Brother Jim sang a solo as a challenge to go over the Harvest Sunday goal. Andrae Crouch gave a testimony and sang at a worship service. English and citizenship classes were given at the church with an enrollment of ninety students from twenty-five countries. A staff of sixteen teachers instructed the foreign-born about American customs and culture, the English language, and, most important, the love of Jesus. Home Missions Week guests included J. D. Ellis, Elesa Straley, and James and Roberta Newell.

Dora Mae Pemberton wrote the following poem to the tune of "On Top of Old Smoky" to describe the process of calling Brother Jim:

The Search of a Church in the Lurch,
or
The Calling of Jim Henry

Our pulpit committee
Has ended its search;
They found us a preacher
To pastor our church.

But it wasn't easy
In case one should ask,
They very soon realized
They had quite a task.

They mused and meandered,
They tested and toiled,
But many a bright prospect
In some way was foiled.

They'd look and they'd listen
Re-assemble and talk,
But when some favored someone
Some others would balk.

They stewed and they studied
They pondered and prayed,
But many months passed ere
A calling was made.

The church prayed unceasing
The Spirit would lead
To just the right person
To fulfill our need.

Then they flew up to Nashville,
This hard-working bunch,
They attended Two Rivers
Then went out to lunch.

They'd heard him—Jim Henry,
That magical name—
And from that day forward
'Twas never the same.

Things started to happen,
Things happy and good,
Like the praying church members
In faith knew they would.

Jim came down to meet us
And to reckon our plight,
Surely God's hand was in it
For 'twas love at first sight!

He's been here a year now
And is never a bore,
And we hope, the Lord willing,
He'll be here many more!

Founder's Day with adult choir—Front row (l/r): Henry Parker, Jim Henry, Henry Symonds, Ragan Vandegriff, and Bill Curl

In 1978, several traditional services were established. Founder's Day was observed to honor or recognize members who had served the church for fifty years or more. Three of those so honored were J. Tom Gurney, Henry Symonds, and Judson Walker. Brother Jim wrote about First Baptist at its 107th anniversary. She is "a church whose shadow of influence is seen in the fourteen Orlando churches she has mothered; the sons and daughters occupying far-flung mission fields and pulpits; the strength she has engendered to the growing Baptist witness in Central Florida; the sustenance she has been for the thousands who have come under her wings in these 107 years." Brother Jim served as a trustee of the Foreign Mission Board of the Southern Baptist Convention for ten years from 1978 to 1988. Also the church began a Month of Missions to celebrate the total mission emphasis of the church. All special offerings for the state, Annie Armstrong for Easter, and Lottie Moon for Christmas, were gathered at this one time. Goals for that ministry were set at 150 volunteers and sixty thousand dollars in gifts. Both of these goals were met. Special Easter programs were begun, originally held at Bob Carr Auditorium to accommodate the numbers of people who attended. A musical drama was developed called "The Day He Wore My Crown." And for Christmas, the Singing Christmas Tree began to be produced. God and Country Days were initiated to be held around the Fourth of July holiday with ice cream or dessert fellowships. At that service, local, state, and national politicians were invited, along with civic and education leaders. Also in 1978, Anita Fisher (later Crews) was brought to Orlando to work with the Recreation Ministry and Single Adults.

On May 29, 1979, the associational building was dedicated. Brother Jim became president of the Florida Baptist Pastor's Conference. He was awarded an honorary doctor of divinity degree from Georgetown College. Our worship service on TV was named "The First Hour." Our adult and Sonlight choirs sang at the Southern Baptist Convention in Houston. Our church began its World Hunger offering. We agreed to sponsor the Orangewood Mission with Jack Fletcher as pastor. A tape catalog was begun. In April the Fellowship Class celebrated its fortieth anniversary with Tom Gurney, its first teacher. Other highlights included Richard Jackson in a revival. Other guests included Beverly Terrell, Tom Lester, Myrtle Hall, Frank Boggs, the Heritage Singers, and the Re'Generation. Training was conducted for deacons and those taking Evangelism Explosion. Other ministries and programs were Faith Expansion, Camp Orlando, No Easy Road Youth Camp, Church Training Fair, and Day Camp, to name a few. There was also an 800 Praying 10 campaign, a service at Lake Eola, Month of Missions called "Go, Teach, Reap," and an Easter presentation called "Hallelujah Celebration." Howard and June Dobson left for a year of volunteer service to Singapore with the newly formed Mission Service Corps. David Ring gave his testimony, which brought tears to the adult choir and most of the congregation as he described his difficult childhood. But he ended with his trademark song, "Victory in Jesus."

In 1980, Tom Draper retired as the director of missions. Our adult and Sonlight choirs sang at the State Evangelistic Conference. Jimmy Knott was called as minister to singles. Prior to that time, Shirley Martin had worked in this fledgling, but vital, department. Reared in northwest Tennessee, Jimmy is short in stature, but long in love, enthusiasm, and Biblical knowledge. He would prove a wonderful addition to the staff with his spiritual gifts of teaching and leadership, subsequently serving in several areas, including outreach, single adults, discipleship training, new members, married adults, and as associate pastor when Bill Curl left several years later for Wales.

The Sonlight Choir went to Israel and England. We agreed to purchase property for the South Orlando Mission and two more pieces downtown. Our Family Dinner Theatre presented "The Miracle Worker." Patsy Russell was WMU president. Rick Blythe and Ken McNutt were ordained. Baruch Goldstein visited. The pastor taught an early-bird Sunday School class at 8:00 A.M. The Singing Christmas Tree was presented. There was a Dream Lake Ukulele band and a Korean choir. Bill Curl and Gerry Leonard were involved in Evangelism Explosion certification. Brother Jim was elected president of the SBC Pastor's Conference.

At various times, the church experienced spiritual warfare. The pastor and many others (Sam Cathey and Jimmy Knott to mention two) gave powerful messages against Satan and Hell, so it was not surprising that the Enemy would attack. Brother Jim remembers, "While I was preaching on a Sunday night on the power of the Name of Jesus and His dominion over everything in the world and universe, suddenly a man stood up near the back to my right and screamed out 'You're supposed to be preaching from II John!' He again shouted at me, began to curse and get very agitated. By this time, a policeman rushed in and subdued him, and our men escorted him outside. It was later found out that he had a long police record." Before and during every service, deacons and others go to various prayer closets in the church and bathe everything and everyone in prayer.

Just as there have been occasions of disruptions, there have been many people who have been encouragers. One in particular was Rev. Mueller. He was a retired preacher who lived at Baptist Terrace. He had a high, shaky voice, and he sat near the front. When he said "amen," it was unmistakable and a blessing! After services, he would collect discarded literature to send to those he felt might need the information.

The church began to experience unparalleled growth. The morning services had increased to three, Sunday School space was "maxed out," and parking continued to be a major problem. There were plans to purchase more property in the surrounding downtown area around the church, but the efforts were unsuccessful. The pastor appointed a "Committee for the Future" to explore options for long-term plans. The members of the committee recommended a relocation and the purchase of at least one hundred acres, with plans for a Christian school, senior retirement center, worship center for five thousand, and other facilities to house ministries of the church. Because of this, a decision was made to look elsewhere, out of downtown. This began a period of upheaval. The church experienced a time of division. Some members wanted to remain in the area for a number of good, sound reasons. The majority, however, saw that it would be impossible to do this if the church expected to meet the expanding needs of its congregation. A tearing process began that was painful for all. Brother Jim remembers: "This was a difficult time for me and many of our people. I wanted everyone to see the vision God had led us so clearly in and go with us on this new adventure of faith. Not everyone was as enthusiastic as I was! My emotions went through a roller-coaster experience for a while; from unbelief, to anger, to grief, and in time, to understanding and peace that the Lord was in control and He would take care of His church. My responsibility was to be faithful to follow His leadership. With the passing of the years, I see more clearly His hand on both churches, but I still miss some familiar faces whose lives encouraged me in the faith."

In 1981, the church voted to purchase 140 acres at I-4 and Thirty-third Street. "The Seventy Day Miracle" was an incredible time when over $2.5 million was committed by the church for the property purchase. A check for $2,620,000 was handed over to the trustees before the deadline by the city of Orlando which bought some of the property the church purchased earlier in her attempt to stay downtown. The church received national attention, including a mention on Paul Harvey's commentary.

In a supplement to the "Beacon," dated November 19, 1981, Brother Jim wrote:

> How do you spell miracle? Only one way: GOD. He is the only explanation. There is no other way to define a supernatural event. The financial miracle we are witnessing is beyond human achievement. It cannot be coerced. It cannot be sentimentalized. It cannot be manipulated. People do not release money, savings, stocks, bonds, land, houses, antiques, jewelry, silver, coin and gold collections, and a host of other prized possessions on a whim. They do it for one reason only. Because they love the Lord, His church, and the advance of His Kingdom more than any earthly prize. They give because they are obedient servants. "Jesus Christ is Lord" is not an empty phrase in their mouths, but a deep-down commitment of their wills. . . . a young couple with tears in their eyes said they had something to give for "Crossing Over". . . and she, with trembling hands, pulled off her wedding rings. "We have nothing else. This is our best. The Lord told us to do it during the service." As I shared that with our congregation, it seemed as if the Holy Spirit used that as a culmination of prayer and the

Sunday School Round-up Day, October 1981. Two cowboys: David Cunningham and Mac McCully

testimonies of others to begin to break us and lift our sights to a higher level of meaningful giving. It was a widower opening his billfold and shaking out two gold wedding rings and saying, "Put 'em in." It was a young Vietnamese mother and wife giving her ring; a young adult giving the papers on a registered Hereford bull; a single-again giving all of her silver and crystal. Truly, the Lord was in control.

Also in 1981, Parkway asked to come back as a mission with Danny Strickland as pastor. Our church voted to help them with much-needed repairs and expansion. Our Sunday School enrollment was 2,495. Brother Jim was elected the president of the Southern Baptist Convention Pastor's Conference in St. Louis. Guests of the church during the year included Myrtle Hall, Vance Havener, Alan Celoria, Jimmy Draper, Tim and Bev LeHaye, Jeannette Clift George, Jerry Clower, and Marge Caldwell. Additions to the staff included Sandy Bozarth, Cindy Franks, Jerry Terrell, and Lois Ann Conoley. Some other noteworthy events and people were a deacon's retreat, an Israel seminar, the "Liberated Wailing Wall" in concert, the first Institute of Church Leadership, forty-eighty weddings, one hundred babies dedicated, forty-one funerals, the Easter drama, two ordained to the gospel ministry, twelve men becoming deacons, the South Orlando Baptist mission dedicated, Vacation Bible School, a visit to the Holy Land, the dinner theater's "You Can't Take It With You," Camp Orlando, Lake Eola Labor Day Weekend, Evangelism Explosion classes, Kay Dunn visit, and the Singing Christmas Tree with five hundred receiving Christ. Brother Jim began serving as a trustee of Palm Beach Atlantic College until 1986.

In 1982, First Baptist purchased 150 acres at I-4 and Thirty-third Street (now John Young Parkway). On January 3, the church offered a "Sneak, Peek & Snack" preview of the following courses of study: Thru the Bible in One Year with Jean King, Dealing with Emotions with Clarence Sichler, God's Economy with Jerry Tuck, E. E. Primer with Gerry Leonard, New Life in Christ (singles) with Jimmy Knott, Preparing for Marriage with John and Sandra Winnie, Spiritual Gifts with Chuck Young, Intermediate Choral Reading with Eileen Weisenbarger and Mac McKinney, The Cults and Eastern Religions with Jim Hansen and Don Moody, Potential Leaders with David Cunningham, Deaf Church Training with Phala Bernhardt, Understanding Youth with Rick Blythe, Ministry of Deacons with Ray Dorman, Basic Sunday School Leadership with Mac McCully, Abundant Life with John Reisinger, New Members Class with Bill Curl, Introduction to the Bible with Jeanette Henry, and Introductory Signing with Bonnie McNutt.

In January two evening worship services were begun. Jimmy Dusek came on staff as minister to senior adults. A stirring revival was given by Sam Cathey and John Shillington from January 27 to February 5. Also in February D. James Kennedy, founder of Evangelism Explosion, electrified fellowship hall with an urgent call. Vernard Johnson, gospel saxophonist, gave a concert. Wayne Johnson was ordained on February 17. Previously he had served for seven years as the preschool/children's minister in the Education Department. Now he became the minister of media with responsibilities including television, radio, print, drama, and public relations. Tommy Gowan was called as minister to adults. The Jean Mallory Scholarship Fund was begun. The senior adult choir (aged sixty or above) began in February. Norma Zimmer sang in March. Perry Sanders and Bill Cox led the church in a great revival. Josh McDowell came for the Super Singles Seminar. David Wilkerson held a citywide youth crusade in our church in

Upon this Rock symbol—Courtesy Ralph Edfeldt

March. Mrs. B. B. McKinney gave a testimony in March honoring her husband's music, including "The Nail Scarred Hand," "Wherever He Leads I'll Go," "Breathe on Me," "Let Others See Jesus in You," and "Have Faith in God." On March 7, the church expanded to three morning services. On Friday, March 12, the church held an "Absolute Auction" of donated items for the church's expansion. Also in March the church celebrated 111 years of history "Look Back with Gratitude." During Easter, the choir and drama presented "The Day He Wore My Crown" to audiences totaling over ten thousand. Christian Home Week was celebrated May 2 through 9. First Baptist and WFTV celebrated twenty years of cooperative efforts in the production of "The First Hour."

The capital funds committee began a fund-raising campaign to raise 12.6 million dollars over a three-year period. Various themes were suggested, but Jim Henry kept coming back to the words "Upon the rock." Finally it was decided to call the campaign "Upon This Rock." The general theme was taken from Jeremiah 33:3. Karick Price, one of the building committee members, thought the church should find a rock to symbolize this event. He spoke with Alex Marsh, another building committee member, and Alex said, "I believe I have just seen the perfect rock." The rock was approximately thirty-three tons and came out of a quarry near Brooksville. Alex was able to get the rock and bring it to the church on a low-boy truck. After one or two moves, the rock was permanently settled at the front entrance at the new campus.

The August 22 "Beacon" welcomed the Charles Bells. He was appointed to the staff as minister of psychology services. September 10 was set aside as a day of prayer and fasting. Evangelism Explosion began its thirty-seventh semester with a current total of 601 professions. Barbara Lee Johnson led the Ladies' Retreat. The Jack Taylor Renewal Conference was held from September 12 to 15. Pledging banquets were held for "Upon this Rock." On October 31, called "Glory Day," the church reported 13.1 million dollars pledged, plus six hundred thousand dollars for an organ. Newspapers all over the country picked up the story.

Other important events took place in 1982. "David, Darius & DeLion" was presented by the children's choir. South Orlando Chapel was constituted as a mission of our church on June 6. The youth choir went to Israel. In July Bill Thrasher became director of technical services. Bob New celebrated twenty-five years on staff. Camp Orlando was held at Stetson in August. Efrem Zimbalist Jr. made a surprise visit. David Clydesdale directed our congregation as we became part of his newest cantata, "How Great Thou Art." Bo Pittman became director of facilities management. Poly Rouse became assistant pastor/junior high. Art Murphy became assistant pastor/childhood education.

Two members remembered a very special all-night prayer meeting on September 10:

> The land had been bought and we had consulted with someone to help us raise the money to build. His thoughts were that we could raise maybe $10 million for the buildings. We were asked to pray for the week before and then to fast on this day of the all night prayer meeting. It was to start at 10 P.M. and end the next morning at 6:00. We met in the sanctuary on Pine Street. There were about 500 people there although it was sort of hard to count because some people would come and then go as they needed to. There were several small tables along the wall of the Worship Center with the roll of the church on them, and people would go and pray for the people by name who were in our church. There was singing, praying, and speaking. We needed about $10 million to build the new Worship Center and Educational Building in a modified way and $13 million for the complete plan. At some time during the meeting, Trevor Hawk began to rise to his feet. His wife, Dot, took his arm alarmed that he might embarrass himself in some way, but he assured her that he had been impressed by the Lord to speak a word. Not wanting to quench the Holy Spirit, Dot was in agreement for him to stand. He stood up and said that the Lord had given him a vision. There are three groups of "givers" in the church—those who could give but wouldn't, those who wanted to give and couldn't, and those who could

Groundbreaking

give and would. But in his thinking about this, he knew that no one could comprehend such a large amount and it seemed an impossibility to raise so much, but that if each person would just give 50 cents a week, there was no reason why we couldn't raise the whole $13 million. He said, "Why can't we trust God for the whole amount?" The "amens" were loud and the clapping continued for a long time. Then Pastor Jim Henry said, "Trevor, do you want to make that in the form of a motion?" With that, the assembly broke free from the prior, more narrow, expectations. It was a wonderful meeting and we ended up having breakfast in the dining hall afterwards. Brother Jim has quoted Trevor several times since that night because it was so electrifying.

The Singing Christmas Tree was presented to twenty thousand with nine hundred decisions. Our property was valued at $10.5 million with a debt of $1.47 million. Resident membership was 5,325 and the Sunday School average attendance was 2,778. Average attendance for the choirs was 1,049.

In 1983, First Baptist had a groundbreaking on January 30 for the new church at I-4 and Thirty-third Street (now John Young Parkway). The music enrollment stood at 1,316. The church's property was valued at $13,610,037, with a debt of $1,438,725. Other highlights took place in 1983. David Cunningham presented the first award from the Kathy Enfinger Memorial Scholarship Fund to Frank Derrick, and Sam Cathey was our special guest in all three services in mid-January. Composer David Clydesdale directed the adult choir in performing "We Shall Behold Him." Jenell Strickland joined the staff as preschool associate. Doug Oldham visited in March with song and testimony. Chester Swor spoke, and Jim Barclay joined the staff in April as the minister to singles. The adult choir and drama produced the Easter program "The Day He Wore My Crown." The Billy Graham Crusade came to Orlando, with Cliff Barrows and Bev Shea visiting our services. Pastor Jim Henry served as chairman for the crusade, and hundreds of our people were participants as ushers, choir members, and counselors. Sandi Patty and Larnelle Harris gave a concert in May, and Larry McFadden became assistant minister of music. Two hundred from the church traveled to Liverpool on a mission trip in June. In July the thrift shop, in its thirteenth year, moved to a new location. Camp Orlando's "Cause for Joy" took place at Stetson University. The Act III Players presented "Our Town" at their fifth dinner theatre. Evangelist E. J. Daniels was honored for his fifty-plus years of ministry. November hosted the month of missions; the cross was raised at the new facility; and John and Cheryl Cox were commissioned as missionaries to Spain. The Singing Christmas

Cupola

Tree was presented to seventeen thousand people.

In 1984, 550 people from the church were involved in mission activities, including the Youth Choir in Israel. On April 5, Barbara Lee Johnson spoke. The nationally known "Joy of Discovery" speaker, Bible teacher, and author thrilled her audience. Rex Frieze came on staff on June 1. "The Day He Wore My Crown" Easter program was given on Easter Sunday. Colonel James B. Irwin, astronaut, author, and humanitarian spoke at the seventeenth annual Mayor's Prayer Breakfast in May at the Sheraton Twin Towers. Bible Day USA collected one-half million Bibles to send to Uganda. In May forty senior adults took a trip to Nashville, Tennessee, and Eureka Springs, Arkansas. Gerry Leonard celebrated her tenth year as associate of evangelism. David Cunningham resigned to become Sunday School director for Florida. In June a new musical drama, "The Option," written by Wayne Johnson and Larry McFadden, premiered in the evening service. On July 1, a God and Country service was given, with our pastor as speaker. A dessert fellowship followed the evening worship service. In July the pastor attended Foreign Missions Week at Ridgecrest, North Carolina. On August 26, forty-four people joined the church. On September 6, Parkway Mission became a church with Danny Strickland as pastor. Three open houses were scheduled for the new facilities. The "Labor of Love" volunteers recruitment was successful. In December, during Sunday School Leadership, members received a total of 427 leadership awards in basic or advanced Sunday School work, ranking the church members one of twenty-five top churches in the state. The Singing Christmas Tree results were 480 professions of faith, 379 desiring more information on the Christian life, and 65 other decisions. The resident membership had climbed to 6,129. Brother Jim's second book, *The Pastor's Wedding Manual*, was published by Broadman Press.

The year 1985 could be called the "Year of the Move." Prior to the actual move, the pastor, accompanied by Bob Talton and Karick Price, drove around the new property in a jeep, praying and claiming the land for the Lord. "We simply claimed this as the Lord's turf and asked Him to build a mighty church to His glory." Strangely, this was another time when spiritual warfare was experienced. The pastor reported:

> One instance I clearly recall happened immediately after the men of the church gathered in the late afternoon to pray over the new buildings, grounds, and ministry of the church we were dedicating and moving into the next day. We broke into groups and with trumpets blowing and

Jim Henry and Karick Price

the Christian flag waving, we marched around the buildings and grounds, even on property we did not own, but wanted to some day. As soon as we left, a man drove onto campus, took a pistol, and tried to kill himself. He was not successful and was able to drive himself to the hospital to get medical help. Later he said he didn't know why he did it . . . something just came over him and urged him to do it. He had never been in our church! The men had just prayed that the Lord would protect all the people from harm who came on the property. We believe Satan tried to rebuke the Lord and our prayer, but he was unsuccessful. Spiritual warfare is a constant in every Christian's experience. Our present church still experiences warfare, but increasingly to a lesser degree. I believe this is because of the growing level of prayer, awareness, praise and maturity in the church.

From Kenneth Muilenburg about the new property:

The building of the new facilities has been an exciting part of my life for the past three years. As Chairman of the Building Committee, it has been gratifying to see the ideas of the church members and staff transferred to drawings and then these drawings becoming a physical reality. It's exciting to be able to have features such as the column free sanctuary, expandable choir space, orchestra lift, television presentation facilities, and a state of the art sound and lighting system. These will allow our creative staff to preach and present the Gospel in many ways that have not been available in the past. It thrills me to imagine such a place where thousands can worship and celebrate together and know that thousands more can have the opportunity to hear God's Word and be saved.

In January evangelist Junior Hill and Tom Lester, of "Green Acres" TV fame, were guests. In February First Baptist officially moved its meeting place to the new facilities on McLeod Road. In March there was a week of celebration including several guests: Sandi Patty, Larnelle Harris, Jerry Clower, Zig Ziglar, Beverly Terrell, Joyce Landorf, Carl Lewis, Willie Gault, Pat Boone, Bill Tanner, Hale and Wilder, and Nielson and Young. A time capsule was deposited in a special container outside the grand staircase. Also in 1985, missionaries Helen and Ray Reynolds returned to Belgium after a furlough. The three stained-glass windows in the worship center building were titled "The Master," "The Message," and "The Ministry." Roger Hogan from California was elected to design, create, and install the windows.

Jim Henry wrote about these windows in the supplement to the *Orlando Sentinel* on February 24, 1985:

> The three stained-glass windows in the new facilities depict the heart of First Baptist and her mission. The center window, located in the worship center over the baptistery is called "The Master Window." It presents the three highlights of the redemptive work of our Lord Jesus Christ and is of Tiffany-type leaded glass. On the left side of the window are three crosses with the ray of light coming down and touching Christ and the thief who will go to Paradise, but not touching the other who refused Christ's love and forgiveness.
>
> To the right is Christ coming from the tomb, which is golden, still full of the power of the Resurrection. Above is the Second Coming scene, with the angels and saints descending with Christ to reign over the world and answer man's long-prayed for peace on each.
>
> "The Message Window" is of faceted glass and is located between the worship center and education building. In the center is the Lamb of God, Jesus Christ on the Bible, the Word of God, with a cross, the theme of salvation behind it. The Lamb has the crown on His head, symbolic of the King of Kings. Beginning on the left and moving to the right, the Bible is pictured in capsules: Adam and Eve leaving the Garden of Eden in shame, below them are Abraham and Isaac with the angel behind them, stopping Abraham from taking this large step of faith.
>
> To the right is Moses with the Ten Commandments and the burning bush where God spoke to him and called him to lead the Exodus.

Below the bush is the Good Shepherd, symbolic of Christ and the Twenty-Third Psalm. The harp is to remind us of David and the Psalms. Here, you leave the Old Testament and move to the New with Christ and the disciples.

The ministry of Christ and the Church is captured in the washing of the feet of Peter; the Eucharist is seen in the grapes and the wheat, which speak of the blood and body of Christ. Moving down, you capture a sense of the Book of Revelation, Christ coming on a white horse as the Victor. A larger image of Christ shows Him reaching back to hold future events from happening until His mission of saving people is complete.

In the right corner is a double symbolism, John writing the Revelation while in prison at Patmos, and the Apostle Paul writing the Epistles while imprisoned in Rome. Sweeping upwards to the top is the idea of the new Jerusalem. The lion and the lamb, the child and the deer show peace and harmony in the new world. Above the rainbow is the new Jerusalem with clear crystals and golden colors.

"The Mission Window" is on the northeast side of the worship center. It portrays the reason for the church's existence. In the center is the dove, representing the Holy Spirit. Below the dove are the continents of the world, done in green. The upper left area depicts Christ commissioning the disciples to 'Go into all nations. . . .' Below the scene of Christ's commissioning is a contemporary scene of a person being baptized. Beneath that scene is a lady in a wheelchair, young people on the ground, a man standing and proclaiming the Word. This speaks of the different types of people we are and of those to whom we minister.

To the right is a picture of two men walking toward the church in an urban environment; one witnessing to the other. As you move across, you see a lady in a chair and behind her is the idea of a tent, a man on crutches—all reminders that the Church offers medical aid and the Word of God at the same time.

Farther to the right you catch glimpses of Third World mission fields in Africa and the Orient. A missionary is seen reaching out to starving people to his right. This is a lesson that the Church feeds the hungry with bread and The Bread of Life is Jesus Christ. The overall sense is that every time we pass the window we are to remember that we are to have the world on our hearts. The Church is always to be a going church to minister to the spiritual, emotional and physical needs of the world.

Also in this 1985 supplement, the following was written concerning the media ministry:

> Just over four years ago, First Baptist Orlando took an innovative step in the creation of an office to handle what is known as the Media Ministry. At that time there were less than a dozen like offices across the 35,000 churches in the Southern Baptist Convention.
>
> The various responsibilities assigned the Media Office were, in part, a consolidation of media related tasks, then handled by other offices and, in part, new expanded areas of ministries.
>
> Television, radio broadcasts, cassette tape ministry, public relations, advertising, layout and design, a full print shop, in house promotion/communication, the weekly church newsletter, the church library, audio visuals and special programming and/or presentations all are the responsibility of the Media Office.

Inside new sanctuary

In the Psalms there is a verse which says, 'make known my deeds among the peoples.' We are attempting just that.

During the last calendar year, 70,000 cassette tapes were ordered from and distributed through our tape ministry. These tapes have found their way literally around the world [Don and Nellie Locke notes].

Every Sunday morning THE FIRST HOUR finds its way into thousands of Central Florida homes. For over 22 years First Baptist and Channel 9, WFTV, have worked together to present, live, our worship service. Telephone calls, letters and personal responses are measurable influences of this program. At 10:30 each Sunday you can join with the First Family with the immediacy and intimacy of a front row seat in the worship center.

A briefer visit with us can be had via radio. Two local radio stations, WTLN and WDBO carry a thirty minute program of Bible teaching and messages at 8:00 a.m. each Sunday. The program entitled WE BELIEVE . . . is heard on 13 major market stations throughout the eastern United States.

Christ was the ultimate communicator. His message, the ultimate truth. A world is searching for these answers. And we are compelled to go into the modern world with the most modern communication tools available.

Roxanne Collins, writing for the same 1985 supplement, gave the following information about the church and its structure: There are nearly two linear miles of pews arranged in a fan-shaped manner around the pulpit. A steel beam enabled the "architects to design a columnless room. The beam is actually one main 140-ton truss girder that spans 180 feet and supports four 70-ton secondary girder trusses that span an average of 170 feet. With the structure of the trusses, the Worship Center is a 164,000-square-foot auditorium that seats 6,000." The sound system has 110 speakers. The total sound system is capable of thirty thousand watts.

In April our 118-rank organ was introduced by Don Hustad.

The most visually dominant aspect of the sanctuary is the pipe organ. Designed and constructed by the Schantz Organ Company, it is the largest pipe organ in the Southeast. In a room with poor acoustics, the best organ would sound only fair. For this reason, the acoustical engineers and organ consultants worked closely together to balance the acoustics with the organ. In size, it is a 118-rank organ. A rank equals the number of rows there are of sets of pipes. The largest pipe measures 32 feet tall and about

Ken Varner and organ

two feet in diameter. The smallest is one-and-a-half inches long and is the same width as a pencil. Two of the ranks are called "en chamade" because of the bright, trumpet-like sound they made. These pipes are made of solid copper and are mounted horizontally to face into the congregation similar to trumpets. (Collins)

Rick Blythe accepted a call to Carmel Baptist Church in Charlotte, North Carolina. In June Vera O'Neill was honored as a volunteer chairman of the thrift shop for fifteen years. Robert L. New retired after twenty-six years of service on the staff. There were mission trips to Salvador, Belgium, Pennsylvania, and New Jersey. Bill Silkman joined the church as business administrator. Vacation Bible School enrollment was 902 with fifteen decisions. In July the church held its God and Country service with Dino Kartsonakis in concert. In August Larry and Ann Verlander left as missionaries to Senegal. One thousand church members and others registered for the Bill Gothard Institute seminar. A thank-you note from Ronald Reagan was received by our fourth-grade Sunday School class for sending him a get-well card.

For a time after the church's move to the new campus, there were joint services at the downtown location. However, "at a town-hall type meeting in the downtown sanctuary earlier this month [June], about 1,000 people many of them retirees who live in or near downtown, voiced their desires to break away from the main body of the congregation.

Some live in a nearby retirement tower built and managed by the church" (Gholdston B1). Eventually, this body did become a separate church called Downtown Baptist. Its Charter Sunday was August 4.

Tammie Dutt joined the staff in the area of activities. In October, 3,437 were in Sunday School. John Bisagno held meetings. The Month of Mission's goal was set at $165,000. In November Brother Jim and his wife Jeanette celebrated their twenty-fifth wedding anniversary. Bill Glass spoke to three hundred men with thirty-one receiving Christ. During some troubling times for the Southern Baptist Convention, Brother Jim served on the Peace Committee from 1985 to 1988. He was awarded "Minister of the Year" by the Greater Orlando Baptist Association.

In January 1986, Adrian Rogers was our special Sunday evening pulpit guest. Ron Sylvia was welcomed as student ministries associate for the junior high ministry. Orange County purchased our Christian Life Center on our former campus. Our bookstore opened for business and evangelist David Ring brought his testimony and message. Commitment Sunday set a $6.1 million budget goal for 1986. Our astronauts were remembered following the shuttle tragedy. The library reopened in its new location on February 9. In March Josh McDowell visited and gave an evening message. In the spring twenty thousand attended "The Light" Easter presentations.

In April the sculpture of Joshua and Caleb commemorating our "Crossing Over" emphasis and move was placed outside the entrance to the Welcome Center A. It was a gift from an anonymous donor. David Wanner, from Roger Hogan's company, sculpted the figures, and the complete work was cast in Italy. A plaque next to the sculpture reads in part: "This original Italian cast sculpture captures the biblical Promised Land as a symbol of God's provision for his people. Numbers 13:21–27 . . . The 'Cross Over' challenge became the motto for the people of First Baptist Church, Orlando, Florida, as more than two million dollars was raised in 70 days of miracles paying for this new land in relocating from the downtown facilities." An anonymous donor paid for the sculpture "in memory of Kathy Enfinger, Marjorie Price, and Andy Yaros, and others who sacrificially gave to purchase this land and possess it debt free. 1982–1983"

Junior Hill spoke at a worship service, with ninety-seven people making decisions for Christ. Over thirty-three hundred were in attendance in Sunday School. Tom Gurney accepted the chairmanship for the raising of gifts to fund our Christian school. Kevin Sweat accepted our call as assistant pastor/preschool education. "Side by Side," a musical, brought

*Crossing Over sculpture of
Joshua and Caleb*

together our senior adults and young people. In May, Rosey Grier, former
NFL star, shared his testimony. Participants in Bible Day USA gave 763
Bibles, and our youth choirs presented the musical "Isn't It Amazing."
Also, Rex Frieze was ordained.

In June our high school graduates were honored. More than 170 First
Folks participated in the Adult Choir Mission Tour to Nottingham,
England. During that trip, three hundred people made commitments to
Christ. Two youth camps were held. Evangelist Dave Roever spoke at our
God and Country service, and Larnelle Harris came for a third visit. Lynn
Kennedy was selected as the first director of our Center for Pregnancy. In
July Vacation Bible School had 935 enrolled. Fred Chase accepted a call as
headmaster of our Christian school.

In August our center for pregnancy became a reality with a new location on Lucerne Terrace with Bill Curl as the pastor in charge. Danny de Armas was ordained to the gospel ministry on August 13. Sonlight and God's Creation went on a mission tour to Portsmouth, Virginia. Evangelist Bailey Smith was the guest speaker for the Evangelism Explosion Kick-Off Banquet. The center for pregnancy held its dedication service in September.

October 25 was our "Vision Two" Commitment Sunday. There was an old-fashioned preaching and dinner on the grounds with our pastor and his wife arriving in a horse-drawn carriage, complete with historic attire. In November we observed our Month of Missions with 718 First Folks committed to trips for 1987. Chief Minister Mangosuthu Buthelezi, leader of the Zulu tribe of South Africa, shared his testimony. The Twin Singing Christmas Trees thrilled our hearts. The children's choirs led the First family in a service of sweetness and praise as they sang "Carols from around the World." Brother Jim received an honorary doctor of sacred theology degree from Southwest Baptist University of Bolivar, Missouri. Our year ended in a solemn and wonderful Candlelight Vesper Service and Lord's Supper on Christmas Eve.

In January 1987, David Ring and his family moved to Orlando to become the church's first staff evangelist. The Florida State Evangelism Conference was held at our site. We celebrated "Super Weekend" with Sam Cathey January 24 through 26. Education Building B and the First Academy were under construction. Chris Hinkle joined the staff as director of technical services. Jay Strack led a crusade with Jack Price as worship leader. E. J. Daniels, great evangelist and warm-hearted pastor, went home to be with the Lord in March. Glenn Davis and Jeff Calhoun shared their testimonies. Larry McFadden, associate minister of music, accepted a call to Calvary Baptist Church in Winston-Salem, North Carolina. Our church continued its moving presentations of the "The Light." On April 19 at 6:00 A.M., Bill Curl lead a sunrise Easter service at Sea World with a dramatic portrayal of Pontius Pilate by Wayne Johnson and a special guest speaker Pat Williams, general manager of the Orlando Magic basketball team.

Byron Cutrer joined the staff as assistant pastor of student music. Our God and Country celebration included Steve Green in concert, Orlando Mayor Bill Frederick and other elected officials, along with Derric Johnson and our adult choir. The Sonlight choir went on a mission trip to Nassau in July. The First Academy opened in August with kindergarten through sixth grade. John MacArthur, pastor of Grace Community

Church in Los Angeles, spoke in October. There was a Larry Burkett financial seminar. Greg Elmquist joined the staff as evangelism pastor. A Scripture Memory Banquet was held to honor 250 first-through-sixth graders. There was a grand opening ceremony of our new education building on October 25. There was a record Sunday School attendance of 4,192 on October 25. Cookie Evans began to work part-time as a wedding coordinator. The Month of Mission's goal was set at $176,000. The total membership of the church was 9,309 with 5,978 resident members; Sunday School average attendance was 3,182; the church's property was valued at $35,200,000; and $1,155,679 was given to missions. During the Twin Singing Christmas Trees' six presentations, 795 prayed to receive Christ, 614 made other decisions, and 35,000 were attendees.

In 1988, five hundred were sent on short-term missions. Danny Wilson was appointed as the new police chief of Orlando's Police Department. January 31 was Super Sunday with J. Harold Smith the pulpit guest speaking on "God's Three Deadlines" and Babbie Mason in song. In January Ed Irey, former minister of music, went home to be with the Lord. He passed beautifully, singing the songs of Zion with his family around his bed. Marti Albert celebrated her twentieth year as the pastor's

Bob Marrero

secretary. Ragan Vandegriff celebrated his tenth year on the staff. On March 1, Martha Edfeldt completed twenty-five years on the staff, working as music secretary and then in the accounting office. March 6 was the Founder's Day Service, with our church celebrating 117 years "young." At that service, the honorary position of deacon emeritus was initiated. The following men received the position: James W. Brandon, Ralph Cottrell, John I. Denson, F. Ray Dorman, Dawson Gunter, J. Thomas Gurney Sr., Alvin S. Hall Sr., George Russell Harper, Marion R. Hunter, Basil B. Hull, Robert L. Marrero, Todd Pemberton, and Millard B. Smith. Poly Rouse left the staff after three years to join First Baptist Church of Merritt

Island. On April 25, Sandra Mullenburg assumed the position of executive assistant to the pastor after Marti Albert had to step down due to her health. On June 5, Parkway Baptist Church, our mission, dedicated its new building.

On July 10, Roger Glidewell was presented to the church for the position of assistant pastor/student ministries. Larry McFadden and his family returned to Orlando, and he became our staff music evangelist. The church's youth went on a mission trip to Nottingham, England, and Glasgow, Scotland, for the Baptist World Youth Congress. Ron Sylvia and his wife left for seminary. On August 15, Terry Winch joined the staff as the first director of instrumental music. Betty Moffatt was recognized for ten years of service in helping to organize and direct the church orchestra, "Jubilation." The Pastor's Guest Reception and Discovery Class was inaugurated on October 2. Pat Hanson celebrated twenty-five years on staff, working as youth director then in the finance office. Wayne Johnson celebrated fifteen years of service with First Baptist, Orlando. From the "Beacon" Pastor Jim Henry wrote of Wayne Johnson as "God's man for these critical years of expansion and probing new areas of visionary outreach through television, drama, radio, and printed material. . . . Carol is equally talented and committed, carving her own niche in teaching and missions." Lucy Pat Curl was elected president of the Florida Pastor's Wives Conference for 1988–1989. Bob Marrero stepped down after nine years as administrator of Baptist Terrace. The adult choir performed at EPCOT. Many of the other traditional events, ministries, and functions of the church continued.

In 1989, the Meadow Woods Church was begun. On January 1, the Intercessory Prayer Room was officially opened. Richard Rettinger and his family began their ministry in Belgium. Two hundred church members were sent on short-term missions. "In mid-December at their annual meeting, the SACS (Southern Association of Colleges and Schools) awarded our church school certification. . . . This achievement makes our school the only SACS accredited institution in Central Florida (private, parochial, public, or Christian) to have achieved this award for its elementary grades. . . . The dream of Mr. Tom Gurney Sr., adopted by our church family in its long range plan for the future in 1981, grows brighter with the years. To God be the glory!" (Henry, "Beacon," January 4, 1990).

In 1990, the church paid off its existing debt and went to two morning worship services. The total membership was 9,020, with Sunday School enrollment at 7,876 and attendance of 3,601. The "Wings of Faith" financial commitment emphasis began its first full year. John Walker assumed

"Christ Crucified"—Courtesy David Naquin

the position of senior director of church finance in January. Also in January, the Ligonier Conference was held on our campus with teachings by Chuck Colson, R. C. Sproul, Josh McDowell, Becky Pippert, and others. The Cathedrals sang in concert. Volunteers of the church were recognized at a February Sunday service. Joe and Gurney Grafton gave a gift to the church: a beautiful crystal and gold eagle sculpture symbolizing the church's "On Wings of Faith" commitments. An anonymous church couple gave the church orchestra a new Lyon and Healy harp.

From the April 5 "Beacon": "How can we at First Baptist support 8,000 home and foreign missionaries, 6 seminaries, 8 commissions and more? Only by cooperating with the other 38,000 SBC churches through the COOPERATIVE PROGRAM. The Cooperative Program was established in 1925 as an effort to extend the mission of the church into the far reaches of our world. Last year we gave $991,620 to the Cooperative Program. That is 14% of the budget tithes and offerings. That sacrificial

Marie Williams Memorial Chapel—Courtesy Ralph Edfeldt

giving certainly has eternal results in the lives of thousands of people around the world. Sunday we celebrate Cooperative Program Day."

In June Headmaster Fred Chase of the First Academy tendered his resignation for health reasons. Sign-up cards were provided on September 16 and 23 for members to participate in the "Call to the Wall Watchman Ministry." Once in operation, 672 prayer warriors, 4 for each hour, every hour, twenty-four hours per day, would pray. Ed and Missy Moses were home on furlough from Bophuthatswana and spoke on September 19. Over five thousand church members gathered outside for a picture taken by a helicopter, Governor Bob Martinez made a surprise visit, and guest speaker Jerry Johnston all had a part in "Friend Day." After one year, the "Wings of Faith" campaign had collected over $1.2 million dollars, so that two of our buildings were declared completely debt free. Bill Curl submitted his resignation from the staff so that he and Lucy Pat could accept their appointment by the Foreign Mission Board to be career missionaries in Wales.

In 1991, the Marie Williams Chapel was dedicated. It was a gift to the church from Art Williams in memory of his late wife Marie. The Cathedrals returned for an evening concert in January. The tape ministry placed in circulation its one millionth tape. The Persian Gulf War impacted the church as some members and their families were called into active military service. Ed Gamble became headmaster for the First Academy. After twenty-three years with Channel 9, the church found out it needed to purchase its own television equipment. A crusade by Jerry Johnston was held February 17–22. At the Sunday evening service on March 17, Marvin Rosenthal presented the Jewish Seder, explaining its historical significance and demonstrating how Christ is actually portrayed throughout the meal. "The Light" was presented to approximately forty thousand. Major Ian Thomas conducted a Bible Conference in April. In May Larry Burkett led a Financial Freedom Conference. In August R. T. Kendall, pastor of historic Westminster Church in London, was our pulpit guest. Lois Ann Roberts and Sandy Lemay celebrated their tenth anniversaries on staff. Greg Elmquist resigned to begin a new work. October 13 was "Law Enforcement Day," and on October 27, Rick Stanley, nephew of Elvis Presley, was welcomed back as pulpit guest. The Singing Christmas Trees celebrated the holiday season and later we had our traditional Candlelight Service on December 24. President and Mrs. George Bush sent New Year's greetings and recognized our youth's New Year's Eve celebration. The value of the church's total property was $38,500,000; total church membership was 9,738; and Sunday School attendance was 3,778.

The year was now 1992. Charles Stanley was the January 5 guest speaker. On January 12, Jimmy Dusek celebrated his tenth anniversary on staff. The church extended a call to Mike McKee as assistant pastor to median and senior adults. Sam Cathey was the pulpit guest on Super Sunday. The Ligonier Conference was held in February with the following as some of the speakers: Charles Colson, J. I. Packer, R. C. Sproul, Charles Swindoll, and Ravi Zacharias. Roy Reaves celebrated ten years as the church's master printer. Charles Bell also celebrated ten years on staff. Mary Sims retired after thirty-five faithful years serving the church in the facilities department. Tim Grosshans joined the church staff as minister for singles. Since that time, the Single Adult Department has grown into a very large segment of the church. There are ten Sunday morning Bible study departments. The ages range from twenty-one to eighty-four and include the never married, the widowed, and the divorced. They represent over twenty-five percent of the church's adults. The singles of the church experience and work in several ministries. Some of them include the annual Labor Day Retreat, Meals on Wheels, Outreach Missions, serving at Sunday Night Fellowships, Mission trips, Weeknight Praise,

Tom Gurney Sr. and Jim Henry

Divorce Recovery classes, and Single Parent classes.

Also in 1992, nearly three hundred members of the adult choir and Drama Department took "The Light" to Coventry, England. The church sent relief teams to Miami after Hurricane Andrew struck south Florida. Sadly, from the September 19 "Beacon": "Tom Gurney, Sr. went home to be with Jesus Monday morning, August 31. He was a pioneer in Florida and left a legacy in the field of law, education, and civic leadership that has influenced and will influence people for generations to come. His life spanned nearly a century. He was an era. . . . He gave generously to the Lord's work and served as chairman of one of our major building fund drives. A strong advocate of Christian education, his dream of a Christian school in our church became the Tom Gurney Elementary School and The First Academy. In death, he yet speaks for he has remembered his church and school in his will. Tom Gurney's influence will live a long time." We had Law Enforcement Day. On November 8, the church broke ground for the new First Academy gymnasium. Bill Mitchell joined the staff. The Singing Christmas Trees gave their presentations in December. The total church membership was now 9,861.

In 1993, the David Ring Ministries presented the "Touch of God Conference" on January 24–28 which included some of the following speakers and musicians: Oliver North, Adrian Rogers, Junior Hill, Ed Young, Sam Cathey, Phil Haskins, Joseph Stowell, Bill Stafford, Gary Taylor, Tim Lee, David Ring, the Cathedrals, the Talleys, the Hoppers, Greater Vision, the Bishops, and Mike and Faye Speck. On March 7, the church celebrated "Miracle Day." Several weeks prior to that date, each church member was given a dollar bill after the pastor read the biblical passage about the talents. Each person was to use the money and see how God would direct him or her to multiply it. The results were to be returned to the church. The members did many things. Some bought seeds and planted fruits, vegetables, or flowers and sold the results from their gardens. Others bought materials for craft items which were made and sold. The congregation was called together on that victory Sunday, and the monetary results totaled nearly three hundred thousand dollars from the four-thousand-dollar to five-thousand-dollar initial investment.

On March 27, the church dedicated the Activities Building/ Gymnasium of the First Academy. The church broke ground on April 23 for the new fellowship hall, later named Faith Hall. Hunter Pittman, one of First Baptist Church's youngest members, and Edna Kelsey, one of First Baptist Church's oldest members, helped in the ceremony. Brother Jim, his wife, and a group of church members visited Israel. For the pastor, some of the highlights of the trip included "baptizing several in our group in the Jordan River and hearing their testimony as people from around the world stood in rapt attention; the Lord's Supper on the Mount of Olives with thirty-to-forty-mile-per-hour winds roaring into our faces and singing 'How Great Thou Art'; preaching and teaching to eager learners in Arab Christian churches in Nazareth, Turan and Haifa; accidentally sitting down in the women's section of the Great Synagogue of Jerusalem and getting the attention of every woman there."

In August the church returned to one morning worship service. Dan Taylor was called as the new minister of education in September. Jon Berry was welcomed as the new director of food services. Michael D. Brown was ordained by the church on August 4. On October 1, Pat Hanson celebrated her thirtieth anniversary of service for First Baptist. In October Percy W. Lancaster was recognized as serving as an active usher at First Baptist Church for forty years. Prior to that, he served as an usher for many years at other churches. During MissionsFest '93, nineteen First Baptist Church people presented themselves as candidates for career missions and nearly five hundred volunteered for special mission projects.

Brother Jim wrote in the November 4 "Beacon":

November 27, 1960 was a significant date for me. A godly group of men gathered on a Sunday afternoon in Nashville, Tennessee to question me concerning my call to the ministry prior to ordaining me. Some of those men are in glory now, but I will always be grateful for their love and trust,

Triple Trees

and that of Dalewood Baptist church in commissioning me to the gospel ministry. As I begin my 34th year as a pastor, I am eternally grateful to my Lord Jesus Christ for saving and calling me to pastor; for that large stream of men and women who prayerfully, lovingly, and faithfully mentored me in the faith; for my parents and family who encouraged me; for Jeanette who has been my understanding and supportive wife; for my children who are not ashamed that their dad is a pastor and preacher; and for the four churches who have given to me the joy of discovering something of the glory and greatness of God together.

Mark Meyer was welcomed as director of facilities in November. The church's total membership broke the ten thousand mark, and Sunday School attendance was 3,501.

In 1994 during March and April, "The Light" was presented in eight services with 545 people accepting Christ. In May Faith Hall was completed and was dedicated debt free. The beautiful stained-glass window in the rotunda was originally in the 1917 worship center. The First Academy graduated its first senior class with twenty-two members. First Academy enrollment had reached 705. Junior Hill led the church in a four-day Harvest Revival. Three missionaries were commissioned from the church: Dan and Mary Agnes Minnich for Taiwan and Lee Flippen for Burkina Faso. Anne Bell's four section murals were being placed in Faith Hall. They depict the 125-year history of the church.

In June Brother Jim received the high honor of being elected as president of the Southern Baptist Convention at its annual meeting, which was held that year in Orlando. He subsequently served two one-year terms. On September 8, the pastor was the invited guest of President Clinton at a prayer breakfast for religious leaders at the White House, meeting personally with the president after the meal. On Friend Day, Jay Carty was guest speaker. The Singing Christmas Trees was presented nine times with 45,000 in attendance and 797 professing new faith in Christ. Total church membership was 10,152, with Sunday School average attendance of 3,740.

Nineteen ninety-five was designated the "Year of Evangelism." Art Murphy celebrated his tenth anniversary of being on staff as the childhood education pastor. Moody Adams was the guest for Super Sunday on January 29. On February 12, the church celebrated ten years at its McLeod Road campus. On March 3–5, our junior highers went on a beach retreat. The First Academy girls varsity basketball team went to district finals in March, winning the finals, the regional championship, and placing second in the state. The tenth anniversary presentations of "The Light" were given April 6–9 and 12–15 with 927 professions of faith. On April 28, Lynn Kennedy was commissioned by the Foreign Mission Board as a missionary to Burkina Faso, West Africa. In May, during "Making Friends Forever," Junior Hill was guest evangelist; Bud Hedinger, anchor or Channel 6, spoke at a men's night; and Marla Weech, anchor for Channel 9, spoke at a women's night. In May the pastor and his wife took a group to the Holy Land. Other highlights for the year included "Mission Orlando" neighborhood Bible clubs in nineteen locations which reached 658 people with the Good News; Brother Jim's election to a second term as SBC president; Camp Orlando's "Carry the Light" theme involving 360 of our young people; 250 of our single adults attending the annual Labor Day get-away; Commitment Sunday recording $260,165 MissionsFest giving, with 305 volunteers for missions and 13 for career missions. On Friend Day the Sunday School set a record attendance record of 5,135, with forty-four professions after Jay Carty spoke in the morning service. Elizabeth Dole, wife of Senator Bob Dole, gave her testimony in November; the "Singing Christmas Trees" performed November 30, December 1–3, and 6–10 in their fifteenth anniversary; and on November 19, Brother Jim received the John Young Award from the Greater Orlando Chamber of Commerce.

On January 7, 1996, the church began its year-long celebration of its history called, "The Year of the Church." The verse for the year was Genesis 28:17b: "This is none other than the house of God, and this is the gateway to heaven!" which focused on the original name of the church, Bethel. A wonderful display of Orlando and First Baptist history was set up in the narthex by a subcommittee of the Year of the Church. During the morning service, a video was run with pictures of our history accompanied by Michael W. Smith's original song, written with his wife Deborah especially for the church, "Our Hearts as One."

Let us offer up our praise to the Maker of our days
To the Author and Perfecter of our faith.
Let us take the road we see, holding fast what we believe
With hope like those who came this way by (before) grace.

Chorus:
Since we have so great a cloud of witnesses around
Let us lay aside the sin that hinders us
Let us run with perseverance in the race that lies ahead
With our hearts as one and our eyes on Jesus.
(Used by permission of Michael W. and Deborah D. Smith)

The following trivia questions were displayed in the narthex and on the screen in the sanctuary: "What was the church's first name and what was the original name of Orange County?" Also in January Scott Randlett came on staff as assistant pastor/students/junior high. First Baptist participated once again in the Life Chain on January 21. Super Sunday was celebrated on January 28 with Ron Dunn pulpit guest and Brad Hansen guest musician. On March 3, the church celebrated its 125th anniversary. For several weeks, the church experienced unprecedented giving to the budget.

Currently, the church's property covers approximately 120 acres with land and buildings of a net worth totalling $40 million. The membership is approximately ten thousand, with the median age set at thirty-nine. The worship center is one hundred thousand square feet, with seating for sixty-one hundred. The full-time staff numbers one hundred, with over

Aerial view of church complex

one hundred part-time workers. There are over ninety-three hundred enrolled in Sunday School, with 203 graded Sunday School classes, preschool through senior adults. As of 1996, one million people have witnessed the Easter and Christmas presentations. "The First Hour," our television program of the worship service, has been redesigned into "The Sunday First Edition" and reaches millions of viewers.

It is easy to see that the body of this church has undergone a series of changes: new people, new buildings, new challenges, and new experiences. The past marks the way we have been, the present presents itself in hope, and the future is exciting to anticipate.

Some further, special moments follow. From a Founder's Day speech by Jim Henry: "A look back reminds us of the fortitude and courage of yesterday's strength which give us stability and strength today. Yet each

Christian generation must chart new pathways if it is to remain a vital force. If it does not, it becomes a religious relic, a mausoleum of past glories, a cemetery of memories. The ability to appreciate yesterday, enjoy today, and anticipate new challenges tomorrow give a church balance, timeliness, and dynamic."

And from other notes, he writes:

> The years at FBC have been exhilarating. We've seen God do miracles in evangelism, giving, ministries, outreach, innovative programs, and missions. We've started four churches as missions directly and two have spun out of our church because of other initiatives. Our church basically has no debt, yet we have 40 million dollars in assets paid for in less than 10 years. We have a dynamic Christian school and a Center for Pregnancy that has saved many babies and souls. We've seen scores of our people called into the ministry and as career missionaries. We've seen thousands saved through the special programs at Christmas and Easter and mission volunteer trips. We've been able to take our youth and adult choirs on mission trips to Israel and England. We've been able to strongly support the Cooperative Program and special mission offerings without cutting back during building programs. Like the Psalmist, we say, "It's the Lord's doing; it's marvelous in our eyes."

Brother Jim loves to laugh, and he related these two stories, one about a wedding, and the other about a baptism: "I married a young couple, new Christians, in our chapel. After pronouncing them husband and wife and after the traditional bride and groom kiss, I turned them to face the audience, introduced them as Mr. and Mrs. ——, and she blurted out for all to hear, 'At last!'"

"I was in the middle of a baptism service, when all of a sudden all of the lights in the church went out. We found a flashlight; one of our baptism committee members held it on the area where we stood while we finished baptizing. With no microphone, I was shouting out the names. All that the congregation could see was one tiny light and all they could hear was the splash. Some years later, we discovered the culprits who had pulled the major switch on our circuit board. They were all students, including one of our staff member's sons. They're all grown now; one is a pastor and another still an active member of our church!"

Another story is not humorous, but it is inspiring: "A well-known business man in the city was killed in an airplane crash. Only weeks before, he had confessed faith in Christ, having been led to Christ by a

Jim and Jeanette Henry at press conference in Orlando where Jim had just been elected president of the Southern Baptist Convention in June 1994. Baptist Press photo by Morris Abernathy—Courtesy First Baptist Church, Orlando

new Christian and member of our church, Rick Fletcher. I asked Rick to give a word of testimony about his personal faith and that of his tragically killed friend. He accepted and with some fear and sweaty palms, he gave one of the most electrifying testimonies I have ever heard. It spoke to all present, and the church auditorium was nearly full. I am confident that many later came to faith through that accident and powerful witness that was shared that day."

The staff of the church has been remarkable. As in any family, there have been many comings and goings, with men and women leaving for a variety of reasons. Most have left at the Lord's call to a new mission. Regrettably, a few have left for unhappy reasons.

When asked for his memory of a support staff member, Brother Jim remembers:

> We have been blessed through the years with some wonderful people on our support staff. Mary Sims, executive housekeeper, worked on our staff for a few years. She ran our crew with an iron hand; worked hard herself

and always had God's place in tip-top shape. She also was a good cook! Several times a year we have a staff lunch together and everyone brings a covered dish. Mary's dish was turnip greens and corn bread fixed the way my grandmother, mother, and wife fix them; a little hog meat, lots of juice, and fresh greens. Mary knew I liked them and she would always get word to me, personally or in a message, that she had "greens and cornbread," where they were located on the table, and "don't wait too long; they're going fast!" I can still see, taste, and smell those greens, and Mary's shy grin when I told her how much I enjoyed them.

His advice to young pastors is the same as R. G. Lee gave him years ago: 1. Stay on your knees. 2. Stay in the Book. 3. Stay close to your people. Brother Jim has some advice of his own: "The older I get, the more I see that knowing God more deeply is the prime reason for living. Family roots are important. Cultivate them. Stay faithful to our Lord! He can handle all arrangements! Walk by faith. Get around wise people who know God and His work. Think big. Be flexible without compromising biblical principles. God's agape is the greatest thing. Give Him your all. Appreciate the rich Southern Baptist heritage the Lord has given us."

CHAPTER TEN

Missions, Missionaries, and Ministries of First Baptist Church

But there is a friend who sticks closer than a brother.
—*Proverbs 18:24*

Two Missionaries
Ed and Missy Moses in Africa

"But as for you, continue in what you have learned and have become convinced of, because you know those from whom you learned it, and how from infancy you have known the holy Scriptures, which are able to make you wise for salvation through faith in Christ Jesus."
2 Timothy 3:14–15

When Ed Moses awoke that morning, the first thing he heard was the sound of the flies buzzing around his head. The heat rising from his floor mat promised a scorching afternoon. He lovingly gazed at his wife Missy asleep beside him. As he did each morning before arising, he prayed for the day ahead. Suddenly, a surge of power seemed to penetrate his body. He felt the Holy Spirit warning him to be on guard. This often happened. The people of Zimbabwe and the thousands of destitute Mozambique refugees filling the camp experienced terrifying attacks from Satan. An evil spirit called "mashave," which was handed down to some recipients from generation to generation, often attacked people about to take a bold step toward the Holy Spirit.

Fortifying himself with God's armor, Ed allowed himself a few more minutes of reflection as glossy starlings and hoopoe birds made their morning sounds.

His thoughts took him back to his own rich heritage. The generations which preceded him were in stark contrast to those to whom he and Missy were ministering. He remembered Grandma Rowe, who had rented a room in her attic and earmarked that money for missions. His Grandma Mary Nat Moses had saved her egg money and family members' pocket change for the Lottie Moon Offering each year.

Next the faces of his parents, E. B. "Doc" and Ruth, came before him to encourage him. In 1920, as a thirteen-year-old girl, Ruth and her family had joined First Baptist Church, Orlando, and were impressed when the pastor, J. Dean Adcock, visited their home in Clarcona the next week. Ruth and E. B. were married by Adcock at a home ceremony, and she served as a Sunday School teacher for over twenty-five years in the Cradle Roll and Junior Departments. She also was very active in the WMU, which might have explained his ultimate calling into the mission field—that and the prayers of his grandparents.

He remembered being told of his early entry, at six weeks, into the church when his name appeared on the Cradle Roll. As a very young lad, he had participated in R.A.s and Sunbeams. As a young boy, his room was decorated with maps, and his eyes seemed to be drawn to Africa. He wrote letters to missionaries and learned to give to mission efforts. Several church families, including the Kelseys, the Riches, the McGuffies, Alex Young, Mrs. Garnett, and E. P. Eggerton with his strong "amens" echoing from the balcony, influenced his young life as he felt the stirrings of the Holy Spirit. He thought of the summers spent at church camps. The many strong Sunday School teachers came to mind as well as the missionaries who visited the church with amazing stories of the power of the Holy Spirit in faraway lands.

Moving ahead in time, he distinctly remembered his call in 1967 and the confirmation of that call in prayer and Bible reading. Trained as a pharmacist, he entered seminary at Southwestern, becoming equipped as a missionary bound for Africa. Now, on the field for a number of years, he and Missy had themselves become witnesses of God's incredible power in the war-torn countries of Africa. They saw the miracle of "baby" Christians, barely able to read God's Word, energized to become church planters and native pastors. Ed and Missy quickly learned that in order for them to be allowed to introduce others to Jesus Christ, they had to first earn their trust. Realizing the people's desperate physical need for salt, vegetables, fruit, and clothing, Ed and Missy set about to help them help themselves.

Alerting their church family and others in the mission effort, Ed and Missy received and distributed eighty-seven tons of salt, taught the people to plant six thousand vegetable gardens, helped in the planting of seven thousand fruit trees, and gave away tons of used clothing. With that, the Moses couple had earned the right to be heard, and the word "Baptist" was translated into the native tongues as "people who care" and "people with open hands." After twenty-five years, these last six had been what Ed called "the strawberry and whipped cream icing on the cake."

Startled by the advancing hour, Ed and Missy ate a hasty breakfast of bread, butter, jam, and hot tea and then made their way to the Baptist church to meet with the pastor and others for prayer. By mid-afternoon on that Saturday, the excitement level was almost electrifying. A crowd of 350 believers had gathered expectantly at the church situated on a prominent hilltop in the center of nineteen refugee "villages." An impromptu marching band had assembled and the "orchestra" was composed of many goat-skin drums, long spiraling khudu horns of the "umpaah" sounds, gourd shakers, and other indigenous instruments from Mozambiquan culture.

With Ed and the pastor in the lead, a big parade started down the main road right through the center of the refugee camp, scattering an assortment of hound dogs, goats, and pigs. It snaked its way to the Mazowe River, often filled with dangerous crocodiles and smelly from pollution. As the procession continued, large clouds of dust rose in the air. With all that noise and jubilant singing, thousands of refugees soon came out of their huts to see this strange procession. They had never seen a group celebrating with such enthusiasm and joy. Because of their idleness, many others joined the swelling parade.

The baptism service as viewed from the river banks was most impressive as the pastor explained the beautiful symbolism of baptism so clearly to the hundreds of observers and the curious. All went well until "mashave" spirits showed that they had possessed eight different women. One woman about to be immersed was violently overtaken by the evil spirit and her body went wildly out of control. Four strong men struggled to hold her safely on the river bank. Church leaders showed remarkable maturity by the calm and orderly manner in which they prayed for this woman and then seven others who were also similarly victimized. Satan was defeated eight times, and peace prevailed as the women submitted to the Holy Spirit and were baptized.

The Moses family

As the last of the 116 believers came up out of the river and the final prayer was offered, the initial sense of joy and victory even intensified as the homeward-bound triumphal parade once more attracted the attention of thousands of curious onlookers. The march home with loud singing and dancing to the various percussion instruments reminded Missy of a similar incident with King David in the Bible.

Sleep was difficult that night because of the exciting day. Sunday proved to be equally impressive, but in a different way. Over 426 reverent worshipers gathered together in the church they had built themselves to solemnly celebrate the Lord's Supper. Over one hundred adult men were present, which was most unusual in an African setting. The choir, not one of whom knew how to read a single note, outdid themselves. Their joyous singing in three languages overflowed so harmoniously from hearts saturated with God's unconditional love. As Ed and Missy retired for the evening, they wondered what the Lord had in store for them and their African friends. Some of the previous material was written by Ed Moses in an interesting article titled "Destitute Refugees Lead a Triumphant Parade."

MISSIONS AND CHURCHES

(Compiled by Mildred Talton, Pat Hanson, and Pat Birkhead,
using church and associational records)

First Baptist Church, from its beginning, has been committed to forming various missions. Out of these missions have grown several churches. The missions and churches from First Baptist Church, Orlando, along with those churches' offspring, include the following:

1922—North Park Mission. On May 18, 1922, a wooden structure was erected in one day by workmen, with women of the church providing dinner on the grounds. On September 6, 1922, there were thirty-four members and this became *North Park Baptist Church.* From this came Barton Shores, 1953; Azalea Park, 1955; Westside, 1984; Longwood Hills, 1977.

1923—Myrtle Heights Mission. In 1923, this mission was established in a tent on Muriel Avenue. Then the name was changed to Link Mission. In 1928, it became *Delaney Street Baptist Church* with thirty-six members with T. E. Waldrup as pastor. From this came Eastside, 1957; Southside, 1962; Forest Park (later called Dover Shores), 1968; Shenadoah, 1976; *Inglesia Evangelica Baptista,* 1992; and various missions in the British West Indies and elsewhere.

1923—Yancey Mission. This mission was established in a garage at the corner of Hughey and America Streets. On January 1, 1926, it became *Lucerne Park Baptist Church* with forty members and J. Bookhardt as pastor. The church disbanded in 1966.

1926—Concord Park Mission. This mission eventually became *College Park Baptist Church* on March 4, 1928, with twenty members and M. M. Bales as pastor. From this came Fairview Shores, 1947; Riverside Baptist, 1961; Edgewood, 1958–1971; Power's Drive, 1962; King's Way, 1987; Horizons Church, 1990; West Orange 1987.

1927—Miller Memorial. On February 27, 1927, this mission was named for W. P. Miller and was established with fifty-nine members. From this came Fairvilla, 1958, and Central Mission, 1971.

1954—Pine Hills Baptist. Began with 109 members and V. N. Maggart as pastor. From this came Sheeler Heights, 1963, and Pine Hills Espanic 1987.

1957—Walnut Street. Began with 159 members and Harold Epperson as pastor.

1961—Tangelo Park. Began with 321 members and Robert Pinder as pastor.

1972—Maitland Baptist Church. Paul Thomas was the first pastor.

1974—McCoy Mission. Began with James R. Hope as pastor. Became Southview with T. J. DeBose as pastor.

1976—Parkway Baptist Church. This church returned to First Baptist as a mission in 1981 and then left in 1984 as a church with Danny Strickland as pastor.

1976—Primera Iglesia Bautista. A few years prior to its establishment as an independent church in 1976, Rafael de Armas gathered a group of Spanish-speaking members in the balcony of First Baptist. There he translated the pastor's sermons into Spanish. Later they moved to the church's chapel to hold Spanish services. Then they moved to their own building in 1976 with de Armas as pastor.

1979—South Orlando Mission. On June 10, 1982, this mission became South Orlando Baptist Church with two hundred members and Jack Fletcher as pastor.

1989—Church at Meadow Woods. No information is available for this church.

In the strictest sense, First Baptist Church of Winter Park might not be considered a mission of First Baptist Church of Orlando. However, in 1913, several members of the Orlando church asked for their letters to form a new church closer to their homes. First Baptist Church of Orlando gave support and, later, an organ to this group.

While not a mission, Downtown Baptist Church has a strong affiliation with First Baptist Church of Orlando. When First Baptist Church, Orlando moved to its new campus, some members felt the need of a continuing Baptist presence in the downtown area. At first a satellite idea was tried. Finally, however, a new church was formed, Downtown Baptist Church.

MISSIONARIES, JOURNEYMEN, AND EVANGELISTS

Missionaries affiliated with First Baptist Church include the following (missionaries with an asterisk were on the field in May 1996): William and Joyce Burkhalter—Indonesia,* Seth and Barbara Collier—Wales, Inez Crane—Burma, Bill and Lucy Pat Curl—Wales,* Lee Flippen—Africa,* Mary Evelyn Fredenburg—Nigeria, William and Alice Gaventa—Nigeria, Richard and Frankee Hellinger—India, Marc and Sandra Johnston—GOBA resort ministries,* Lynn Kennedy—Africa,* Dan and Mary Agnes Minnich—Taiwan,* Ed and Missy Moses—Africa, Lin Pinter—Africa,* William Powell—Africa, Nora Rakes—foreign and home missions, Ray and Helen Reynolds—Europe,* the W. F. Sharps—Cuba, William L. and Carolyn Smith—Brazil, D. T. and Elizabeth Stamps— China, Larry and Ann Verlander—Senegal,* and Graham and Jeanne Walker—Singapore.*

On July 24, 1949, Mary Evelyn Fredenburg sent the following letter to the church from Nigeria, West Africa:

> Dear Friends: After a year and three months of teaching, I have finally returned to medical work but in an entirely different section of the country. I am now in the eastern section, a country of rivers, rubber trees, saw mills (mahogany), and four or five different tribes of people. We are opening a new hospital in this area in about three months when Dr. and Mrs. Gaventa come. It is to be a big hospital and well equipped, but a tremendous task for a new doctor. I know that you will assure Alice and Bill [Gaventa] of your love and interest as you have me. Orlando will have a big share in staffing Eku Baptist Hospital, and we covet the prayers of those at home for our work. Pray with us that our ministry might be entirely that of Jesus, healing not only those in physical need but those in spiritual need as well—the thousands in this area who have never heard of our Saviour. With love and prayers.

The following, from the July 19, 1990, "Beacon," written by Bill Curl, gave a flavor of missionary work in Kenya:

> They walked single file along narrow, dusty paths from village to village—sharing God's love to the listeners. Occasionally a barefoot woman with a large jug of water balanced atop her head would smile and step aside as they passed. Or maybe they would need to stop a moment, allowing a young boy with a small herd of goats to cross the way.
>
> Often the footpath would lead beside a small cornfield or through low growing bush with a few big trees. The sun was hot—but a cool breeze made the arid climate pleasant.
>
> As the entourage of four or five would enter a village, the first to notice would direct them to the coolest spot, usually under a shade tree. Often this greeter was a mother, busy with several young children. She would summon the elder of the village, the man who commanded highest respect. The visitors were welcomed, and brought something to sit on— a small stool carved from a tree trunk, a simple log, a mat woven from

straw spread on the sandy dirt. Occasionally a low cot was pulled out and once or twice there was a wooden chair to offer the guest.

Friendly conversation would begin—introductions and exchanging of greetings. Soon the owner would be told of the purpose of the visit—to share with him about the good news of Jesus. Would they be allowed to continue? Seldom would the elder one refuse.

One of the group would eagerly proceed to share God's purpose for us, our need for repentance and salvation, and God's provision for eternal life through Jesus. By now most of the others in the village had gathered around. A mother listened as she nursed her little one. A young boy whittled intently. In the background a woman was heartily pounding her grain. A younger lady came out from her hut made of sticks and clay and straw, resting from her task of grinding with two large round stones. Chickens wandered among the gathering. There were few sounds except of people's voices, asking Jesus to forgive them and take control of their lives.

The Holy Spirit had obviously prepared the hearts of the people in these villages. It was like walking through an orchard at harvest time, gathering an abundance of ripe fruit while being careful not to pick the green as well. There were 16 teams of three from FBC/O (of a total SBC troop of 256) who worked with a translator/pastor long hours every day. Get one of them to tell you of the different foods, the music, the sights and smells, the gracious way they were received—the thrill of leading people to Jesus!

Ask David Causey what it was like to establish the very first Baptist church for deaf—and to be instrumental in seeing 300 deaf come to Jesus.

Thank you, church family for praying and for supporting us in various other ways! The well-prepared missionaries and local pastors have the names and addresses of 20,814 people who prayed to receive eternal life. Twenty new congregations were begun. They count on your continued prayer for the follow-up as these precious people are encouraged, trained, and brought into the fellowship of the churches.

Lucy Pat and I will share our Kenya experience at this month's WMU meeting.

William Burkhalter

Joyce Burkhalter

Seth and Barbara Collier

Bill Curl

Lucy Pat Curl

Lee Flippen

Mary Evelyn Fredenburg

William Gaventa

Alice Gaventa

Marc Johnston

Sandra Johnston

Dan Minnich

Mary Agnes Minnich

Richard and Frankee Hellinger

Lynn Kennedy

Ed Moses

Missy Moses

Lin Pinter

Nora Rakes

Ray Reynolds

Helen Reynolds

William L. Smith

Carolyn Smith

Larry Verlander

Ann Verlander

Graham Walker

Jeanne Walker

The following people affiliated with First Baptist Church served as journeymen: Shawn Cashion—South America, Sheila Clarke—Africa, Debbie Francey—Africa, Jane Gouge—Africa, Marvina Perez—Panama, Bonnie Petrus—Switzerland, Merrie Petrus—Africa, Karen Severino—Africa, and Aubrey Truex—Africa. People associated with First Baptist Church who were called to be full-time evangelists include: Jon Bos, Paul Freed, Roger Glidewell, Tim Kaufman, Larry McFadden, Jim Ponder, David Ring, Billy Speer, Jay Strack, and Jim Wilson.

BIBLE SCHOOL/SUNDAY SCHOOL AND SUPERINTENDENTS

In 1874, Bethel Baptist Church voted to have a Sunday School, but it was not until twenty years later that a Bible School superintendent was mentioned. The first few superintendents and the years they served are as follows: 1891–1894, E. R. Rice; 1895, M. J. Hull; 1897, E. H. Rice; 1898–1904, E. A. Heffield; 1905, J. W. Prentis; 1906, F. M. Baldwin; 1909–1911, W. T. Haizlip; 1912, F. N. Boardman; and 1913–1914, C. M. Tichenor.

In 1914, the Wekiva Association bulletin said this about Sunday School: "We feel that Sabbath School is the right arm of the church and any Minister of the Gospel will tell you that a good wide awake Sabbath School is half of the work done in his charge." Superintendents at this time included: 1915–1917, Sam A. Newell; 1918, Alfred Link and Mrs. J. O. Ward; 1919, J. H. Keller; and 1920–1923, O. S. Lang.

In 1923, First Baptist Church was recognized as having the largest Sunday School in the state. The superintendents who carried on this legacy were: 1924, J. Tom Gurney; 1925–1926, W. D. Napier; 1927, M. K. Van Duzor; 1928, Lee MacDonald; 1929–1930, G. W. Broyles; 1931–1932, W. R. Smith; 1933–1934, Robert L. Hodges; 1935–1936, J. D. Peck; 1937–1939, E. G. Rich; and 1940–1941, Alex Young.

The 1941 associational bulletin reported: "At a time when the world is torn with strife, modernism and skepticism are leveling their heaviest attack on the church; therefore, the church of Jesus Christ is needed as never before. Only when we teach the Word of God to our men, women, young people and children under our influence will strong Christian character be developed. This is the challenge of our Sunday School." Rising to this challenge were the following superintendents: 1942–1945, Judson B. Walker; 1946–1948, D. E. Denson; 1949–1950, Winston B. Smith; 1951, E. G. Rich; and 1952–1961, C. A. West.

For many years, the Sunday School Department used the *Broadman Record Book* "Six Point System of Credits." These point values were twenty points for Sunday school attendance, ten points for being on time, ten points for bringing a Bible, ten points for making an offering, thirty points for a prepared lesson, and twenty points for preaching attendance. All these together totaled one hundred points. Bringing the office of superintendent into the present were: 1962–1968, Ralph Edfeldt; 1969–1970, Bo Mitchell; and 1971–present, Mac (W. E.) McCully.

In 1978–1979, the church was recognized for its outstanding Sunday School growth in the Southern Baptist Convention. In 1980–1983, First Baptist was recognized for its outstanding Sunday School growth in the Florida Baptist Convention. Shirley Bos, Sunday School secretary, reports there are approximately 9,390 currently enrolled with 203 age-graded Sunday School classes.

Glenda Mowdy, fifth-grade coordinator, wrote the following about her work in the Children's Division of Sunday School:

> My husband and I been here for sixteen years. The key Children's Ministers since we've been here have been Wayne Johnson and Art Murphy. At present there are three Children's Coordinators: First and Second Grade, Third and Fourth Grade, and Fifth Grade. We have Children's Altar Counselors who are specially trained to deal with children who come forward at the invitations during church services. There is a Children's New Members Class that is excellent and helps the children to be grounded in their faith.
>
> The church provides many activities for the children:
>
> 1. Sunday School (Sunday Mornings)—We have some of the most dedicated and loving teachers you'll find anywhere. They have shared experiences of going to visit prospects or children who have not attended Sunday School in a long time and leading their parents to the Lord. There are more men involved in teaching and leading our children than ever before. It used to be a service of women, but not so much any more. This is wonderful in this day and time because so many children in our society today don't have a spiritually strong male that they can relate and look up to. In our Sunday School classes, we have an emphasis on memorizing weekly memory verses, and we also have a Scripture Memory Plan for each age group.
>
> 2. " 'N Gear" (Sunday Evenings), formerly called Church Training, is a time of spiritual growth, personal encouragement, and recreation.

3. "TeamKids: Kids in Discipleship" (Wednesday Evenings, May–August), formerly called Girls in Action and Royal Ambassadors.

4. Children's Choirs (Wednesday Evenings) led by Lois Ann Roberts and a volunteer staff.

5. Children's Bible Drill (Wednesday Evenings, January–April)—The children learn Bible verses, key passages of the Bible, books of the Bible, etc. It is an excellent way to give them the tools they will need to witness to others and to get guidance in their own lives. When children learn Bible verses at any early age, the verses become a real part of their lives.

6. Children's Mission Club (Wednesday Evenings, September–November). This club provides the children with an opportunity to study missions and meet local, national, and international missionaries as well as learn about the church's ministries.

7. Half-Time (Wednesday Evenings) is a discipleship program just for preteens in grade six.

8. Vacation Bible School—Each year we have hundreds of children in VBS that might not come to any other function at the church. We have also had Backyard Bible Clubs during summer months. These clubs are held at some of our members' homes and are very similar to VBS. Also, for the past two years, we have reached many children through Mission Orlando (Bible Clubs) which were held in many of our homes and neighborhoods all over our city. We had both VBS and Mission Orlando this summer of 1996.

9. Preteen Camp—This is held each summer for fifth and sixth graders. Many decisions have been made at these camps.

10. Children's New Members (Sunday Evenings), a six-week class for new Christians preparing for baptism.

11. Children's Adventure Club is a recreation ministry during the summer for children entering grades 1–5. They take special trips.

12. Special emphasis days like Friend Day, Children's Day, First Grade Bible Day (in the fall when first graders are given their very own Bible), Children's Choir Worship Service, Bible Memory Awards, and special rallies for children.

Our children are one of the most precious blessings we have. They are going to be our leaders of tomorrow and, if we don't reach them when they are these ages, it will become more difficult to reach them as they grow older. They *are* our future. We dare not neglect them.

One occasion that stands out in my mind happened one Wednesday night after Prayer Meeting when we were still located downtown. My husband, Wil, and I had out-of-town guests with us who wanted to meet Brother Jim. As always, there was a long line waiting to talk with him. Two places ahead of us was a little boy about six or seven years old. When he became the first one in line, Brother Jim knelt down to be at eye level with him. He told Brother Jim that he had hurt his leg. Giving him his full attention and not rushing him through the line, Brother Jim had prayer with him and talked to him. I was reminded of the many scripture verses that tell of Jesus' love for these precious little ones.

BOOKSTORE

The bookstore of First Baptist Church had its beginnings around 1983 at the Pine Street facilities. It was located in the church library when Barbara Thigpen was librarian. Alan Rasmussen and Beverly Daniels helped on the volunteer staff. The bookstore sold Bibles, tracts, and other books. The pastor in charge at that time was Wayne Johnson. Later, when the church moved from its downtown location to its present facilities, the bookstore was discontinued for a few months. Then it reopened in the fall of 1985 in a corner of Welcome Center A. Since that time, a number of pastors and volunteers have manned this vital, nonprofit ministry. Some of them have included Scott Hertzler, Brian Broome, Mike Murray, Tim Grosshans, Jimmy Knott, Dan Maffett, and Ron Graham. Currently a staff of approximately fifteen people volunteer their time. The bookstore sells Bibles, other books, tapes, videos, and gifts. It also has available church service tapes from the tape ministry. Often, the bookstore donates old or surplus stock to various other ministries of the church including the Children's Department, Students' Ministry, Senior Adults, and Women's Ministries.

BUS MINISTRY

For many years, First Baptist had a thriving bus ministry that went throughout the small community providing transportation to the citizens. Now that Orlando has grown and is so spread out and because of the ready availability of private cars, the numbers using the church's bus services have drastically decreased. One or two buses currently make regular runs to Baptist Terrace and Lutheran Towers. Formerly,

Westminster was also on the route. Sometimes Lake Shore Landing is serviced during the Easter and Christmas presentations.

CHILD ENRICHMENT CENTER (CEC)

In her notes on kindergarten, Betty Carow wrote:

> Because there were few kindergartens in the city of Orlando, Dr. Parker decided that First Baptist should offer this experience to church preschoolers. At the time, this ministry was not called Child Enrichment Center. A committee, headed by Mrs. Roy Kesler, was appointed to work out details. Policies and guidelines were drawn up and a class for five-year-old children began in the fall of 1960 with Mary Nell Byrd as Director and Teacher, Rosalie Cox as Assistant, and Louie Wilkinson as Staff Advisor.
>
> After the Byrd family moved, Rosalie was made Director and Betty Carow came in as Assistant. Then Rosalie returned to college to begin graduate work, so Delores Rutlege assumed the Director's position. After her resignation, Betty Carow became Director and worked in this area for thirteen years. Betty Peterson was Teacher and then Frances Massey as Assistant for several years.
>
> About this time, day care, under the supervision of Lorene Lumpkin, was set up, meeting the many needs of working mothers. Later, a class for four-year-old children was begun with Faye Straw teaching, and shortly after another class was begun. For a time Gloria Rigdon was Director and Darinda Cheatham was also in leadership. Cindy Franks served briefly in 1982–1983, followed by Shirley Dusek as Director from 1983 through 1993 with Carol Johnson as Assistant Director.
>
> In 1988 there were 139 children enrolled with a staff of 19 employees. The curriculum used was Wee Learn Curriculum published by the Southern Baptist Convention. The school was instrumental in helping establish other work with sister churches (Baptist) and First Presbyterian Church of Orlando. The Kindergarten maintained an excellent reputation in Orlando.

In 1993, Gloria Rigdon returned to serve again until 1995. Currently, Helen Stowell is director and Faye Straw is the assistant director. Now, the CEC is a prekindergarten program for children ages two–four during the morning hours, with afternoon care offered for children of working parents. The CEC's purpose is to provide a positive and happy learning experience for preschoolers (Dusek notes).

COUNSELING CENTER

This "center was started in 1982 and provides counseling for church members and non-church members alike. There are no fees for church members, and non-church members are asked to pay a modest fee based on a sliding scale. Counseling revolves around a variety of topics, including depression, anxiety, marital and family difficulties. . . . We reach over 1000 family units each year through this ministry" ("Beacon," February 15, 1990).

Charles Bell is the director of the center. He is assisted by Jane Brown and a staff of part-time counselors. Currently this staff provides assistance in a number of varied areas, such as career assessments; learning assessments, including learning disability testing; Christian counseling; and custodial evaluations. The center oversees a number of support groups such as weight control, drug and alcohol misuse recovery, survivors of sexual abuse, and employment support. The center also shares responsibility with the Singles' Department in divorce recovery classes.

DEAF MINISTRY

As early as 1947, the church was interested in a ministry to the deaf. From the September 8 deacons minutes: "Bro. Van Whatley [writing unclear] was present and presented matter of our Church providing some means for reaching and teaching the deaf . . . people of our community, pointing out that such a program was in effect at Central Baptist Church, Atlanta, Ga., that the Southern Baptist Home Mission Board does this work, and that Rev. Frank Philphott, St. Cloud, Fla., occasionally leads a class at First Methodist Church, Orlando." It is unclear if any action was taken at that time.

The annual report to the Worship and Pastoral Committee, dated 1978, stated that in June 1978, "under the leadership of Bonnie McNutt, our church launched a ministry to the deaf" with the attendance of two deaf people, Gary and Victoria Tegg. From that humble beginning, the ministry has steadily grown through the addition of Bible study, discipleship programs, deaf revivals, fellowships, and other activities reaching into the community.

In October 1978, Bonnie began the first sign-language class with fifty-one attendees. This group was invited to sign "Silent Night" at our churchwide Christmas program, and thus a beautiful and heartwarming tradition was begun which is carried on by the children's choir program today.

First Baptist Church, always on the cutting edge, enabled this ministry to begin reaching out to other churches in a cooperative effort to reach more than six thousand deaf in the central Florida area. The Greater Orlando Baptist Association for the Deaf was begun with three churches—Delaney Street, College Park, and First Baptist Church—sending representatives. Out of a desire to reach the deaf community for Christ, the first deaf revival was held. Clifford Bruffey, a deaf pastor considered to be one of the founding fathers of deaf ministry in America, accepted our invitation to lead this inaugural meeting. He has returned on several occasions to speak to this group or lead in some manner to encourage their growth in the Lord.

During the summer of 1978, Phala and Don Bernhardt began attending our church. They soon joined and added Phala's knowledge and interpreting skills to this growing ministry. She and Bonnie interpreted the first Singing Christmas Tree program. Periodically, she led a deaf choir for the congregation. Phala and Don served diligently in so many different ways until her resignation in 1993.

There has been a long and steady line of faithful soldiers serving as interpreters, teachers, and deacons through the years. Pam Kersey, Tom Bridges, Mary Ellen Brewbaker, Stacey Strickland, Bruce Tegg, Kathy Campbell, Penny Tegg, and Bryan Terrell are only a few. David Causey was the first deaf man to teach the Bible study class on Sunday morning. Gary Tegg and George Garcia were the first deaf to participate in dramas for Christmas and Easter. Norm Korbin was the first deacon for the deaf, and he continues to serve as teacher for the early Sunday morning Bible study. Under the Korbins's leadership, that class has grown steadily. Linda and Beth Cody have served faithfully for several years in the preschool ministry.

Our ministry has touched the lives of so many deaf. They have come here for growth and training and then the Lord has moved them to other areas for his service, or they have gone home to be with him. They have been faithful in community service, drama presentations, music, visitation, and so many other avenues of communicating the love of Jesus to

Deaf ministry

those who could not "hear" without their willing feet and hands carrying his message.

After the Teggs came Walter (who turned ninety-eight in November 1995) and Jonie Hauser, Keziah McDowell (who has now gone to be with the Lord), Mickey and Jackie Corson, George Garcia, Ken Gould (who now serves in a singing/signing group—Silent Touch and the Door), Gary Smith, Ron and Paula Poultney, Linda Cody, Beth and Dennis Cody, Eva Harris, Tom Schneider, Carol Jackson, Robert and Julia Jackson (both gone to be with the Lord), Elizabeth Serrano, Greg and Jenny Flynn, Jack Summer, and Eric and Julie Cruz.

All of these persons have graciously and generously given of themselves to help this ministry grow and reach other deaf for Jesus Christ. As in any other ministry, the people who love Jesus serve as His hands and feet, loving and caring for those who so desperately need to know someone understands their heartache and needs and is willing to reach out and touch.

DRAMA MINISTRY

Virginia Parker remembers helping to start this vital part of the church. Several years ago, she was attending a planning board meeting at the state's Florida Baptist Convention in Jacksonville. An idea formed in her mind of portraying biblical characters in a three-to-five-minute sketch at the forthcoming evangelistic conference. She asked what others thought about her idea, and they encouraged her to try it out. When she came back to this church, she and Wayne Johnson "put their heads together" and tried the idea out here. It was met with much success and enthusiasm, so it was also begun at the conference. This was in the days before drama was really recognized as a part of worship. And the rest, as they say, is history.

From that point on, they began trying out drama for special occasions, such as Christmas and Easter. After a while, as the drama group became more structured, and as the members increased under Wayne Johnson's capable direction, more and varied presentations were given. Barbara Hawxwell remembers joining Wayne as a volunteer in this department before finally joining the staff. A family dinner theater was begun and some of the plays were "You Can't Take It With You," "Don't Drink the Water," "The Miracle Worker," and "Our Town." Later, the Easter drama was called "The Day He Wore My Crown." In 1984, at the state drama festival at Stetson, First Baptist's drama group were guest artists and presented three plays.

In 1986, the first presentation of "The Light: The Story of Our Christ" was given. That began a tradition of magnificent Easter celebrations that have continued to the present. The drama group and the choirs of the church combined for this dramatization, as they have for the stirring Singing Christmas Trees. Derric Johnson has written and directed many of the Christmas presentations. He is director of the "Voices of Liberty" at EPCOT.

At the present time, the Light Company is a year-round program for church member involvement and training in the dramatic arts.

Evangelism Explosion

This ministry was begun in 1974 by Gerry Leonard and Bill Curl under the instruction of D. James Kennedy. Gerry Leonard was in the area teaching united training courses. Bill Curl attended one of these and asked her to come to First Baptist to train a group of committed deacons in the Evangelism Explosion program of witnessing. After some prayer and God answering in a specific way, Gerry came to First Baptist for a six-week crash course. Some who were trained were Dr. Parker, Bill Curl, John Carow, Ed Irey, and eighteen deacons, including Charles Skinner, Ralph Edfeldt, and Bob Vickery.

When this class was finished, the church called Gerry to begin what became her eleven years on staff as evangelism associate. For those years, she and her helpers had two semesters a year, with sixteen weeks each semester of training. In all, about fifty deacons and fifteen hundred church members were trained while Gerry was on the staff. In addition to First Baptist members, pastors of other churches and their members were invited to be trained in this effective ministry. As members were trained, the Lord opened doors to train teams to share this evangelism in Holland, Germany, Australia, and Africa.

A typical training session would comprise training on one night with visiting homes on another. Usually three would go as a team: one trainer, one intermediate, and one trainee. After an evening of witnessing, the team would come back to church, and all teams would report their results. Leonard was retired by the church in 1985 and has begun a ministry in south Florida. Stu Tully was hired as pastor of evangelism, followed by Greg Elmquist. Currently, Bill Mitchell is the minister of evangelism.

THE FIRST ACADEMY

As an outstanding citizen and extraordinary businessman, J. Thomas Gurney Sr. was loved by young and old alike. He had a dream some years ago of a church-sponsored school where children could not only learn the principles of life but could grow spiritually as well. A church committee was set up to look into the feasibility of such a school. After planning and investigating, a school staff began to be hired. The first headmaster of The First Academy was Fred Chase, who wrote, "The Cornerstone of The First Academy is its singular commitment to the Lordship of Jesus Christ. We have been called to show forth His excellencies in every area of life as we assist children to move toward Christian maturity." He continued the dream of a Christ-centered school by hiring a team of visionaries who were totally sold out to building a dynamic school environment, all to the glory of God. The school began with two hundred students and thirty-three faculty and staff. Within two years, The First Academy received SACS accreditation and initiated several unique academic programs in an exemplary structural facility.

Fred Chase also believed that "to fit sons and daughters for living the abundant life, The First Academy makes a mighty reach for excellence in the whole aggregate of human life—intellectual and moral, physical and

The First Academy—Courtesy Ralph Edfeldt

spiritual, and domestic and social. The Christian life and world view bring all of the diverse elements of life into harmony."

In 1991, after Fred Chase's resignation, Ed Gamble came to The First Academy as its second headmaster. Larry Taylor was assistant principal and did much work in the Athletic Department. Currently, Ralph Walton is principal of the upper school, and Barbara Johnson is principal of the lower grades. Headmaster Gamble penned the current mission statement of the school: "Preparing children for life as Christian leaders who choose character before career, wisdom beyond scholarship, service before self, and participation as a way of life." The staff increased and a computer technology program was instituted. The current enrollment is over eight hundred, with special recognitions and awards being received by the students in academics, athletics, and the arts. In 1994, the school held its first graduation of seniors.

The campus is comprised of a growing number of buildings. There is an education building, an administration building, a gymnasium, and two modulars which house after-school care, art, and a weight room. The school also uses the church's second educational building for some of its classes.

FIRST LIFE CENTER FOR PREGNANCY

The center began in September of 1986 when God inspired Suzanne and Rick Fletcher to do something to help the hurting women who were faced with a crisis pregnancy. Bill Curl asked Lynn Kennedy to be the director. The first building was on Lucerne Terrace. The area became unsafe with many break-ins and property stolen, so in 1990, the center moved to its present location at 4053 L. B. McLeod Road. It was at this time that Sandy Epperson became the director because of Lynn's leaving to go to Bible college, seminary, and the foreign mission field.

Each year the center ministers to over two thousand clients. Approximately one-half of the clients come in for a free pregnancy test, and the other half come to be enrolled in the "Hope" program. This program enables them to earn coupons to spend toward the items they will need for their families. The center has clothes from newborn size to 4T. It also has baby furniture, formula, and diapers, along with a food pantry.

In the nine and one-half years since it was founded, 1,182 women have come to know Jesus as their Lord and Savior. In addition, 1,789 babies have been born, and 337 babies who would have been aborted have been spared.

Of the hundreds of stories which could be related, Sandy recalls a couple who visited the center in their search for food for their family, which included three children. As the center ministered to their physical needs, it also saw the couple come to a saving knowledge of the Lord Jesus Christ. Realizing their need to be married, the couple was aided in that endeavor through the gifts of numerous people. Now this family is being fed by their hunger for the Word of God.

GOOD THIEF COFFEE HOUSE

In 1969, First Baptist began a coffee house to minister to what were then called "hippies and flower people." Raphael de Armas, along with Charlie Brown, assistant pastor to Dr. Parker, and Hugh Tarsai worked together with volunteers at the Good Thief Coffee House. During its beginning, some First Baptist Church members did not like the church's involvement with the clientele, many of whom were runaways and drug users. But through the years, as lives were transformed and letters were received from grateful parents, approval of the ministry increased. The Reverend Jim Wilson recalls: "When the young people came into the coffee house, many were hungry. The rule was that they could not eat until after 'the God rap' given by either Hugh or Charlie. Then peanut-butter sandwiches and Kool-Aid and coffee were served. After that the people working at the coffee house witnessed and counseled those who came in. The coffee house was open from 7:30 to 11:00 P.M. every weekday evening. The attendance averaged about thirty to thirty-five each night" (interview with Doris Morgan and Emily Meiner).

In 1970, after Brown's departure, Jim Wilson became director/staff liaison at the coffee house. Some of the volunteers included Don and Billy Taylor and Roy Manning. Later John Carow was named director. In 1971, there were three hundred professions of faith at the coffee house. Around 1972, Arthur Blessitt, a well-known evangelist, came to Orlando and spoke at rallies which included the coffee house. That seemed to help further the acceptance of the coffee house by the church. In addition, a favorable newspaper article claiming the Good Thief had done much to help curb the use of drugs in Orlando also contributed to the good will. Records kept in 1972 showed thirty-four conversions, three rededications, one lettered, twenty-one thousand sandwiches made, seventy-two hundred cups of coffee served, twelve hundred gallons of Kool-Aid made, hundreds of articles of clothing given out, and one hundred Bibles distributed.

The house changed location twice and finally closed in 1975, reporting a total of six hundred saved souls. As in any mission field, the "missionaries" were blessed as well. Many of the church's young people felt called to volunteer, and their lives were touched. However, now the tide had changed; flower children were replaced by older men as Orlando's leading transients.

HOMEBOUND MINISTRY

Many of the dear people of the church are not able to attend services. These precious individuals are not forgotten. The Wednesday night newsletter continuously publishes their names so that the church body can pray for them, call them, send them cards and letters of encouragement, and visit them.

Presently, the church has approximately sixty homebound members, ranging in age from twenty-nine through the nineties. Because of various handicaps, sometimes physical or mental or both, these people are unable to be mobile enough to attend services. Mike McKee is currently their pastor in charge. Together with Gail Brown, his associate, and a core of fifteen volunteers plus the deacons, the pastor is able to minister to the homebound. They are each visited once a quarter, and two times a year they are given flowers: at Easter and Christmas. Visitors often take them church literature and, once a year, they are sent birthday cards. When a homebound person requests it, a deacon will visit to administer the Lord's Supper. Periodically, the Lord's Supper is celebrated on Sunday mornings so that these shut-ins can participate via television. Each widow who is homebound is assigned a deacon for special attention. The volunteers are given as many names as they wish. They make calls once a week and visit once a month, on average.

Those who desire to attend the special Easter and Christmas presentations are given a free ticket. With the growing number of Alzheimer's disease sufferers, some family members also become homebound in a sense, because they must stay home with their afflicted loved one.

INTERNATIONAL MINISTRIES

The International Ministries was begun in our church as English classes for foreign-speaking people in the summer of 1967. Gayle Leininger began with one student, a Cuban lady. Later, June Bradley made puppets, banners, and helped organize the curriculum, and Jim Hansen taught American history classes.

Citizenship classes were added to the ministries in 1968. From 1967 to 1974, six hundred internationals were helped by the English and citizenship classes. Literally thousands have been helped in the twenty-nine years they have existed. Many have found Jesus as Savior and have been baptized. The classes have continued at Downtown Baptist with 357 enrolled in the 1994–1995 session.

Primera Iglesia was begun with Cuban people from the English classes as a Bible study class. Out of that was formed a mission of First Baptist which later developed into a church.

From the "Beacon" of October 23, 1968:

> It has only been a little over a year since our church began English classes for foreign-speaking people and in that length of time this ministry has grown from one student to over seventy-five. Beginning with just one teacher, there are now over twenty volunteers. The fall session began September 12 with classes meeting each Thursday morning from 9:00 to 11:00 and Thursday nights from 7:30 to 9:30. In addition to the regular language instruction, a citizenship class was started for those preparing for their United States citizenship. This class is led by June Bradley and has an enrollment of over ten with many nationalities represented.

Many of these classes are already too large and every Thursday there are more students enrolled. Almost every student has brought a friend or relative and therefore our classes continue to grow. Teachers are always needed and if you are interested you can be trained to help. . . . The Laubach method of teaching English as well as other materials and information concerning the students will be taught by Gayle Leininger. From *The Southside News* of May 13, 1981:

It's been 14 years since the first English class for the foreign born met at First Baptist church of Orlando. There was one teacher and one student in that first class. Now there are 20 teachers and 100 students. Students from 38 countries were enrolled in the program last year. Gladys Partin, one of the directors of the program, gives these personal glimpses of students who have attended the classes. Elisa San Julian was the first student and she now is the hostess for the night sessions. Manuel is 81, a Cuban lawyer. Another student from China is learning to speak English. The program's purpose is to help people learn the English language, adjust to life in the U. S., and to "show them the love of Jesus as we do it." In addition to the lessons, there are also coffee and juice breaks, a monthly birthday cake, and a songtime led by Ed and Alberta Irey with students being taught "fun songs" like "Row, Row, Row Your Boat," "Three Blind Mice," and choruses "God Is So Good" and "I've Got The Joy, Joy, Joy." Volunteer teachers are given a 16-hour workshop. Students only pay for the books they use.

A BRIEF HISTORY OF THE JAIL MINISTRY IN ORANGE COUNTY
Marshall M. Wilson

Early in the 1970s Robert M. Vickery asked me to join a group of men from First Baptist Church who were responsible for a monthly Sunday evening church service in Orange County Jail. Alex Marsh, R. K. "Pat" Rhyan, and Bill Curl participated, among others. The service, held in a room of steel walls into which we were ushered after having three steel doors locked behind us, was attended by twenty-five male inmates. Music, acapella and spirited, was followed by a clear gospel message by Bob Vickery. He challenged the men who wanted to confess their self-willed ways to stand and to receive Jesus as Savior and Lord. Fifteen of the twenty-five did so, praying as Bob led them.

One of those inmates began a tremendous spiritual growth during the months that followed. At his trial, he was found guilty of his offense and was sentenced to twenty-five years in prison. He emerged from the courtroom praising God for the sentence; his testimony was that he could serve God in or out of prison.

This team from First Baptist, deeply impacted by those events, accepted responsibility from the chaplain for a second monthly Sunday evening service and a weekly Bible study to disciple those who were coming to know the Lord. Several men also began one-on-one counseling of inmates during the week.

The officials of Orange County Jail had arranged in the late 1960s with Good News Mission, a jail and prison ministry organization training and placing chaplains, to locate a chaplain in the county to coordinate and supervise the religious program in the jail. Several men from First Baptist Church were asked by this chaplain to serve on the local board. First Baptist began monthly financial support of Good News Mission of Arlington, Virginia.

Shortly afterward, the jail ministry was incorporated independently as Florida Chaplaincy Service. Tom Gurney completed the legal documents. Alex Marsh and myself were officers and directors, with Pat Rhyan a director. Several years later this organization ceased to exist when Good News Mission again gave direction to the jail ministry.

In 1978, following a formal request from the chaplain in Orange County, First Baptist Church ordained me to the gospel ministry. I had already been functioning as a chaplain in the jail for two years, having resigned as director of the Graduate Program in Education at Rollins College.

Two important changes took place, significantly affecting the jail ministry. By state statute, separate county and city detention facilities were assigned to counties in Florida. The jail ministry, therefore, had responsibility for religious programs for all inmates in Orange County.

The second change was initiated by Lawson L. Lamar. When he was elected sheriff, he requested that Frank Costantino, president of Christian Prison Ministries, Inc., "evaluate, upgrade and propose a jail ministry for Orlando that would incorporate volunteers from the local churches, Christian organizations, and concerned laity." Sheriff Lamar further stated that it was his intention "that Rev. Costantino set up an interdenominational framework that will provide programming for all Christian doctrines, as well as providing the spiritual support for non-Christian prisoners where reputable representatives of their religions are available in the community." The jail ministry is not supported by tax monies but from donations received from the local community.

Orange County Jail Ministry, established as an arm of Christian Prison Ministries initially, was incorporated in 1984 and has an interdenominational board which sets policy. I joined the staff as chaplain and was designated senior chaplain in 1985. I served in that capacity until retirement in December 1994. I was recognized by Stetson University as Chaplain of the Year in 1993.

Good News Mission continued to function in Orange County Jail, essentially providing two jail ministries for a rapidly expanding inmate population. Each ministry had designated buildings to facilitate administration of respective religious programs.

First Baptist Church has continued financial support for both jail ministries.

J. Seth Collier was ordained by First Baptist Church after Orange County Jail Ministry indicated by letter that Seth would be called as a chaplain. Seth served as chaplain until his call to missions in Wales.

The challenge of the jail ministry is enormous. In recent years in Orange County, more than fifty-five thousand individuals have been arrested and booked annually into the jail. Daily inmate population housed in Orange County Jail is over thirty-five inmates. Orange County Jail Ministry has responsibility for twenty-five hundred of those.

Current staff of Orange County Jail Ministry includes four chaplains and a secretary, all full-time. Over four hundred volunteers have security clearance and assist in conducting church services and Bible studies, doing one-on-one counseling, and teaching in specialized areas. One volunteer from First Baptist grades most lessons completed by inmates who participate in an extensive Bible correspondence course. An extensive corp of volunteers from First Baptist assists in ministry to male and female inmates in Orange County Jail.

The Administrative Board of Orange County Jail Ministry established two objectives for the ministry: 1. lead inmates to a saving faith in Jesus Christ, and 2. disciple those who come to know Him. Each year over four thousand inmates have professed Jesus as Savior and/or have renewed a relationship to Him.

LIBRARY

The 1895 Wekiwa Associational bulletin reported that our church had three hundred volumes in its library, although no mention in our records was made as to when the library was formed. Some time during Rev. Adcock's pastorate, a Mr. Johnson was recorded as the church librarian. During 1946, some of the following were listed as librarians: Mrs. E. A. Bales, Mrs. Earl Clay, Doris Kelsey, Elizabeth Gertner, and Mrs. Buddy Felter. Mrs. Hillard Johnson gave the report.

From the 1947 Wekiwa Associational bulletin: "Without any doubt, the greatest need in the world today is education, Christ centered and filled with His ideals. False education can blight and curse an individual, a home, a church, or a nation. Germany had an abundance of Godless education. We are in danger in this country of the same Godless education. Our churches are needing and demanding a better educated ministry because of a largely increased membership who are not only high school graduates but college graduates as well. Many books are good. They should be read. Many are questionable and many are evil. Our people need to acquaint themselves with the character of the books they are reading and choose only those that are uplifting—No. 1—The BIBLE!"

In 1951 Mrs. J. A. Stinson was the librarian. Then in 1956, Mrs. Bernard Plummer became librarian, and an inventory of the books was conducted by Mildred Talton, who gave the final count of books as 2,071. Others who have served as librarians have been Minnie West and Jean King. Sometime later, when Barbara Thigpen complained to David Cunningham that the library wasn't open, he handed her the keys. She served for nearly ten years from approximately 1976 to 1985. As librarian, one of the feats Barbara was most proud of was the starting of a mini-bookstore which sold Bibles, small Scriptures, and Bible story coloring books. The room for the library in the downtown facility had beautiful wooden tables and chairs in a rather cramped setting, but the staff made it very inviting. For a little over one year, 1985–1986, Pat Birkhead, helped by Carolyn Wilson, was in charge of setting up the library on the new McLeod campus. It was a monumental task, but Barbara Thigpen had done a wonderful job of boxing up all the contents for transfer. Since the mid-1980s, the library has grown and expanded its technology and services. Videos and cassettes are also loaned as well as thousands of books. Sheryle White followed Pat Birkhead as librarian, and currently Martha Maslin is the head librarian with a staff of dedicated volunteers.

MUSIC

F. N. Boardman came to Orlando from New Hampshire in 1887. He was a musician and connected with all the orchestras and bands in the early days. He organized the first municipal band. His instrument was clarinet.

In 1895, the church had one mission band, as recorded in the Wekiwa Associational bulletin. A choir director was not listed until 1923, when W. H. Bixby held the position. In 1924, H. Andre Schmidt was choir director, and Elsie Shealy was organist/pianist.

From Linda Reddick and Mac McKinney's history of the choir:

> In 1925, a man came on the scene who was to influence First Baptist music for many years to come. It was Henry Symonds who first came to Orlando in 1908 from Elmira, New York, with his parents. He was baptized at First Baptist when he was 12, began singing in the choir, and taking piano lessons. Church music was his love. . . . Later, he studied with Stanley Pope, a music teacher at Rollins College. Henry shared much of what he learned with his fellow choir members.

> Up until this time, there had not been an organized choir program in the Church. Henry approached Dr. Dean Adcock, the pastor, and asked for permission to organize a choir. The permission was granted with Dr. Adcock's blessing—and the Lord's blessing, too. The program grew until there was a need for an expanded choir loft. An elevated choir loft was built extending in a semicircle out from the organ. . . . There were a number of pianists and organists who helped Mr. Symonds build the

music ministry. Among them were Will Branch, Mrs. C. H. Kennedy, C. A. Stewart, Louise Graham, Jessie Baker, Pauline (Polly) Tiller, Herman Siewert, Elsie Shealy, Ruth Jernigan, Mildred Adair, Iris Engle, Jo Kesler, and Patsy Powell.

Under Henry's leadership, the First Baptist music ministry grew so that, in 1934, it was decided to call Martha Shearouse as the first full-time Minister of Music. Martha was well-liked and served until her resignation.

1925	Henry Symonds	Elsie Claire Shealy and C. A. Stewart
1926		Mrs. C. H. Kennedy
		Mrs. John Baker
1930		Herman Siewert
1931	Martha Shearouse	Ruth Jernigan and Mildred Adair
1932	Martha Shearouse	Mildred Adair

Mildred Talton, in an early list, gave the following as music directors: H. Andre Schmidt, Evelyn Mason, Pauline Tiller, Henry Symonds, Mrs. J. B. Shearouse, the Earl Jollses, Mrs. Marvin Powell, Mrs. Roy Kesler, and the Edwin Ireys.

On November 18, 1932, the following letter from the board of deacons was sent to the director and members of the choir of First Baptist Church:

God in his infinite wisdom has endowed mankind with manifold talents. Fortunate indeed is that individual who recognizes these blessings and seeks to develop and give expression to same. More glorious is it when that individual, so blessed, voluntarily uses these blessings to the glory of God in loving service.

Realization of the large part that music plays in public worship and the value of such a contribution has prompted this tribute to our Choir.

We deeply appreciate the loyalty of the members of our Choir which prompts the regular participation in this important service. We know that back of the splendid programs of music are hours of consecrated effort, spent in preparation. The high quality of your music, and its excellent rendition, plays such an important part of our service and is evidence of this service of love.

Knowing that all too often proper recognition is not given those rendering faithful, loyal support, we are taking this means on behalf of the church of expressing appreciation of your splendid music and telling you the Church is counting on this support.

Thanking you every one and praying God's blessing will attend your efforts in His behalf. Sincerely.

Martha M. Shearouse served as full-time minister of music from 1934 to 1943. During this time, Pauline Tiller and Walter Kimball were the organists/pianists. The following beautiful letter of resignation was written to the deacons by Martha Shearouse on January 25, 1943:

Dear Sirs: Since the dawn of creation, when God set the stars and planets into rhythmical motion, music has been an inseparable part of worship of the Creator. The history of God's people reveals music as the natural expression of worshiping man—whether singly or collectively. Much of the world's greatest music has been inspired by and set to the texts from Holy Scripture. So we have counted it a great privilege to have ever so small a place in such a vital part of the services in the Lord's sanctuary.

For many years now you have granted me that place in this grand old church and I wish to assure you, I have accepted that responsibility in deep humility, praying always that I might give of myself unsparingly under the guidance of God's Holy Spirit. I count it among my choicest blessings to have touched lives with so many of the finest young people in all the land—many of whom are now scattered all over the earth, in many instances carrying the gospel in song. Rich, also, has been the experience of associating with two of God's chosen servants, your pastors, who have been wise counselors and friends.

We have enjoyed seeing your choir grow from a small band of twelve or fourteen to an average enrollment of forty-five members with auxiliary choirs bringing the number being trained to well over one hundred. It is not an empty statement to say you now enjoy the distinction of having one of the best choir organizations in the state. The complete harmony and good will among the personnel of the choir has been a constant testimony of the Christian spirit that prevails among us.

. . . I find I cannot go further without jeopardizing my health, so I must in some way reduce my activities. My personal problem has been whether to give up the church music, which is so dear to my heart, or my private class of pupils.

So it is, I am offering you my resignation to become effective February 15.

As a member of the church and one who loves each individual member of all the choirs, I wish to offer a request that this educational program, which has been developed the past eighteen months, will be carried on so that the latent talent of the young people may be saved and trained for most effective service to our Lord. Respectfully submitted.

Henry Symonds returned to the position of choir director in 1944 and remained as such until 1949. Pauline Tiller was organist/pianist in 1944. Also at some point during this time, Tiller began a children's choir.

After his resignation as choir director, Henry Symonds opened up a "new phase of his musical life—that of composer. Over the next three decades, he wrote hundreds of hymns and spiritual songs which he published using his own special music typewriter. Volume after volume he turned out and sent to missionaries around the world. Sometimes he would have a First Baptist choir or ensemble perform his music, and he would send the recordings" (Reddick and McKinney).

During the 1950s, several people served as choir directors for a year or two. Earl and Peggy Jolls served in 1950–1951, Evelyn Mason in 1952–1953, Pauline Tiller in 1953–1955, Jo Kesler in 1955, and in 1956, Earl and Peggy Jolls returned. During this time, Louise Graham and Iris Daniel Engle played organ and piano. Patsy Powell directed the children's choir in 1955.

In 1956, Edwin S. and Alberta Irey were called as ministers of music. Edwin Irey was the minister of music, played the organ, and did the office work—writing letters, Sunday bulletins, records, and such. His wife, Alberta, directed the choirs. Earlier, "their careers and their lives merged at Bob Jones" (Reddick and McKinney).

Martha Edfeldt wrote the following about the Ireys:

They really had a true choir program for all ages, starting with the Celestial Choir—ages 4 & 5; then came the Cherubs—grades 1–3; Crusaders—boys grades 4–6; Carols—girls grades 4–6; Choralier—junior high school; and Concord—senior high school; and the Sanctuary Choir. The Ireys directed all of these choirs and when a young person had gone through 14 years of their choirs, that person knew music and appreciated how to praise God through the music. Our son, Richard, never had any music in his life except what he learned in the choir program at First Baptist. When he was in seminary, he was the choir director of a church in Texas and did a good job, doing simple cantatas, etc. at Easter and Christmas, all with the knowledge of music that he learned in the choir under the Ireys. Ed used to tell the new members classes that the children and young people received $100's of dollars worth of music as well as the religious and praise learning. All of the choirs would sing in an Easter and Christmas program as well as Thanksgiving and other holidays. The Ireys also started what they called a pantomime group which was made up of seven or maybe nine girls in white satin flowing robes where they would interpret the music that was sung. Very often at Christmas the girls would pantomime "O Holy Night" using living people for the parts of Mary, Joseph and the Christ Child. This group was invited to the Southern Baptist Convention and also to Ridgecrest. The Ireys used an award program to encourage faithfulness, giving a hymn book with the person's name on it for the first year of perfect attendance, and small busts of music composers for other awards. The high school winners would also get to go to Harmony Bay, a Baptist camp, at that time near Panama City, for a week of music camp.

The Ireys always selected good, traditional music for their presentations. Sometimes a string quartet from the symphony would accompany the choir. Some of the cantatas that were given were "Elijah," "Messiah," and "Job." I will never forget when "modern days" overtook and they used a tape for a "modern" musical. They really didn't enjoy that kind of thing because they wanted to use the real instruments, but sort of felt they needed to keep up. In this musical "Celebrate Life" which really had a swing to it, the choir clapped hands.

The Ireys had three daughters: Carolyn, Joanne, and Kathleen. Alberta Irey, in addition to being a devoted mother and wife, was also an accomplished violinist who could have been a first chair of any symphony, but she used her talent to praise the Lord in our church. The Ireys took the Concord choir and some college youth to Israel and sang in Bethlehem Square on Christmas Eve in 1973. Also during their time as choir directors, the choir made two recordings.

The Ireys left a real music legacy when they retired. They were loved by everyone who came in contact with them, and many of the young people kept in touch after they were grown and married. When Edwin Irey died, he was in the hospital. All of his dear family surrounded him and quietly sang hymns as he stepped over into eternity.

Jo Kesler said the Ireys were a wonderful couple, very dedicated, worked well together, and they "had rules to improve the looks of the choir for the television broadcasts." From Martha Edfeldt: "Sometimes I would come into the music office where I worked all flustered and upset. Edwin would say, 'Martha, your salvation doesn't depend on it.' That would seem to calm me down."

The Ireys served First Baptist from 1957 until 1976. In 1962, choir enrollment was 442. In 1970, Youth Pastor Dennis Baw and Dr. Parker took the New Wind Choir on a Jamaican crusade and nearly nine thousand decisions were made for Christ. "Even in the midst of a national state emergency, His worship, the Honorable Florizel Glasspole, spoke and participated in the Stadium Crusade Sunday afternoon, June 20. More than 2,000 people were saved at that service" (New Wind publication). Also, "Mayor Ralph Brown, leader of Jamaica's largest city (700,000), began his greeting at the National Arena with those words 'Thank you, Jesus.' On the first day of a state of national emergency, he said Jamaica's greatest need was Jesus. The 6,000 in the audience showed an extremely warm response to these words." In all, there were eighteen services with song and preaching.

In 1977, Forrest Thompson and Ray Holcomb took over from the Ireys. "Forrest Thompson was an excellent, well-trained musician with a warm, outgoing personality which endeared him to the First Baptist choir members. He occasionally sang solos and would be joined by his wife, Pat, for duets. . . . Ray Holcomb had a powerful, beautiful voice and frequently sang solos. He had many years of experience as a vocal music teacher and spent some time in each choir rehearsal teaching the principles of voice production" (Reddick and McKinney). Ragan Vandegriff became the minister of music in July 1978. Ragan Malone Vandegriff III is a native of Atlanta. His parents were in the dry-cleaning business in Atlanta with a fire station across from their establishment. Since the station was so near, Ragan developed an interest in fire prevention. His family was active in Atlanta Baptist Tabernacle. At a young age, Ragan became interested in music, playing the oboe in his high school orchestra, taking piano lessons, and singing in choirs. Typical of most students, he enjoyed his music lessons, but he didn't like to practice. However, he soon decided to become a minister of music. He graduated from Bob Jones University with a B.A. in sacred music, a master's degree from Southwestern Baptist Theological Seminary, and a Doctor of Ministry degree from Luther Rice Seminary.

W. A. Criswell preached Ragan's ordination sermon. Ragan interned at First Baptist, Dallas. Later, Ragan joined the staff of the Roswell Street

The brass section

Baptist Church in Marietta, Georgia. He married Patricia Lynn Wells, whom he met at First Baptist, Dallas. At Roswell he began his chaplaincy ministry with the fire department which has continued here in Orlando. In 1978, Ragan accepted the call to come to First Baptist, Orlando. "Through the years, Ragan has led us a merry chase. He often says, 'Get lots of rest, take your vitamins, and hang on!' He instituted such traditions as The Singing Christmas Trees and, with Wayne Johnson's help, the Easter musical dramas which have evolved into 'The Light.'. . . [The choir has] sung in airports, in shopping malls, on the city streets, and at Walt Disney World" (McKinney booklet).

There have been trips outside of Orlando. The youth choir has gone to Israel; Opryland; Nottingham, England; Virginia; and the World's Fair in Knoxville. The adult choir has gone to Houston; Atlanta; and Liverpool, Nottingham, and Coventry, England. There have also been numerous recordings, three with prolific composer and arranger David Clydesdale.

Ragan, as chaplain of Orlando's Fire Department, goes to the scenes of fires and accidents and ministers to injured firemen, victims, and their families. Ragan's own family includes his wife Pat and their sons Van and Adam. "Ragan is loved for his sense of humor, his funny little comments during rehearsals, and his sly looks and winks during performances" (McKinney booklet).

When Ragan first came to First Baptist Church in 1978, a small instrumental ensemble was used as needed to accompany the adult choir, student choirs, and other special musical presentations of the church. With a desire to be personally involved in the ensemble and with his trumpet in hand, Bob Roycroft approached Ragan and presented his vision to someday have an orchestra that would participate not only in special programs, but the Sunday-by-Sunday services. It was this desire that encouraged the real beginning of our modern orchestra. Bob played faithfully until his death in 1995. That orchestra has grown, first under the direction of Betty Moffatt and currently with Terry Winch, who brought to First Baptist Church an illustrious record of ministry and music talent as an arranger, composer, producer, and trumpet player. He was the arranger of the Super Bowl XIX half-time show, televised on January 20, 1985. He was also the arranger/conductor of a Fourth of July Spectacular at Disneyland and has arranged for a multitude of music personalities such as Sandi Patty Larnell Harris, Dave Boyer, Bob Bailey, the Spurrlows, and the Continentals to visit the church. Currently at First Baptist Church, he has done a number of arrangements, has been very important in the Easter and Christmas events, and plays his trumpet during some services.

When Ragan began as minister of music, there were thirty-five choir members. He began a program of care group leaders as the numbers increased, and he personally called new members to welcome them. A number of staff, directors, and accompanists have aided him in the music ministry through the years. Among them have been Pat Shackelford, Hadley Fuller, Shirley Estes, Lois Ann Roberts, Larry McFadden, Bill Thrasher, Lucy Pat Curl, Larry Verlander, Marcia Carow, Teresa McFadden, Stella Cottrell, and Betty Moffatt.

When the church moved to the new facilities in 1985, a new organ was purchased with funds from an anonymous donor. Ragan said, "We were awed by what God was doing, but we weren't surprised." It is a Schantz pipe organ handcrafted for the worship center, 118 ranks with 6,757 pipes. The orchestra lift measures fifty-five feet by twenty feet, one of the largest in the state; second only to NASA lifts. The stereo sound system cluster in the worship center is seventy feet by fifteen feet by fifteen feet.

In a 1985 supplement to the *Orlando Sentinel*, Roxanne Collins wrote about this lift. "The orchestra lift, built by Gagnon-LaForest of Canada, is approximately 1,100 square feet with dimensions of about 55 feet long and 20 feet wide. This makes it one of the largest lifts in the state and second only to lifts at NASA. The lift is actually two lifts in one. The organ console and piano are on one lift, while the rest of the orchestra is on another. Each lift can act independently or together, providing extra versatility."

Currently, there are twenty graded choirs for ages four through senior adults. Speaking of senior adults, the Golden Heirs, a singing group of senior citizens, was started in the fall of 1987 with Lois Ann Roberts directing and Pat Shackelford accompanying. Lois Ann and Pat saw a group of senior citizens at Ridgecrest and said to each other, "We can do that!" And they did. The Golden Heirs have presented a musical, "Count on Us." They have attended Music Week for Seniors at Lake Yale and have sung at many locations around town. Their big forte is to sing in smaller churches and, as Lois Ann said, "That is probably their mission." Currently they meet on Tuesdays at 10:15 A.M., and have a glorious time singing together.

The Singing Christmas Trees (which began with one tree in 1981) were discussed in an *Orlando Sentinel* article written by Adelle M. Banks. One section of her article was titled "Behind the Scenes" and listed some "insider information," such as volunteer "tree rats" massage the legs of those who must stand and sing in the tree for approximately one hour and forty minutes. Singers who want their legs to be massaged to prevent leg cramps write "yes" on a piece of white tape which is then attached to their pants leg. Those who don't write "no." To make the singers of a uniform height, they stand on wooden boxes. Singers standing on the sides of the tree are able to see the director via TV monitors. The red and white capes are only waist length and the greenery hides the pants. Because of climbing, singers must wear tennis shoes. Elsewhere in the same article, she wrote about the eleven thousand computer-controlled lights on the trees which are synchronized to the music.

Each tree is approximately forty-five feet tall with fifteen rows of singers. A full orchestra accompanies the choir. For a number of years, Derric Johnson has been instrumental in the composing and arranging of the music. While thousands of church members enjoy attending this annual event, the primary focus is on evangelism and reaching the unchurched. Many people feel the Singing Christmas Trees are a fitting tribute to our Lord when the rest of society has turned Christmas into a secular occasion.

"Rivaling the Tree has been the Easter musical drama. Ragan and Wayne [Johnson] have created moving presentations of the Easter story in a setting designed by Jim Tyckoson of Walt Disney World. With wonderful lighting and sound effects and beautiful costumes, these presentations, too, attract thousands and result in hundreds of meaningful decisions each year" (Reddick and McKinney). Of course, many others have contributed to the success of the Easter presentations since the time discussed in this 1984 article.

NURSING HOME

Some years back, maybe twenty, the Sunday School classes of the church took on as a project visiting the nursing homes in Orlando and giving a program or short worship service on Sunday afternoons. Ralph Edfeldt was asked to go with a retired chaplain, Frank Riley, and to lead the singing. From that beginning, Ralph led the singing, had devotions, and gave hugs to the people there for some seventeen years. It became more organized when Jimmy Dusek came on staff, with Grace Sanford sending our reminders to the people who were going. Some of the homes visited were Florida Manor, Americana, and the Orlando Convalescent Center. Now, there is usually a devotional, singing, prayer, and sometimes there are soloists. The service usually lasts from thirty to forty-five minutes. There is a great need for this ministry as some of the people confined there have few visitors and really enjoy a little attention being paid to them—a hug, a pat on the shoulder, a comment on how nice they look, and just anything that lets them know they are loved. The story is told by one of the people going to the homes about a lady there who was always so glad to see the visitors and particularly enjoyed the hugs. One Sunday afternoon when the visitors arrived, the lady handed one of them a piece of paper with these numbers on it: 1, 4, 3. She asked the visitor if she knew what it meant. Not knowing, the visitor guessed—room number, street number, part of a telephone number? The visitor couldn't guess. With a twinkle in her eye, the lady said, "How many letters in 'I'?" "One," the visitor answered. "How many letters in 'love'?" "Four," the visitor responded. "Now, how many letters in 'you'?" the lady asked. "Three," the visitor answered. The lady explained in triumph, "1, 4, 3, I love you!" That's just one of the many precious stories that can be told by nursing home visitors. There is a real need here for people who care to go and show Jesus' love to the people there.

PRAYER MINISTRY

First Baptist Church has always been a church of prayer. Throughout its history, there have been a number of specific prayer ministries. Most recently four segments have come to the forefront. The first is called Intercessory Prayer Ministry. There is a special room set aside in the church for this outreach. Our goal is to staff the Prayer Room in thirty-minute or one-hour segments. It is staffed sixteen hours a day, between 6:00 A.M. and 10:00 P.M., seven days a week, 365 days a year by volunteer prayer warriors. This ministry serves as a prayer support system for our church staff, our church family, and for people throughout our city, state, nation, and world. Often the person prayed for is sent a card letting them know about this special touch.

A second area of prayer is called the Watchman Prayer Ministry. It is made up of "prayer warriors praying in their homes. The Watchmen are commissioned to pray in thirty-minute or one-hour segments each week. The importance of this ministry is that our people are praying twenty-four hours a day, 7 days a week, 365 days a year."

Thirdly, the church maintains a twenty-four-hour Prayer Information Line which is available to receive specific prayer requests. The prayer requests are updated weekly by Bill Mitchell, prayer pastor. And fourth, in January 1996 our church mailed out its first monthly newsletter, called "Praying It Through," to provide information about prayer concerns in our "Jerusalem . . . and the uttermost parts of the earth." In addition, the Wednesday night church paper lists prayer needs.

PRAYER MINISTRY FOR THE SICK

> Is any one of you sick? He should call the elders of the church to pray over him and anoint him with oil in the name of the Lord. And the prayer offered in faith will make the sick person well; the Lord will raise him up. If he has sinned, he will be forgiven. (James 5:14–15)

The prayer ministry for the sick involves men of the church being available when the sick call upon them. Usually the sick person contacts them, although sometimes an elder may approach someone who is ill. Several pastors, deacons, and others are trained in this vital work. If the person who is ill is able to travel, that person comes to the church. If not, the men will go to the afflicted.

The first step is prayer. Both the men and the ill person pray for cleansing of any sins. Next the men ask questions of the sick, such as "Are you the spiritual leader of the home?" (if a man) or "Is your husband the spiritual leader of the home?" (if a wife); "Have you ill feelings about anyone?"; "Will you give a brief testimony?"

A third step is to read the Scriptures, especially the verses from above. Finally, the men apply oil to their fingertips and explain that there is nothing mystical about the oil. Then this oil is placed on the afflicted's head, and the men again pray. Then the one who is sick prays and accepts the healing.

The Lord always answers their prayers. Sometimes the person is immediately healed, sometimes the person is healed later, and sometimes the person is not physically healed in an earthly sense, but goes to be with the Lord.

Bob Vickery remembers a time when after the final prayer he immediately felt the Lord speaking to him that the person would be healed. Bob told the man's wife that she might as well go home from the hospital. Her husband was already made well.

Loren Mallory recalls a man who was so ill he was unable to come to the church. Hooked up to oxygen, he gave a wonderful testimony to his tearful wife. He went home to be with the Lord soon after.

While this practice has been experienced since the beginning of First Baptist, and while hundreds of men are on the list of people in this ministry, a few names are given to represent the entire group: Jim Henry, Jimmy Dusek, Bob Vickery, Loren Mallory, Ray Dorman, Jim Stagg, Randall James, Tige Fletcher, Charles Skinner, Ralph Edfeldt, and Jack Pratt.

TAPE MINISTRY
George R. Downes

The tape ministry at First Baptist Church Orlando was started by Al Amos and Bill Haynes in 1970 when Henry Parker was pastor. Not long after it was started, Al Amos and his wife Doyce moved to Tennessee, and Bill Haynes made the recordings and did the duplications by himself. Bill was having trouble with his back, and in 1975 he had to resign the ministry altogether. Richard Downes, who had begun helping Bill, then took over the recording and duplicating. The ministry at that point consisted of recording the services on a small portable recorder using a feed that Walter Reed would provide from the sound booth and making copies as they were requested. Much earlier, beginning in the 1950s before this more sophisticated technology, Reed had been instrumental in the sound and mike areas of the church. A small closet outside the church library was provided for housing the duplicator, which could make two copies of a tape in about three minutes. The ministry also had a small manual type-writer on which one could type two labels about as fast as the duplicator could copy the tapes. People would come by the library and turn in requests for tapes which would usually be ready to be picked up at the library the next week. Occasionally a special series of meetings or guest speakers would cause a backup of a week or two. Mark and Karl Fennimore volunteered to help in taping the services and the number of volunteers tripled.

Orlando was growing, First Baptist was growing, the tape ministry was growing. With the arrival of Jim Henry as pastor, the tape ministry began to grow even faster. Soon the volunteer help was not sufficient to meet the requirements of taking tape orders, phone calls, and walk-ins during regular business hours, and the first paid staff member assigned to the tape ministry was hired in 1981. This required a little rethinking of the goals and aims of the ministry. Up until that time, the ministry had been a strictly "faith ministry." No financial support from the church had been received or asked. Tapes were provided to anyone who asked for them, and contributions had met the needs of purchasing the blank tapes and other needs of the ministry. It was decided to keep the min-istry as one of faith, with the church paying the salary of the new position of tape supervisor. The church would also make some office space available, but the day-to-day operation of the ministry would remain as a faith ministry—tapes would be provided to anyone requesting them and would be paid for out of contributions. No item in the church budget was to be included for operation of the tape ministry.

Richard Downes continued to work as a volunteer to help coordinate the schedules of volunteers who taped the services and helped with the technical aspects of recording and duplicating. Other major milestones occurred when a "standing order" list was formed for mailing out tapes on a regular basis; a catalog of the available tapes was published; the church services were broadcast over a number of radio stations, resulting in numerous letters and requests; volunteers began tran-scribing the tapes, making messages available in written format; the Christian Endowment Foundation included some of our catalogs in one of their shipments of Bibles to Africa, resulting in a deluge of letters and orders for tapes; in 1991, the one millionth tape was distributed; and through August of 1995, over 1.4 million tapes have been distributed in twenty-seven countries on six continents.

An early decision in founding the tape ministry was to retain all the original recordings. This has provided the church with a valuable archive of thousands of recorded messages. The tape ministry has provided opportunities for a host of volunteers to serve the Lord in many different capacities. Over thirty volunteers are currently involved in addressing envelopes, packaging tapes for mailout, transcribing and editing messages for print, duplicating and labeling tapes, preparing returned tapes for reuse, reading letters, providing tapes after the services, recording messages, and generally being available to help people who want to know the Lord and study His Word. The tape ministry is currently managed by three paid part-time staff people, including the tape supervisor, Dan Maffett and two assistants, Theresa Hopcraft and Beverly Downes. The following have served or are serving in supervisory and assistant capacities: supervisors—Gail Alligood, Lou Anne Davidson, Paula Sapp, Linda Cody, Nellie Locke, Dan Maffett; assistants—Beverly Downes, Don Locke, Theresa Hopcraft.

THRIFT SHOP

The thrift shop was started in 1968 by Rafael de Armas to meet the needs of lower income families and to supply affordable clothing to the homeless. At that time it was called the Good Riddance Shop. The pastoral staff was first represented by Bill Curl. Jean Mallory and Vera O'Neill managed the shop, enlisting around forty volunteers to work a half-day each week on two, three-hour shifts. The shop was open five days per week and for a while on Saturdays. In later years Jimmy Dusek and Bill Mitchell represented our staff, with Jim Goodwin and Nancy Glenn as managers.

Customers come into a spiritual atmosphere and purchase a selection of clothing. Typically, prices are shirts for one dollar, pants two or three dollars, suits five dollars, socks twenty-five cents, ladies' dresses two dollars and fifty cents to five dollars, blouses one dollar, slacks two to three dollars, and shoes one to five dollars, depending on condition. Towels, soap, toothpaste, and other necessities are provided along with the clothing. A blanket is given to those living on the streets.

In 1970, Rev. Parker had this to say about the thrift shop: "We have an excellent committee in charge of the work. They, along with a number of assistants, have given untold hours of time and hard work in this specialized ministry of our church. The Thrift Shop has given an opportunity and an avenue of service to some of the older members of our church. These people, with their experience, love of the Lord, and desire to serve, are making an invaluable contribution" ("Beacon," August 27).

A counselor is on duty each morning to talk with the people who request free clothing. The plan of salvation is presented, and many have made a profession of faith and started a new life in Christ.

When First Baptist Church moved to its new location, we combined our efforts with Downtown Baptist and now share the income. The shop's first location was on Pine Street, but it moved to larger quarters on Central Avenue in order to handle miscellaneous items.

The thrift shop is considered one of the exemplary missions of the church, meeting the physical and spiritual needs of hundreds of people each year. The shop's mission statement is to help people with special needs, both physical and spiritual; to be a Christian witness to the downtown area; to give tracts and Bibles to further the outreach of the Gospel; to show our love and concern for others who may not be otherwise reached for Christ; to provide fellowship and a listening ear to those who are lonely; to provide opportunity to give to the mission program by donating time in the shop. We are not in this ministry to make money, and any profit goes directly to our church mission program.

Summary of Financial Report, 1995

	Receipts	Expenses	Disbursed	1/2 to each church
1st quarter	12,707.44	5,461.45	7,245.99	3,623.00
2nd	11,141.34	5,466.71	5,674.63	2,837.32
3rd	9,370.53	5,710.74	3,659.79	1,829.90
4th	12,095.68	5,449.03	6,646.65	3,323.33
	$45,314.99	22,087.93	23,227.06	11,613.55

Each church has received $11,613.55 for 1995 to be used to further missions throughout our community and the world.

Free Clothing	Disbursed	People Counseled	Saved
1st quarter	1,787.60	279	20
2nd	1,352.35	266	11
3rd	1,410.70	290	13
4th	2,145.00	335	23
	$6,695.65	1,170	67

OTHER MINISTRIES

The ministries inside the church are so numerous and varied that many could not be written about at length. Some of these include the engagement classes, the men's ministry led by Bud Hedinger, the women's ministry led by Beth Smith, the young married adult ministry, the married median adult ministry, men's Sunday School classes, women's Sunday School classes, the education ministry, bed babies, extended care, mom's day out (originally called Children's World and begun by Rafael de Armas), Mothers of Preschoolers (MOPS), financial planning ministry, Becoming One (Marriage Enhancement), parking, ushers, deacons, basketball camp, Centre for the Arts, videotape ministry, wedding services, funeral services, Wednesday night dinners, Sunday night fellowships, culinary services, and a host of others.

The people of First Baptist have always had a commitment to those outside the doors of the church. Some of these other ministries include the Orlando Union Rescue Mission, the Christian Service Center, World Hunger Relief, Edgewood Children's Ranch, Frontline Outreach, Central Florida Fair, Meals on Wheels, House of Hope, Daily Bread, Central Florida Helpline, Disaster Relief Program (Amateur Radio Operators), Human Crisis Council, Lakeland Children's Home, Missionary House, Resort Ministries (through Greater Orlando Baptist Association), and First Hands Benevolent Ministry, to name a few.

Baptist Terrace was a HUD-funded project that our church sponsored. Charles Horsley was the first administrator, followed by Martha Snipes, Bob Marrero, Anna Sharp, and Jim Merchant. The original building committee, which started looking for land in 1967, consisted of George Stuart, who oversaw the entire operation; C. B. Davis, who secured the property and handled all the real estate concerns; Bob Marrero, who was involved in the budget and personnel; Dick Lassitter, who handled all government and loan matters; and Eugene Kelsey, who served as clerk of works and managed all the construction. Finished in 1970, the building contains 101 efficiency apartments and 96 one-bedroom apartments. When it was built, the terrace was the first high-rise in Orlando that was 100 percent fireproof with a sprinkler system. In 1970, a loan for the building was taken out for $2.5 million at three percent interest for fifty years. At the end of that time, Baptist Terrace will become the property of the church. Currently, on the board of directors are members of First Baptist Church and Downtown Baptist Church.

As of 1996, the church gave $1.5 million annually to mission causes, with five hundred volunteers in missions projects. The annual Singing Christmas Trees and the Easter program, "The Light," each minister to eighty thousand visitors, with six hundred members in preparation and production. Over one million people have attended the presentations of our Singing Christmas Trees and Easter presentations of "The Light: The Story of Our Christ."

The thrift shop shares with the Christian Endowment Foundation managed by F. Ray Dorman. They send Bibles around the world and bring Bibles to the thrift shop to give to those in need. Excess clothing is provided to the Amazing Grace Ministries in Baldwin, Florida, managed by Wesley Mosely, and the Christian Veterans Association, managed by Ben Walker, in Jacksonville, Florida. These organizations bring blankets to the thrift shop for issue to the homeless. All four organizations work together to fill shipping containers of Bibles and clothing for shipment to overseas missions and churches.

Epilogue

"Therefore, since we are surrounded by such a great cloud of witnesses, let us throw off everything that hinders and the sin that so easily entangles, and let us run with perseverance the race marked out for us. Let us fix our eyes on Jesus, the author and perfecter of our faith."
Hebrews 12:1–2

Sunny skies greeted the dawn of a special day. It was March 3, 1996, the Sunday closest to the anniversary of the church. A joyful crowd of six thousand people, First Baptist members and guests, came together for "The Homecoming." They were celebrating 125 years of church history. Distinguished guests from around the country came to help the church celebrate its anniversary.

A hush fell over the sanctuary as Steve quickly took his seat. Slowly, sounds of nature stirred the air. Birds sang and crickets hummed. Suddenly shots rang out, and two hunters came on the platform. Andrew and John discussed the plentiful game. Wild turkeys were there for the taking, and Brother Jernigan had recently been rewarded with a panther

253

on his foray into the surrounding pine forest of their little settlement
known as Orlando. Other animals weren't as obliging, namely wild hogs
and rattlesnakes.

Conversation drifted to the coming visit of the Reverend William
Miller from the village to the northwest called The Lodge. His presence
was requested by a band of believers here, wanting to start a church. At
John's statement about "Good preachers are hard to find," spectator
Steve noted a burst of laughter from Brother Jim, which rippled through
the congregation. Andrew wondered, "Do you think anybody'll ever
move here?" There was more laughter as the two men made their way off
the stage.

Next, Steve's attention was drawn to two other men making their way
to the front. There were Bob Marrero, chairman of deacons for 1968, and
Dieter Matthes, present deacon chairman. They asked the Lord's blessings on the church. "May we not lose our first love, may we continue in
prayer, missions, and godly teachings."

The sound of water signaled Jimmy Dusek's entry into the baptistry.
He was followed by Eddie and Mary Jo, husband and wife, who were
baptized in a brief ceremony.

Next, Steve's voice joined the congregation and choir in a medley of
praise songs: "Jesus is the Cornerstone," "Rock of Ages," and "How
Great Thou Art." Two distinguished gentlemen, captured on video,
flashed on the overhead screen. John Sullivan sent his greetings and
reminded the church that she was the first in Florida to give one million
dollars to the Cooperative Program. The second man, John Bisagno,
kidded Brother Jim about being 125 years old, "Oh, no. It's the church,
isn't it!"

The camera then traveled to a wonderful group of senior adults sitting
at the front, representing all those long-time members. Steve glanced at
his bulletin, which named those who had been members for sixty or more
years: Alene Gatch, Myrlee Hearn, Versa Hendrix, Edna Kelsey, Eugene
W. Kelsey III, Waldo Lord, Howard Lott, Robert Marrero, Emily Meiner,
Ruth Moses, Elizabeth Pacewicz, Gennivee Rich, Edna Sanders, Lelia
Sneed, Carolyn Trumbo, Jewel Walden, and Ruth Ward. From the second
group of fifty or more years, some of the members honored were Jack
Boring, Barbara Braswell, Charles B. Brown, Eva Belle Brown, Norman
Brown, Charles E. Crews, Jean M. Crews, William C. Denson, George
Russell Harper, Helen P. Harper, Nancy Hull, Barbara Kelsey, Donna
Marrero, Margaret Smith, Millard B. Smith, W. P. Thomas, Joan T. van
Akin, Doris McCully, and Shirley Mallory.

Steve watched as other visitors made their way on stage or were honored where they sat. It was like a joyful reunion to see them: David and Nancy Cunningham, Bob and Sally New, and Ed and Missy Moses. Mildred Talton was recognized as the church historian for over twenty-five years. Virginia Parker made her way to the front. While her husband was pastor, she started the senior adult work in the church. She gazed up to heaven as if looking at her husband and the rest of the church triumphant. Ed and Alberta Irey, who have since gone to be with the Lord, were fondly remembered as former music leaders. Their three daughters were present and were introduced. Finally, Glenda E. Hood, mayor of Orlando, came forward to read and present a resolution of the church's distinguished history.

Steve heard the familiar voices of Bill and Lucy Pat Curl coming by phone from Wales with their greetings. Steve sat up straight as the church posed for a picture to commemorate the occasion. If cameras had been available to the eighteen charter members, a picture of them would make a startling contrast to the current, enlarged photograph.

The voice of the Reverend Wayne Johnson narrated a brief film of the church's history highlighting pictures from the four murals in Faith Hall. Then it was time for more old-fashioned singing: "The Church's One Foundation" and "We Are Standing on Holy Ground." Bob Vickery, accompanied by his wife Miriam, led the offertory prayer.

After more music, Steve watched as Brother Jim came to the podium to give a brief message taken from Acts 4:1–31 called "The Church—Profile of Courage." He began by saying, "Courage has been a mark of the church for twenty centuries." He enumerated several instances of courage, climaxing in a brief summary of the courage exhibited by a young warrior for the faith, Kathy Enfinger, who bravely fought cancer and witnessed to hundreds before joining her Lord in heaven some years ago. Steve noticed his neighbors wiping their eyes as he brushed some tears from his own.

At the close of the service, the invitation was given for those who felt a stirring of the Holy Spirit to accept Christ and come forward. Steve knew over the past 125 years, this act of obedience had been answered thousands of times as members of the church watched. Mac McCully led the closing prayer. Steve slowly left the sanctuary, almost sorry to disturb "this holy ground."

Others who witnessed that day have written about the occasion. Pat Brandt:

> It was wonderful to sing in the choir on our 125th birthday celebration.
> And what a celebration! The choir loft was filled to overflowing

(I oughta' know—I help seat the choir members as they come in, and they kept coming and coming and coming). My heart was overflowing also as we sang one of my favorites—"Cornerstone." Memories of singing that song downtown went through my mind. I thought of how far our choir has come and the ministry God has allowed me to be a part of. God has truly blessed us, as a choir, under Ragan's leadership to literally reach the world for Christ. Happy Birthday FBC/O!

Dan and Lin Maffett:

"The Lord has done great things for us, and we are filled with joy" (Psalm 126:3). What a fitting verse, as on March 3, 1996, we as a church celebrated the 125th commemoration of the vision of eighteen people whose desire to do God's will resulted in the establishment of First Baptist Church, Orlando. An overflowing congregation greeted friends of long-standing and welcomed back brothers and sisters who returned to First Baptist Church for this wonderful event. Our hearts were stirred with love and wonder at what God has done over the years because of the faithfulness of a few. Thousands, not only in Orlando, but around the world have come to know Christ as Saviour and Lord.

Now, as we are on the threshold of the twenty-first century, can we do less than those saints of God who preceded us? Our prayer is that God will continue to use First Baptist Church, Orlando to proclaim the Good News accurately and boldly. What a great joy to be part of this "river glorious"—God's Church on the Move.

David and Nancy Cunningham:

Wow! The Founders Day service was an unbelievably magnificent testimony and witness to the presence of our living Lord Jesus Christ through His church, First Baptist, Orlando. The choir and music sounded and felt like we had ascended to the presence of angels in heaven.

The phone conversation with missionaries Bill and Lucy Pat Curl, the presence of retired missionaries Ed and Missy Moses, and the realization that 37 missionaries have been commissioned from First Baptist Church/Orlando was a testimony that the sun and the Son never sets on the mission of this congregation.

The videos of gratitude from Dr. John Sullivan acknowledging the gift of over one million dollars to world wide missions through the Cooperative Program and the personal warm fraternal salutation and blessing from Dr. John Bisagno in Houston, Texas recognizes the stewardship and fellowship of this wonderful body.

The reception of former staff and the presentation of former First Lady Mrs. Virginia Parker represented your kind heart and appreciation for those who have labored with you over the years.

The honoring of longtime members and their presentation was a just tribute to their faithfulness and commitment over the years.

The message by Brother Jim, highlighting the witness of Kathy Enfinger and the witness of unknown Christians in the former Soviet Union pointed out the Alpha and Omega of your witness.

We left your presence with the song of praise "Worthy, you are worthy, King of Kings, Lord of Lords, you are worthy" flooding our hearts. May His presence keep you faithful in the days ahead until He returns for the triumphal celebration!

Theresa Hopcraft:

The two things that I especially remember that morning that made me chuckle are: ONE) I came to the church that morning as a weary counselor on-board a chartered bus that was returning from Cocoa Beach where we had held a "Spark" weekend which was a youth retreat for about 300+ teenagers. Boy, were we tired (and it showed). As I was shepherding the kids off the buses and directing them into Welcome Center B, the kids stumbled out of the buses with bleary eyes, "way too casual" clothing, and clutching pillows and stuffed animals for creature comforts.

All of a sudden, I noticed two teen boys, half-asleep, getting off the buses WITHOUT SHOES ON! I asked them, "Where are your shoes?" and they meekly replied, "In our luggage on the bus that broke down." I just remembered rolling my eyes and wondering if these boys had given any thought about their arrival to church. In a moment's hesitation, I told them to go into the church, quickly find a seat with the youth, cover their feet, and NOT TO GET UP. As they staggered into Welcome Center B, I just said a little prayer that they would make it to their seats without anyone really noticing, especially Brother Jim. And then I thought that even though all the kids were not in their Sunday best clothing (and shoes), Jesus had preached to multitudes who were probably not wearing shoes, so I was sure that Jesus probably didn't care how any of the kids looked that morning—He was just glad that we were all there!

TWO) After all of the youth had taken their seats, I rushed off to the Choir Room to put on my robe and prepare for the service. Since it was Anniversary Sunday, ALL the choir members were in attendance, and consequently I did not have my usual seat due to my late arrival.

I was on the front row in the 1st Soprano section where I had never sat before. When we filled the Choir loft, it turned out that the first row was behind the dividing wall of the orchestra pit, and once we sat down, we could not see the pulpit at all except if we strained and sat up as high as we could (and for this short person, that position was not too comfortable at all).

Well, despite my lowly seat that morning, we had a wonderful service of song, praise, and special presentations honoring our 125th Anniversary.

Later, there was a lovely luncheon at Lee's Lakeside honoring some of the guests and the longtime members. That evening Steve returned to church for the evening service. It began, as it so often had done, with baptism. Several saints of God entered the waters with Jimmy and Art.

Next, there was singing by Craig and Jill Anderson, visitors who had ministered to the youth at the camp in Cocoa Beach that weekend. Ed and Alberta Irey's three daughters, Carolyn Rogers, Joann Hand, and Kathleen Albert, came to the front to present a quilt to the church. It had been stitched by thirty women of this church as a going-away present to the Ireys after their twenty years of service in the music ministry. Now, it was returned to be on display as a living memorial to these great leaders. Ragan thanked the Lord for the "joy of music and for Ed and Alberta Irey."

The Ladies' Ensemble, Heart Song, sang "Embrace the Cross," an appropriate selection for the evening. Baby Joseph Gregory Driberg was brought forward to be dedicated by his parents and other family members, symbolizing the church's future and work with children. The evening's service culminated in the celebration of the Lord's Supper and a reminder of our Lord being a willing Lamb led to the slaughter for the remission of our sins.

And so, the celebration of the church's anniversary ended. The halls of the building echoed with the sounds of the saints as they left. There were tears and laughter of remembrance. Steve touched the grapes of the sculpture of Caleb and Joshua near the front door. He lingered for a few minutes, shaking the hands of his departing fellow members. As the night sky began to darken, he glanced up to the clouds and noticed a sunbeam connecting the heavens to the earth. He imagined the faces of the eighteen charter members and hundreds of others smiling down. How great a cloud of witnesses!

Appendixes

Appendix I

It would be an understatement to say that Florida has had a checkered and very interesting history. In a way, things have not really changed since the early days: there were many visitors seeking a variety of elements from gold to better health to a great climate. One of the best ways to get an overview of this state's history is by providing a timeline combined with a short narrative. Most of the timeline has been constructed by using six sources: Bacon's *Orlando: A Centennial History*, Gore's *From Florida Sand to "The City Beautiful,"* Kendrick's *Orlando: A Century Plus*, Del and Martha Marth's *Florida Almanac 1995–1996*, "Discover Orlando! A Student Walking Tour," and an article in the *Orlando Sentinel*, "Orange County, A Ripe Old Age of 150."

Florida was originally inhabited by various tribes of Indians, most notably the Muskogans, Tomokans, Caloosas, Creeks, and Seminoles. Some were peace loving, and others fought among themselves and with other tribes. Some wandered from area to area, and others settled in one place to farm.

"When Ponce de Leon claimed Florida for Spain in 1513, the peninsula was occupied by . . . Indian groups. . . . The Orlando area was the southernmost part of [Timucuan] territory. . . . Nearest the Orlando area were the Acueras, farmers who lived along the Oklawaha chain of lakes" (Shofner, *Orlando* 18–19).

Since the first inhabitants, Florida has been a land of contrasts. Some noticed and appreciated its beauty. "On March 27, 1513 Ponce de Leon sighted land, which he called in Spanish *Florida*, meaning 'feast of flowers'" (Garrison 14).

Others preferred to dwell on its negatives. In a letter by Thomas Heyward, Florida was described as a haven for refugees and renegades. "Everyone knows that the place is good for nothing else" (quoted in Garrison 28). Many of the Spanish explorers after Ponce de Leon made note of the lakes which swelled or receded with the alternating rains and droughts, the sand which could impede progress and swallow up man and beast, the hurricanes which brought destruction and death, and the vile pools of water which became the breeding ground for one of Florida's cruelest tricks—the mosquito.

SOME IMPORTANT FLORIDA DATES

1500—Seamen from Europe explored the water and islands around Florida.

1513—Ponce de Leon landed in present-day Florida, probably between St. Augustine and the mouth of the St. Johns.

1586—Sir Francis Drake razed St. Augustine.

1803—Louisiana Purchase was made. The U. S. claimed west Florida.

1816–1818—The First Seminole War was waged. "Aligned with refugee Creeks from Georgia, native Apalachees, and runaway slaves, the Seminoles battle Andrew Jackson's troops while Florida is still a Spanish territory" (Bulkin 2).

1821—Florida was purchased from Spain by the U. S. and Andrew Jackson was the first territorial governor.

1823—Tallahassee selected as the site for the capital.

1831—John James Audubon made his first visit to Florida. He "made no secret of the fact that he killed birds in great numbers. Many of them he shot to get their skins that, mounted on wire frames, provided the models for his famous paintings" (Garrison 51).

1835–1842—The Second Seminole War was fought with the Dade Massacre marking its beginning. Native Americans migrated to central Florida.

1845—Florida became the twenty-seventh state. William D. Moseley was selected the first state governor.

1855–1858—The Third Seminole War was waged.

1861—January 10, Florida seceded from the Union and became a haven for Union and Confederate deserters.

1868—Florida was readmitted as a state.

1883–1885—The era of railroads began.

1898—The Spanish-American War was waged. Afterward, military men returned to their northern homes extolling the virtues of Florida.

1912—The railway extended to Key West, connecting the entire state.

1917–1918—World War I was fought. Florida was used as a place for training camps and shipbuilding.

1918–1919—A worldwide flu epidemic killed many in Florida.

1920s—Florida's land boom sent Miami property selling for fifty dollars a lot to ten thousand dollars in a matter of months. Sometimes land changed hands several times in one day. But the time of prosperity was short-lived. On September 17, 1926, a devastating storm hit the area. With virtually no weather forecasting, the area soon resembled a war zone. Hundreds of buildings were destroyed by the 125-mile-per-hour winds, along with a tragic loss of life estimated to be nearly four hundred, with over seven thousand injured. Moore Haven, in a cruel irony, became the antithesis of its name.

The boom was over. Just as quickly as they had risen, land prices plummeted.

The final blow came in 1928, when a second—and even worse—storm struck Florida. This one—hurricanes were not given names then—had winds of 160 mph.

As it moved through South Florida it pushed a wall of water 12 feet high. Around Lake Okeechobee, nearly 2,000 people were swept to their deaths.

The true death toll will never be known. Years after the storm, remains were still being discovered. . . .

The 1928 storm killed off what remained of the boom and the Great Depression came to Florida a year before striking the rest of the nation. (Clark 4–5)

1929—President Coolidge dedicated Bok Tower on February 1.

1933—During an attempt on Franklin D. Roosevelt's life, Chicago Mayor Anton Cermak was killed in Miami.

1941–1945—The U.S. involvement in World War II affected Florida with 250,000 Floridians serving in the armed forces.

1958—*Explorer I*, first satellite, went off from Cape Canaveral.

1959—Fidel Castro came to power in Cuba, sending many Cubans fleeing to Florida.

1960—Hurricane Donna came to the Florida Keys and central Florida.

1961—Alan B. Shepherd Jr. completed "first U. S. manned sub-orbital space flight from Cape Canaveral on May 5" (Marth 55).

1962—John H. Glenn became the first American in orbit on February 20.

1963—John F. Kennedy visited Tampa days before his assassination.

1964—Hurricane Cleo destroyed $115 million in Florida property.

1967—Cape Kennedy—three U.S. astronauts were killed in a fire aboard Apollo I.

1969—In July, first men walked on the moon.

1982–1983, 1985—Hard freezes killed much of the citrus industry.

1986—Seven astronauts were killed at Cape Canaveral when the *Challenger* exploded.

1989—Miami suffered three days of riots.

1992—Hurricane Andrew devastated southeast Florida and other parts of the U. S.

SOME IMPORTANT CENTRAL FLORIDA DATES

According to French and Spanish records, present-day Orlando was once an Indian hunting ground. There were probably several large Indian settlements in an eighteen-mile radius of the area (Breakfast 5). But just as he did throughout the country, the white man began to infringe on these grounds. Trying to maintain peace became impossible after a time.

1821—Jacob Summerlin, "King of the Crackers," was born on February 22 in Lake City. "The first white baby born in Florida after its acquisition by the United States in 1821, [he] was raised in the cattle business and could crack a whip before he was seven years old" (Breakfast 15).

1824—Mosquito County was established from St. Johns County by the state legislature on December 29.

1835—There were at least two Indian villages in the Orlando area. One Indian chief, Coacoochee (also known as "Wildcat") lived in the Orlando area prior to the Second Seminole War (Shofner 28). Orlando Reeves was killed near Lake Eola. Some feel the city bears his name. Near Lake Eola, a fierce battle was fought between the Seminole Indians and the U.S. Dragoons.

1838—Fort Gatlin was established in 1838 between present-day Orlando and Pine Castle. The soldiers' job was to round up the troublesome Indians and move them out of the area. Surrounded by three lakes (Gem Mary, Gatlin, Jennie Jewel), the fort was nearly impregnable.

> There is a tradition that a council of representatives of the government and Indians met here under a huge live oak tree, and this oak, now no longer existing [but identified by a marker], was long known as the "Council Oak."

> Whether Ft. Gatlin was named for the lake, or the lake for the fort, is not known. However, in a recent letter to the author [Blackman], General Lutz Whal, Adjutant General of the army, says: "Referring to your inquiry, nothing is found in the official records here to show for whom Ft. Gatlin, Florida, was named. It is highly probable, however, that it was named in honor of Dr. John S. Gatlin, assistant surgeon, United States army, who was killed in the Dade massacre in the present Sumter County, Florida, December 28, 1835, at which time nearly 100 soldiers were killed by Indians. That officer was born in North Carolina, and was appointed from that state. Fort Gatlin was established November 9, 1838, and was abandoned November 22, 1849." (Blackman 83)

1842—Central Florida was covered with pine forests and lakes and not much else. The federal government, in an effort to attract settlers and eliminate the Indians, enacted the Armed Occupation Act. People coming to the area would be able to receive land on which to build. They were called "citizen-soldiers" and would continue the work of trying to settle the Indian problem. Some of these intrepid individuals chose the Fort Gatlin area (Shofner, *Orlando* 29).

Aaron and Isaac Jernigan came to the Fort Gatlin area. They were typical of the early settlers, who were mostly cattlemen. With some protection provided by the fort and the army and a ready buyer for their meat, these sometimes unscrupulous men made their home. Once they explored an area, they would bring down their families from the north and set up homesteads. Only an occasional dent was made in their herds by wandering Indians. "Several of the [cattlemen] stole entire Indian herds, then burned the dwellings of their owners, after kicking the Indians out of doors. The practice brought reprisals from the badgered Seminoles which greatly prolonged the Indian Wars, much to the profit of the cattlemen" (Breakfast 13). It is believed that Colonel Henry Washington, nephew of President Washington, spent some time in his uncle's previous profession as a surveyor in the Orlando area.

1843—Aaron and Isaac Jernigan settled on Lake Holden. Aaron is considered by many to be the first white settler of present-day Orlando, although Mr. Mendola of the Orange County Historical Museum believes Aaron Jernigan at first settled further south and later moved to Lake Holden.

1845—Mosquito County became Orange County on January 30.

1846—John Perry, a Methodist circuit rider, ministered to the area.

1849—Fort Gatlin was abandoned on November 22. Settlers continued to carry guns for protection, and Jernigan built a stockade on the west shore of what is now Lake Holden, large enough to hold all families in the vicinity in case of trouble (Breakfast 15). "Three whites were killed by Seminoles during a series of raids in south Orange County" (Andrews, "Landlocked" K-2).

1850—The first log house was built in Orlando by John Worthington. Martha (Jernigan) Tyler wrote about Orlando: "The first little log house ever built in Orlando was built out of pine poles with the bark left on them. It was about 12 feet long and eight feet wide and one had to stoop to get in the door. There was a counter at one side, and a few cigar boxes full of sand with candles stuck in the sand, which stood on the counter. A box of tobacco and a barrel of whisky stood in one corner. That was in 1850" (quoted in Kendrick 6). A post office was established and named Jernigan. Orange County's population was 466.

1855—William Benjamin and Emily Hull moved to Orlando from Cobb County, Georgia.

1856—Orlando was named the county seat through the influence of Judge J. G. Speer. An early settler said: "There was nothing to the place but a sawmill operated by John Worthington." Present-day Apopka was named "The Lodge" until 1887.

1857—The village name became Orlando. There has been much controversy as to how Orlando got its name. Some feel it was named to honor Orlando Reeves, a soldier in the Second Seminole War who was killed near Lake Eola in 1835. Others feel it was named after a character in Shakespeare's play, *As You Like It*. Still others say it was named after a Mr. Orlando, an ox-cart driver who died of appendicitis and was buried in the area. As travelers passed by they would say, "There's Orlando."

"On September 19, 1857, the United States Post Office officially recognized the name of Orlando and named John Worthington as postmaster, with the Worthington store as post office. The location of Orlando as the county seat was the most feasible site since it was the intersection of the road from Fort Mellon to Fort Brook east and west, and Gadsden's Trail from Fort Butler to Fort Lloyd, north and south" (Bacon I, 16). Prior to this, Aaron Jernigan had received his commission as postmaster on February 9, 1857. The following is a list of early Orlando postmasters and their dates of service: John R. Worthington—September 19, 1857, to September 20, 1859; Henry Overstreet—September 20, 1859, to March 6, 1859; Henry Robeson—March 6, 1860, to January 10, 1861; and D. K. Hall—January 10, 1861, to March 19, 1861. There was no official service until 1866. Postmasters after that time have been: Mary A. McGinnis—December 4, 1866, for one year; William Whitted—December 13, 1867, to June 6, 1870; Robert O'Conner—June 6, 1870, to February 27, 1871; and Edward W. Speir—February 27, 1871, to 1887. Speir was commissioned as postmaster and served for sixteen years. A one-story frame building on the corner of Main and Pine streets was erected to serve as post office (O'Neal 50).

For several years, cattle raising remained the chief means of support for the settlers, with farming done mainly on family plots. When vegetables were scarce, scurvy was a threat, but wild orange trees provided a ready remedy. Most families were able to sustain themselves with few trips necessary for supplies. Game was in abundance. Staples were pork, beef, fish, deer, grits, sweet potatoes, syrup, milk, whisky, and butter. They bought wheat flour and salt.

One particularly troublesome animal was a wild hog, or razorback. It roamed free in herds and terrorized the early settlers. It was a very large beast, probably descendants of hogs brought by DeSoto in the 1500s. When aroused, it was dangerous. The head and nose were long, the ears were small, and the tusks were from three to four inches, capable of inflicting much damage. The Indians had used the meat of these animals for food and the hides for a variety of other purposes (Breakfast 18–19).

A deed was given to the county commissioners by Benjamin F. Caldwell of Alabama for four acres of land for a town plot to be known as the village of Orlando. Mr. Mendola said this land was given for a courthouse.

"On November 23, 1857 John Patrick deeded to Captain Aaron Jernigan, Thomas H. Harris, and Henry Hodges, a committee appointed by subscribers to a Free Church to be built in Orlando, one acre of land in the SE 1/4 of Section 26, TS 22, South of Range 29 East, for the purpose of building a Free Church" (Bacon I, 16).

1860—As soon as Abraham Lincoln was elected president of the United States, Florida joined her sister southern states in the process of secession. A secession convention met in Tallahassee. Residents of Orange County were mixed in their opinions of leaving the Union. However, they elected William Woodrull, who was a Unionist, to travel to the convention and represent them. He was only one of seven to vote against secession with the final vote recorded as sixty-two to seven.

Most people in central Florida put their differences behind them and vigorously upheld the decision to withdraw from the United States. When Florida joined forces with the Confederacy, many men marched off to engage in the conflict. Although no battles were fought in the Orlando area, the war's many hardships were felt here. As supply lines were destroyed, our citizens struggled and overcame some of their privations through numerous innovations. For a time James P. Hughey made trips into Gainesville for supplies for his store and community.

Others put their home gardens to use and shared their produce with their neighbors. Some took trips to the coast to harvest salt for themselves and as a money crop, which they sold to the Confederacy for fifty dollars a bushel. Military wives picked up the reins of their absent husbands and fought a different kind of war on the home front, trying to stave off famine from conquering their families. For a time, Mrs. William Hull ran a boardinghouse while her husband fought in the war, and she became an unofficial postmistress.

While many Florida communities dwindled and some died out, Orlando's population actually grew. Several people came to seek relief from war-torn Georgia. Among these were William and Charles Hansel and Nathan and Hiram Beasley. William H. Holden arrived from northern Florida to buy up twelve hundred acres around present-day Lake Holden. Later he cultivated a citrus grove (Shofner, *Orlando* 32).

1861—The Orlando post office was discontinued on March 19.

1862—The small group of Baptists that had formed in 1858 was forced to disband due to the war and the absence of most of its male members.

1863—A log two-story courthouse was built on Main Street (now Magnolia Avenue). This building replaced the first courthouse, which "was an abandoned log cabin—with no windows and a dirt floor—on or near what is now Church Street" (Robison and Andrews 224).

1865—Dr. Whittle, one of Orlando's first physicians, arrived.

1866—The Orlando post office was reestablished. The downtown area of Orlando was still quite small with only a log courthouse, a few stores, and a boardinghouse or two. The Homestead Act of 1866 was passed which enabled former slaves to buy land, some of them settling in the county. Surprisingly, there was little racial tension in the town (Shofner, *Orlando* 34).

1867—Francis Eppes, a mayor of Tallahassee, arrived in Orlando. He was a grandson of Thomas Jefferson (Shofner, *Orlando* 34). "Uncle Dan Prescott" arrived. An ardent fiddler, he often played at weddings (Kendrick 11).

1868—The courthouse was burned down, probably to destroy evidence for an impending trial.

1869—A two-story frame courthouse was built. "Capt. Bluford M. Sims built it for the county at a cost of $1,250, according to the Orange County Historical Society" (Robison and Andrews 224). The courthouse was used for church meetings. Gore in *Florida Sand* writes, "The men sat on one side of the room and the women on the other. The floor was covered with sawdust for the convenience of those who chewed tobacco or snuff and many brought their babies and dogs to meeting" (139).

On December 11, 1869, A. C. Caldwell, W. A. Lovell, Z. H. Mason, and W. C. Roper met at the courthouse to organize a Board of Public Instruction. Earlier, children from wealthy white families were educated in private schools. Superintendent W. A. Lovell and three board members began work to organize education for the county. "Existing school were incorporated into the public system, and all grades were taught by the same teacher. The separation of church and state was not an issue. School was later held in Orlando's first church building, pastors often were teachers during the week, and teachers were required to be well-versed in the Bible and to pass on instruction in proper morals" (Andrews "Establishing" K2).

1870—Cattle and citrus replaced cotton as Orlando's main industry.

Union Free Church and School meeting place, 1872–1882—Courtesy OCHM

1871—Bethel Baptist Church was organized on March 5 and probably met in the courthouse. In August, a storm of hurricane force dumped over a foot of rain in forty-eight hours. E. W. Speir was postmaster. Orange County had nine election districts. D. B. Stewart was sheriff.

1872—Orange County was a very violent place to live, with forty-one people slain that year. Not surprisingly, then, Orlando's first jail was built.

As families arrived, survival was difficult due to all types of adverse conditions. They chose a piece of high ground and began to raise the typical crops of sweet potatoes, corn, greens, sugar cane, cotton, and hogs. Many also came to raise citrus, which was nicknamed "Florida Gold."

"The Union Free Church, planned in 1857, finally was built in 1872, financed by contributions and fund-raising social events. It did double duty as church and school house. The one-acre lot given by John Patrick was located on South Main Street (Magnolia) between Pine and Church streets, now the site of the First Federal Savings and Loan Association and the old Baptist Sanctuary. The Free Church was built 150 feet south of Pine Street and 100 feet east of Main. The section where the old Baptist Church stood was used as a cemetery—Orlando's first official burial ground" (Bacon I, 46). The structure was built as a combined effort of the Baptists, Methodists, and Episcopalians. It was wooden and L-shaped, with a shingle roof.

Orlando had thirty school-age children attending school three months a year. Blackman writes that Cassius Boone came to Orlando in 1872 and became the first teacher for Orlando schools. He was also an early storekeeper along with W. A. Patrick. In addition, Boone was the county clerk for six years. He set up a hardware enterprise, was on the town council, and served as mayor in 1883. A busy man, he also ran a dairy and nursery (88).

1873—Jacob Summerlin moved to Orlando and helped establish peace among the cattlemen. Orlando's first hotel, the Summerlin, opened at a cost of fifteen thousand dollars. Daily rates were two dollars. Milk was furnished by cows grazing behind the building. A storm damaged cotton and citrus crops.

1874—Razorback hogs ran amok through the village of Orlando. They especially enjoyed rubbing their backs against the steps of the courthouse and slept underneath it at night. The floor was covered with sawdust so tobacco chewers did not have to bother to spit out of the windows. The room was used on Sundays for religious services, and the fleas were so thick no one went to sleep during church (Gore 84).

1875—Orlando was incorporated with one square mile of land and a population of eighty-five on June 23. At the town council's first meeting, held at the courthouse on August 4, the first officers were William J. Brack, mayor; James P. Hughey, clerk; J. W. Williams, marshal; James R. Montague, Jacob Summerlin, E. W. Speer, W. C. Stubblefield, E. A. Richards, C. A. Boone, and J. R. Cohen, aldermen; Jacob Summerlin, president; and Colonel R. W. Broome, attorney (Breakfast 23–24).

James Delaney came to Orlando. He had nine children and was postmaster, storekeeper, and builder. One of his daughters, Claudia Delaney, gave her life to the Orlando Postal Service. Another daughter, Eunice Delaney, was a teacher and administrator. Delaney Avenue was named for this pioneer family. They were very active in the Baptist faith. Delaney Street Baptist Church was named as a memorial to this early family who did so much to build a greater Orlando.

Cattle baron Jacob Summerlin donated ten thousand dollars for the building of a new courthouse so Orlando would remain the county seat. Captain T. J. Shine arrived. He was married to Virginia Eppes, great-granddaughter of Thomas Jefferson.

1876—The *Orange County Reporter* was founded on June 6 with Rufus Russell as the publisher and Mahlon Gore as the editor. Citrus trees grew wild and the first commercial grove was begun. Joseph Bumby made semi-weekly trips on horseback between Mellonville (Sanford) and Orlando to bring in the United States mail. The First Presbyterian Church of Orlando was organized.

Samuel A. Robinson wrote, "When Mrs. Robinson and I landed in Orlando in 1876 the population of the town did not exceed 100 inhabitants counting all ages. Hog raising was the chief industry, as they ran at large they were ever present, many congregated and slept under the court house steps, much to the inconvenience and distress of worshipers who attended church service which was held in the court house" (quoted in O'Neal 16–17).

1877—J. H. Allen was elected mayor.

1878—Charles H. Munger was elected mayor.

1879—S. A. Robinson surveyed the first railroad through Orlando, but this one was never completed because a major backer died suddenly in New York.

Then Samuel Robinson surveyed for the South Florida Railroad to run from Mellonville to Orlando, and construction was begun. A. M. Hyer was elected mayor.

Late 1870s—There was a blacksmith shop near Lake Conway that made and repaired the two-wheeled ox carts and wagons then in use. Other items made were pocket, butcher, and bowie knives; hoes; rakes; plows; harnesses; saddles; and bridles.

1880—The First Methodist Church officially organized. In November, South Florida Railroad was completed from Mellonville to Orlando. This enterprise brought growth and prosperity to the area. Joseph Bumby was the first agent, and trains stopped at his grain store on the northwest corner of Church Street. "The downtown was two and a half blocks long, north to south, and four blocks wide, east to west" (Logsdon 3). The real estate office of John G. Sinclair and N. L. Mills was in the downtown area. A funeral parlor was run by Edgar A. Richards.

Mount Zion Missionary Baptist Institutional Church was established as one of the first black churches. R. L. Summerlin was elected mayor. The *Orange County Reporter* was purchased by Mahlon Gore, and the paper listed one dentist for Orlando, H. M. Granniss. Orlando was reported to have a population of two hundred.

1881—A wooden railroad station was built. Orlando's first telephone was a line which ran from Major P. A. Foster's livery stable to his home. C. D. Sweet was elected mayor.

1882—C. A. Boone was elected mayor.

1883—Orlando's first bank was organized. "The telegraph office was opened Jan. 1, 1883. The first message was sent out by Mr. Lewis H. Lawrence and read, 'To my friend, Chester A. Arthur, President of the United States, Washington: Happy New Year, first message from office opened here today. No North, No South'" (Blackman 181). The railroad was extended to Tampa. J. L. Bryan was elected mayor, serving for two years. Orlando's first sidewalks were laid from the depot to Orange Avenue and then north on Orange. A volunteer fire department was organized by W. C. Sherman.

Jacob Summerlin donated land for a public park at Lake Eola. Lake Eola was "named by Robert Summerlin for a family friend. Originally called 'the lake' the shores on the south and east sides were known as Sandy Beach" (Bacon 1, 56). The lake was twenty-two feet deep.

Eva Bacon also wrote about the beginning of the naming of a number of Orlando streets. For example, Church Street was named because it was the site of the Union Free Church during the early days. Pine Street recalled the dense clusterings of said trees of long ago (1, 379–81).

Orlando voted itself dry during the temperance movement that swept the nation. This order was largely ignored by most of the cowmen who raised havoc in the streets of Orlando on the weekends. However, early Saturday mornings were more peaceful but equally busy as farmers came to town for "Cracker Day." "Families gathered from miles around to trade and exchange the latest news.

Sometimes the entertainment took unusual forms. One popular activity was watching Bunk Baxter wrestle his pet alligator at the corner of Orange Avenue and Pine Street. On another weekend, the main event was the public hanging of a murderer, Henry Stokes" (Shofner, *Orlando* 46). Some sources have a different name for Bunk Baxter—Bud Yates.

1884—The city's first major fire occurred on January 12, with much of the downtown area destroyed. Orlando's population was 1666, sixty of them Baptists. The Episcopal Church was officially organized, although it had been meeting in homes since 1869. The first circus came to Orlando.

The *Orange County Reporter* displayed ads for a practical embalmer, lightning rods, plows, cook stoves, and chemical manurers. Tavares was called "the Gem of the Lakes!" An ad for a store read "W. G. White's—the Old Reliable. Leads all the while to greater and better bargains—dry goods, groceries, hardware, shoes, hats, clothing, furniture, etc." (a February issue). An opera house and community hall held weekend performances of plays, musicals, traveling performers, and minstrel shows (Shofner, *Orlando* 46).

From a map of the business district, the following are listed: South Florida Foundry Works, Dr. Hicks Residence, J. H. Mooney Pianos and Organs, Magnolia Hotel, Peter Mack's Winery, South Florida Railway, Water-house and Russell Feeds, pump, White-Knox-Grady Ins. & Real Estate, B. B. Cambells Restaurant, Chas. Rock Bakery, A. D. Bernway Barber Shop, Sinclair Mills Real Estate, Carpenters Shoe Repair, Deadrick Tin Shop, Mathes Shoe Shop, Joseph Bumby Feeds, N. C. Motley Grocery, J. A. McDowell Grocery, Rollins Fish Mkt., J. S. Mairson Dry Goods, Cuban Cigar Mfg., C. A. Cartino Fruits, F. A. Lewter Dry Goods Groc., Ives & Ferguson Groc. & Express, Kuhl "KKK" Candy, DeLaney & Heard Groc., Merneagh Groc., Christophers Boarding House (Fruit Stand-Thanashaw), So. Fla. Rly. Depot, Dr. J. N. Butt Drugs, N. P. Nimo Dry Goods, Campbell Pump & Wells, Cohn Bros. Clothes, Randolph Cafe, Jewl. Store, W. C. Sherman, Mathews Barber Shop, Green Front Groc., W. P. Kyle Tin Shop, Danns Groc., Price Harness Shop, Skillman Well Driving, W. G. White Gen. Merchant, Peek & Williams Drugs, Duckworth Shoe, Smith Jewelry Store, rooming house, DeLaney & Heard Groc., Birmbaum Dry Goods, Alligator John Curio Shop, Billie Williams Saloon, E. P. Hyer Saloon, C. A. Boone Hdw., Ives & Rowland, Big Tom Shine Auction, Mrs. Kollock Boarding House, J. N. McElroy Drugs, Rice Bros. Dry Goods, E. A. Richards Undertaker Gunsmith, Charleston House, A. M. Hyer Saloon, Milo Cooper Barber, O'Connell Paints & Signs, A. M. Hyer Livery Stable, mule lot, city well for fire, band stand, First National Bank, C. G. Butt Lawyer, Dr. Chapman Drugs, C. F. McQuage Real Estate, Mrs. Holloway Residence, J. H. Livingston Real Estate, Barber Shop (Col.), Price (Bee Hive), W. M. Oglivie Hardware, jail, court house, Summerlin House, Cohens Bros. General Store, Armory (Shine Guards) Lord & Taylor Groc, English Club, post office, J. V. Duke Grocery, Ed Gunby Lawyer, Orlando Record, C. A. Wimer Post Office, Ed Speer, cemetery, Geers Photo, Opera House, Spot Cash Davis Mkt., Dave Russell Res., Dr. Rowland, Scott Allen & Co. Feeds Store, H. H. Berry Wagon Works.

1885—The first city hall was built. The Catholic Church erected a church building (Bacon 1, 87). F. J. Reel was elected mayor and served for two years. Orlando's first flower show was held. Henry S. Kedney of Minnesota came to Orlando and built, with A. H. Cary, the San Juan Hotel at a cost of approximately $150,000. Rollins College was established. The zoo was opened. The Orlando Ice Manufacturing Company was listed in a directory.

1886—A cold wave damaged citrus. The Orlando Opera House was able to seat eight hundred. The railroad fare from Orlando to Chicago was $36.85. The Orlando Colored School was established.

The English Club (also called the Cosmopolitan Club) was formed specializing in festive parties, tennis matches, and yacht regattas. For a time they met in the "Rogers Building" (current site is 37–39 South Magnolia Avenue), which was built in 1886 for Gordon Rogers. Later, other businesses occupying this building were a grocery, the *South Florida Sentinel*, a beauty shop, a dance studio, and several eating establishments (Logsdon 8).

There was an earthquake. A streetcar franchise was granted. Mule-drawn cars had speed set at six miles per hour, and drivers were ordered to stop at all intersections to allow pedestrians to cross. The armory building was built.

"Bumby Hardware Building" (currently 100–102 West Church Street) was constructed for Joseph Bumby. During his life, Mr. Bumby was an active businessman who ran Bumby's Express Line from Orlando to Sanford and a feed store; he also became the first freight and passenger agent for the railroad (Logsdon 10).

Orlando Water Company was given a charter. The Board of Trade (later Chamber of Commerce) was organized. Phone lines connected Orlando to Sanford. A wood-frame grocery store was built which belonged to H. H. Dickson and Sydney Ives (Logsdon 18). Daily mail was established.

O'Neal gave a humorous account of travel to Orlando. The journey began with a traveler leaving his home north of St. Mary's River in July. The author joked that it would be wise to make out a will before leaving on this "dangerous" journey. The first leg of the trip would utilize the Savannah Florida and Western train coming to Cow's Ford (later renamed Jacksonville). Next you had your choice of boats, either the Frederick DeBara or City of Jacksonville. If no calamities struck, like fog or sandbars, you would land in Sanford around noon. Stopping for refreshments at the old Sanford House hotel, you would arrive in Orlando in the early evening. Probably the afternoon rains would have submerged the street planks, making city travel difficult but not impossible, especially if the traveler had a thirst which he could quench at a number of saloons. "You would probably register at the Charleston house, corner Orange and Pine, where Charlie Gooding would properly assign you to your room. . . . The bedroom had a one-piece cotton mattress on slat springs, a mosquito bar over the bed, a bowl and pitcher on a small stand, and a mirror on the wall. . . . In the dining room . . . you probably had hot biscuits, grits, cow peas, sorghum and stewed meat, with sweet potato pie and coffee with long sweetening, and milk out of a can" (163–66).

Another humorist, Will Wallace Harney, enjoyed writing about the scourge of central Florida, the mosquito, along with other pests: "Everything that buzzes or flies, everything that bites or stings is familiar in Florida. The red bug, of the loathsome chinch genus, I think, buries itself under the cuticle, and makes a purulent sore. Mosquitoes and sand flies, of course. . . . [The mosquito] flies in clouds, darkening the air and fouling the dishes. . . . They have forceps that will plug through a two-double army blanket" (quoted in Shofner, *Orlando* 33).

Insects weren't the only pests of concern. The razorback hog was also a menace. "There was no animal more aptly suited to cleaning the streets of early-day Orlando than the razorback hog for . . . the animal was good for very little else" (46). Mahlon Gore in 1895 said, "Architecturally, the razorback is built on four legs—the two hind ones at the rear corners; the front ones just far enough in front of center to prevent the long snout from tilting the tail end into the air. . . . The Creator never made anything in vain and no doubt there was a wise purpose in providing the razorback with tails on his jaws, but man has never yet been able to penetrate this veiled mystery. There is an excess of tails and paucity of brains. He has no sense and his instincts are perverse and lead to destruction. . . . He eats anything that comes his way. . . . He is mostly made up of bowels and sin" (quoted in Shofner, *Orlando* 46).

1887—Orlando was nicknamed "The Phenomenal City." The Lodge was renamed Apopka. F. S. Chapman was elected mayor. Edward and Burchard Kuhl, along with James Delaney, had built the "Kuhl-Delaney Building" (currently located at 69 East Pine Street) which housed, in succession, the Orlando Post Office, Arnold's Grocery, the Knights of Pythias, and, much later, Mather Furniture (Logsdon 9). Lake and Osceola counties were separated from Orange.

F. N. Boardman moved his family to Orlando from New Hampshire and bought the Sinclair/Mills building, moved it, and established it as his residence. He started a small shoe store which developed into a general store. "His goal was to make $50,000 and then retire. By industry, investments in property when it was cheap and selling at a profit, he soon achieved his goal." (Bacon I, 164). He gave large sums of money to charity and to the First Baptist, Winter Park, and College Park Baptist churches. He was one of the founders of the College Park Baptist Church and before his death paid off all its outstanding indebtedness. It is said he gave as much as fifty dollars a month to the church.

Jacob Summerlin made the land surrounding Lake Eola into a fairgrounds, with a racetrack circling the lake and a bathhouse convenient for bathers (Breakfast 31). Lake Eola was also the site for the first golf course. "The play was constantly in the rough and alligators and snakes occasionally acted as caddies. 'Shinney,' a game played with hockey sticks and with a ball or a block of wood for a puck and an indeterminate number of players on each side, was most popular among the growing boys. . . . Baseball, sandlot or school style, was always popular—and as added attraction, when Orlando played Sanford in one town or the other, was a glorious fight which nearly ended every game" (Kendrick 50).

1888—Mathew R. Marks was elected mayor and served three years. He began a program of planting shade trees in the city.

1889—The Baptist church deeded land to the city so that Orlando could extend Pine Street from Main to West streets. A city order stated that all gates which opened on a city street were to swing inward (Bacon 1, 174). The Catholic Church built a school and convent (Bacon 1, 174). The Orlando Railroad Depot (currently located at 76–78 West Church Street) was completed by Henry B. Plant for the South Florida Rail Company (Logsdon 12). A second fire in the downtown area would prompt the use of bricks instead of wood for future buildings.

1880s—Until the late 1880s, ice was a luxury which few people could buy. Salt was a staple everyone needed. It was used to preserve nearly everything: beef, quail, duck, wild turkey, venison, boar, rabbit, and fish. Salt was extracted by boiling either saltwater or the roots of the saw palmetto.

1890—The old railroad station was torn down and a brick building was erected. The county's first clay thoroughfare, Iron Bridge Road, was constructed. The first local polo team was organized by the Orlando Polo Club.

1891—Pine Street became the first really paved road in the city. Clay was used, and a race was held for firemen. Orlando High School graduated its first class. W. L. Palmer was elected mayor and served for three years.

1892—The fair association was organized. Orlando purchased Greenwood Cemetery. A bicycle club was formed with members using the race track and wooden paths. The county built a red brick courthouse with a large clock. The old courthouse was moved and became part of the Tremont Hotel. The Cottage Hospital Association was founded.

1893—The Sorosis Club, a women's study group, started the first lending library. Harry Beeman purchased the San Juan Hotel and added two more stories.

1894—Mahlon Gore was elected mayor for three years. On February 15, twenty-three ladies met to form the Rosalind Club, a social group. A big freeze in December 1894 (and February 1895) destroyed most of the citrus industry. Hundreds of people who had moved to Florida to seek their fortune in citrus were wiped out. Blackman wrote that the freeze came as a "thief in the night." However, he saw some good which came from the calamity. Farmers were forced to diversify into other areas of agriculture and horticulture (75–76). Seven out of eight banks located in Orange County closed (Logsdon 3).

1895—The county's population was 12,549. The Church and Home Hospital was organized.

1897—J. B. Parramore was elected mayor, then served for six years. The Orlando Water and Light Company was organized.

1898—Orlando's first fire house was established on Oak Street (now Wall Street).

1900—Orlando's population was 2,481. Orange County's was 12,582. Electric service was introduced. Hunting, especially for wild cat and fox, was a major sport.

1902—Orlando's first automobile, a "one-lung steamer," was owned by J. J. Harris. The speed limit for cars was started at five miles per hour, then raised to seven.

1903—The *Evening Star* began publication. E. H. Gore came to Orlando from Michigan on January 21. He worked for the *Evening Star*, carried mail, was a partner in a grocery, was a post office clerk, and a foreman. Later, he wrote *History of Orlando: From Florida Sand to "The City Beautiful"* and a booklet of First Baptist Church's history. Zora Neale Hurston was born in Eatonville. B. M. Robinson was elected mayor and served for two years.

1905—Orlando's first mail delivery began. The old schoolhouse burned. Orlando suffered a three-month drought. Then, strangely, a rainy season flooded all lakes. The "Elijah Hand Building" (currently located at 15–17 West Pine Street) was built by Elijah Hand on the former site of the Magnolia Hotel, which he had moved. Mr. Hand was the first embalmer in the city (Logsdon 14). J. H. Smith was elected mayor and served for two years.

E. H. Gore, postal worker—Courtesy OCHM

1906–1907—"In 1906–07, occurred a severe and protracted drought. For more than a year, scarcely any rain fell. Crops of fruit, grain, and vegetables were destroyed; citrus and ornamental trees and shrubbery were injured; water courses and lakes were dried up, live stock suffered for want of both water and grass; and from ten to fifty per cent of the pine trees of the state were killed, except on the lower and moister lands, and many other varieties of forest trees were injured or destroyed. Naval store operators, lumber men and owners of timber lands suffered great loss" (Blackman 75).

1907—There was a ban on cockfighting, dogfighting, and prizefighting. Orange Avenue was paved with brick. Braxton Beacham was elected mayor. P. Phillips opened the first packinghouse.

1908—The city's nickname changed from "The Phenomenal City" to "The City Beautiful" suggested by contest winner Mrs. W. S. Branch. William H. Jewell was elected mayor and served for three years.

1910—The first airplane to fly from Florida soil was flown by Lincoln Beachy. The first Orange County Fair was held. Swans for Lakes Lucerne and Eola arrived from England purchased by Charles Lord.

1911—W. H. Reynolds was elected mayor, serving for three years. Forty-one people were pictured as attending the first annual meeting of the Pioneer Association of Orange County at the fairgrounds on October 11.

1912—Barney, a buffalo with Buffalo Bill's show, escaped and charged down Orange Avenue coming to rest in Duckworth's store.

1913—Seminole County was formed from Orange. Orlando's first "air-cooled" building, the Empire Hotel, was constructed.

1914—*Romance in Orlando*, a film about the city's fire department, played at the Grand Theater. E. F. Sperry was elected mayor, serving three years.

1915—The first traffic light was put up in Orlando.

1917—James L. Giles was elected mayor and served 1917–1919 and then from 1924–1925. The "Yowell-Duckworth Building" (currently located at 1 South Orange Avenue) was completed. Newton Yowell and Eugene Duckworth were partners in the department store for two years. Later it became Ivey's department store (Logsdon 16).

An amusing story was told about a prominent woman in Orlando who hosted a bridge club party at her home. Somehow, even though there was rationing going on due to World War I, she was able to procure a salmon, which she made into a salmon loaf to serve for lunch to her female guests, all "creme de la creme" of Orlando society. As she went out to the kitchen to fetch the dish, she discovered her cat had eaten a portion of the fish. Not knowing what to do, but having nothing else to serve and wanting to impress her guests with the expensive meal, she shooed the cat outside, smoothed over the salmon, and served it without telling anyone about the incident. Her guests raved about the delicious food, especially the fish loaf.

After the meal was over, she returned to the kitchen and discovered her cat, dead on the back porch. Thinking the cat died of food poisoning, she faced a dilemma: should she swallow her pride and tell, or should she risk harming her guests? She soon realized her duty and informed the women of the necessity of their going to the hospital to have their stomachs pumped out. Returning from the hospital, she met her neighbor outside. He said, "I noticed you had company earlier, so I didn't want to disturb you, but now I can tell you my sad news and ask your forgiveness. I ran over your cat with my car, and I'm afraid he may have climbed back on your porch to die" ("Orlando Natives Luncheon" 1990 video).

1918—A worldwide influenza epidemic closed down all churches, businesses, and schools in Orlando for several days in October by order of Dr. S. McElroy. On Sunday, October 27, the *Orlando Morning Sentinel* published sermons from various pastors since the churches were closed. The Board of Education voted to continue teachers' salaries through the period of quarantine. Families were advised to avoid visiting with others, and children were asked not to play outside.

1919—There was one Baptist church with 442 members.

1920—Orange County's population was 19,890. E. G. Duckworth was elected mayor, serving 1920–1924. A new fire station was completed. The census revealed that Florida had a population of 980,000; there were 175,000 Baptists.

1921—The "Dickson-Ives Building" (currently located at 2 South Orange Avenue) was built as a department store (Logsdon 18).

1922—Tinker Field was opened. Orlando's first high school was built.

1923—The public library opened.

1924—On March 27, the Orlando chapter of the Daughters of the American Revolution unveiled a granite marker to celebrate the site of Fort Gatlin (Gatlin Avenue and Summerlin). A new city hall was built. The San Juan Hotel was rebuilt with an additional 250 rooms.

The Woolworth Building (currently located at 135–141 South Orange Avenue) was built by Franklin J. Mason. Prior to this, "the Guernsey family operated a hardware store on this corner. They had Mason build a new building and then leased it to the Woolworth Company" (Logsdon 24).

1925—Orange County's population was 38,325. "Thomas Gilbert Lee starts T. G. Lee Dairy with a lot of faith in one cow named Hopper. By 1925 he has another cow and a calf. He feeds his small 'herd' in a pasture where Colonial Plaza will stand. Lee and his wife Elizabeth work long hours" (Poole 5).

The "Tinker Building" (currently located at 16–18 West Pine Street) was built for baseball legend Joe Tinker of the Chicago Cubs. He ran a real estate business in the building and, for a time, shared the site with the Singer Sewing Machine Company (Logsdon 23). Calvin Coolidge stayed at the St. Charles hotel. Orlando had three Baptist churches with a total membership of 1400.

1926—Buck Field, Orlando's first airport, opened. A new depot was opened. The Municipal Auditorium was built. L. M. Autrey was elected mayor, serving 1926–1928.

1927—The $1-million-dollar Orange County Courthouse was opened. The Municipal Airport was established. The Orlando Coliseum was built.

1928—P. Phillips built what was at that time the world's largest citrus fruit packing-house.

1929—"An invasion of Mediterranean fruit flies devastates Orlando's citrus industry. Its ruined economy is capped by the stock market crash" (Bulkin 3).

1931—Orlando's first Sears store was opened.

1932—S. Y. Way was elected mayor and served 1932–1934 and 1938–1940.

1934—The First National Bank of Orlando opened.

1935—V. W. Estes was elected mayor, serving 1935–1937.

1936—President Roosevelt visited Rollins College.

1937—An armory was built, which became an army camp during World War II.

1940s—From "Cracker Girl" by Nadine Dixon:

Two yearly events we looked forward to were hog killing and cane grinding—both done in the winter time. The pork needed the cold to keep it from spoiling while it was being prepared, and the furnace under the syrup kettle was very hot so the cold helped guard against the heat. The cold also prevented the cane juice from spoiling before it could be cooked, and the cold temperature made the cane juice sweeter.

Everyone helped with these large tasks as there was much work involved in both. The hogs had to be shot, bled, calked, and the hair scraped off before they could be hung up, gutted and sawed in half. Next they were placed on a large table, cut up to be processed into smoked hams, sausage, headcheese, live cheese, and pickled pigs feet. The fat was cut into small pieces and fried in the wash pot to make lard. The lard was stored in large cans to be used later. (14)

Other chores were shelling corn for feed and pumping water. Orlando was called "Florida's Air Capital."

1941—William Beardall was elected and served as mayor 1940–1952.

1942—The Orange County Historical Society was started. The "McCrory Building" (currently located at 101 South Orange Avenue) was built when this company moved its Florida/Georgia headquarters to Orlando (Logsdon 29).

1949—President Truman dedicated Andrews Causeway.

1952—J. Rolfe Davis was elected mayor, in office 1952–1955.

1955—Elvis Presley visited.

1956—Robert Carr was elected mayor, serving 1956–1967.

1957—Martin Marietta came to Orlando. The Orlando Centennial Fountain spouted for the first time in Lake Eola, built by W. C. Pauley.

1964—President Johnson visited Orlando. Walt Disney began buying up land.

1965—John Young and Gus Grissom orbited the earth. I-4 was completed through Orlando. The Walt Disney World plan was announced.

1966—The Naval Training Center was established.

1967—Carl T. Langford was elected mayor and served 1967–1980.

1968—Florida Technological University (later renamed the University of Central Florida) was opened. Kennedy Space Center became the site for space missions.

1971—Walt Disney World was opened.

1973—President Nixon addressed the graduating class at Florida Technical University. Sea World was opened.

1975—The San Juan Hotel was closed.

1977—Snow fell in Orlando.

1980—William Frederick became mayor, serving 1980–1992.

1981—The Winter Park sinkhole made its appearance, causing quite a stir.

1982—EPCOT was opened.

1989—The Orlando Arena, which cost $85 million and contained fifteen thousand seats, was opened. Walt Disney Amphitheater opened, and two Shakespearean productions began to be performed on an annual basis.

1990—Universal Studios was opened. The Orange County Public Schools Educational Leadership Center opened.

1991—The new City Hall was completed and occupied.

1992—Glenda E. Hood was elected mayor.

1995—The new courthouse construction was begun.

Appendix II

LISTS AND OTHER INFORMATION

Appendix II includes a list of senior pastors of First Baptist Church, the church's meeting places, First Baptist firsts, a list of full-time staff, some past and present members, and statistics.

SENIOR PASTORS OF FIRST BAPTIST CHURCH
(Compiled by Mildred Talton and Pat Birkhead)

The following have served as senior pastors during the years indicated.

William Miller, 1858
G. C. Powell, 1871–1872
A. C. Tindall, 1872–1873
J. A. Parker, 1873–1878 or 1879
L. J. Simmons, 1878 or 1879
Sam F. Gove, 1879-1882
J. S. Mahan, 1883
J. W. Butts, 1883–1884
A. Barrelle (Barelle?), 1884–1885?
A. L. Farr, 1884–1885, July and
    August 1886
Rev. Bebee, 1885
William Powell, 1885–1886
N. A. Bailey, 1887–1890
C. S. Farris, 1890–1892
S. M. Hughes, 1893–1894
W. J. Bolin, 1894–1896
J. W. Gillon, 1896

J. C. Massee, 1897–1898
Claude Raboteau, 1898–1900
C. H. Nash, 1899 (interim)
M. A. Clounts, 1900–1901
A. E. Crane, 1902–1905
W. A. Nelson, 1905–1907
T. F. Callaway, 1907–1911
Frank W. Cramer, 1911–1912
E. T. Poulson, 1913–1918
Kerr Boyce Tupper, 1918–1919 (supply)
E. J. Bingham, 1918 (supply)
J. Dean Adcock, 1919–1937
T. V. Crawford, 1937 (supply)
J. Powell Tucker, 1938–1956
W. R. Clark, 1956 (interim)
Henry Allen Parker, 1956–1977
William Curl, 1977 (interim)
James B. Henry, 1977–present

First Baptist Church, 1882–1897—Courtesy OCHM

CHURCH MEETING PLACES
(Compiled by Mildred Talton and Pat Birkhead)

1858–1862—The first meeting place is uncertain, but legend has it at the Hull home in the Lake Fairview area. Another place could have been a log courthouse, but this one would have to have been built prior to the well-documented log courthouse constructed in 1863.

1871–1872—This was a two-story frame courthouse built in 1869 by Bluford Sims. The floor was covered with sawdust. The location is thought to have been on Central and Court Streets.

1872–1882—For ten years our church met at the Union Free Church and School building on South Main (now Magnolia) Street between Pine and Church Streets. The current location would be around 56 East Pine Street. Another source said the location was between Main and Rosalind. Our church met once a month, alternating with other denominations.

1882–1897—A frame church we built on the northwest corner of Pine and Garland Streets was our first private meeting place.

1897–1915—The church met in a painted white frame with a steeple (one of the first to rise in Orlando) at the southeast corner of East Pine and Main.

1915–1961—The congregation built a Greek-style building with cream colored brick and columns and stained glass windows on the corner of Pine and Main.

1961–1985—The building, which has since become Downtown Baptist, has large columns, and a brick structure with a million-dollar sanctuary.

1985–present—Our current campus is at John Young Parkway and McLeod Road.

First Baptist Firsts
(Compiled by Mildred Talton, Pat Hanson, and Pat Birkhead)

1858—Baptist church became the first church of any denomination in Orlando. It was perhaps started in the home of William and Emily Hull, by William Miller of Apopka (another record said Lake Eustis Settlement) with twelve members. It was disbanded during the Civil War

1871—March 5. The church was begun again by G. C. Powell of Oviedo with eighteen members and has been continuous since then. W. John Brack, mayor of Orlando, was a charter member and the first church clerk. Church discipline was

First Baptist Church, 1897–1915

First Baptist Church, 1915–1961

difficult. Members were dismissed for nonattendance, playing billiards, dancing, horse racing, drinking, heresy, nonpayment of debts, and un-Christian conduct.

1872—A Negro woman was admitted to membership: Annie McDuffie. Three other blacks of the Glover family are listed in the early records. W. B. and Emily Hull joined.

1879—The first lady committee member was Emily Hull on the Vigilante Committee.

1880—The first trustees were Len Tyner, John Wofford, and W. B. Hull.

1881—The first to be licensed to preach was J. B. Graves. The first Woman's Missionary Society president was charter member Narcissa Lovell. The first to be remembered, by name, in death was John Young.

1882—The first Baptist church building was completed, located at the northwest corner of Garland and Pine Streets. The first Sunday School began sometime between 1879 and 1882 with Sam Gove as pastor.

1884—Our first full-time pastor was A. L. Farr and was given a salary of forty dollars a month.

1906—The first pastorium was built east of the church facing Pine, at a cost of twenty-eight hundred dollars. T. F. Callaway was the first pastor to occupy the pastorium.

1913—The church purchased its first pipe organ. Up to this time, a reed organ had been used.

1923—Dr. Adcock was the first pastor to live in the next pastorium on Livingston. The first mention of a choir, directed by W. H. Bixby. The first mention of an orchestra, directed by F. N. Boardman.

1928—Bobby O'Rork became the first boy of the church to pass the Royal Ambassador's test, and the seventh in the state.

1931—The first radio broadcast over WDBO.

1944—The first full-time church hostess was Leona Swain.

1949—The first churchwide pageant at the Coliseum was held at Christmastime.

1950—The first officers' and teachers' meeting.

1953—First G.A. Coronation. Travis Plummer was the queen.

1958—The New Member's Department was begun.

1959—Our church became the first Standard Sunday School in Florida.

1961—The first kindergarten was established.

1962—The first television telecast of worship services occurred on April 29 over WLOF.

1963—Dr. Parker was elected president of Florida Baptist Convention. This was also the first time First Baptist Church gave over fifty thousand dollars to the Cooperative Program, the most ever given, up to that time, by a Florida church.

1967—In February, Senior Adult Week began to be celebrated.

1968—Construction of Baptist Terrace was begun. The first literary class was held. The first ladies prayer retreat was held at Camp Joy.

1969—The Good Thief Coffee House was begun.

First Baptist Church, 1961–1985

First Baptist Church, 1985–present

1970—The Baptist Terrace was completed, and Charles Horsley was the first administrator. The thrift shop opened (originally called Good Riddance). Mom's day out program was started. The tape ministry was begun.

1971—The one hundredth anniversary of First Baptist Church was celebrated in March.

1973—The youth choir had its first trip to Israel with the Ireys and Dr. Parker.

1974—Virginia Parker became the first woman president of the Florida Baptist Convention. Evangelism Explosion was begun, with Gerry Leonard leading.

1975—The old sanctuary was demolished to make way for the Christian Life Center.

1977—The Christian Life Center was dedicated.

1978—The first English and citizenship classes were held. All mission offerings were taken together during the Month of Missions. Easter and Christmas dramas were begun. Founder's Day was begun. God & Country Day was begun for July 4th celebration.

1980—The Seventy Day Miracle for Crossing Over raised $2,620,000 in seventy days. The Singing Christmas Trees were begun.

1982—The church purchased 150 acres at I-4 and Thirty-third Street. We pledged $13.2 million, plus six hundred thousand dollars for an organ, toward a new church building. Three A.M. worship services and two P.M. worship services were begun.

1983—Groundbreaking for the new church. The first bookstore for the church was opened in the library.

1984—The first Bible Day USA: First Baptist Church collected six thousand Bibles to go to Uganda.

1985—The church moved to the new church site.

1986—The Crisis Pregnancy Center was started by Bill Curl.

1987—The First Academy was opened. We hired our first staff evangelist: David Ring. The first baby was born as a result of the ministry of the Crisis Pregnancy Center.

1988—The deacon emeritus program was initiated. We established the Current Issues Council to serve as political information clearing house. The pastor's Discovery Class and Guest Reception was begun on Sunday mornings following the worship service.

1989—The first poinsettia tree was placed in Welcome Center A at Christmastime.

1990—The church paid off its existing debt and became debt free. The Easter presentation, "The Light," was televised live on WFTV Channel 9. The Watchman Prayer Ministry was begun, instituting round-the-clock prayer.

1991—The church purchased its own TV equipment

1992—The church takes "The Light" to England. First Baptist Church produced, directed, and engineered TV service on church equipment, with church staff and volunteers. We led the SBC in Cooperative Program gifts with $931,224. Mary Sims, executive housekeeper, retired after thirty-five years of service.

1993—Church membership reached ten thousand. The church purchased the first Family trolley.

1994—Jim Henry was elected president of the Southern Baptist Convention. Sunday School reached nine thousand enrollment. The First Academy achieved its first graduating class.

1995—"Mission Orlando" neighborhood Bible clubs took the place of Vacation Bible School. Jim Henry was elected to a second term as president of SBC. Four murals were painted for Faith Hall, depicting the history of First Baptist Church. First Baptist Church became the first church in Florida to give one million dollars to the Cooperative Program.

1996—The "Year of the Church" was a celebration of 125 years of First Baptist Church history.

FULL-TIME STAFF OF FIRST BAPTIST CHURCH OF AT LEAST SIX MONTHS AS OF MAY 22, 1996
(Compiled by the Personnel Office)

Name	Current Job Title	Date of Full-time Employment
Aldrich, Alan L.	Security Supervisor	3/4/88
Alfaro, Jose Manuel	Custodian	4/30/94
Ates, Darrel Dean	Custodian	7/24/95
Bailey, Patricia	Custodian	8/22/94
Bailey, S. Michael	Custodian	4/6/82
Bauer, Stephanie	Operator of Facilities Secretary	1/9/95
Bell III, Charles	Assistant Pastor/Counseling Center	10/15/82
Berry, Jeffery S.	Printer/Darkroom	6/15/94
Bordonaro, Raymond	Runner/Fleet Maintenance	6/20/95
Bos, Shirley	Education Administrative Assistant	8/7/89

Brantley, Shelva	Cash Receipts Clerk	6/25/84
Brown, Gail	Median and Senior Adult Secretary	8/28/89
Brown, Jane	Counseling Center Secretary	8/13/84
Bynum, Carol	Membership Assistant	11/29/93
Collingsworth, Joe	Assistant Pastor/Young Married Adults	8/29/89
Diffey, Linda	General Accounting Clerk	12/17/90
Driggers, Darla	Singles Secretary	7/3/95
Dusek, Jimmy	Assistant Pastor/Pastoral Care	1/1/82
Dusek, Shirley	Preschool Associate	4/1/85
Edge, Mary	Custodian	8/6/80
Emerick, Paul	Security Guard	10/26/92
Epperson, Robert	Assistant Business Administrator	7/27/88
Epperson, Sandra	CFP Coordinator	4/4/88
Estes, Shirley	Music Ministry Assistant	11/17/80
Eudell, Corey	Third Cook	7/31/95
Fletcher, Barbara	Food Service Office Manager	8/3/95
Fort, Connie	Preschool Secretary	10/9/95
Fuller, Hadley Jean	Music Assistant	6/20/86
Garces, Gloria	Custodian	5/17/79
Godin, Roger	Executive Chef	1/1/94
Green, Deborah	Banquet Culinary	12/3/95
Grosshans, Tim	Assistant Pastor/Single Adults	4/29/92
Guilfoyle, Francis	Custodian	5/4/95
Hale, Lisa	Evangelism/Prayer/Missions Secretary	3/28/94
Hale, Virginia	Second Cook	9/4/94
Hanson, Patricia	Facilities Secretary	10/1/63
Hawk, Dorothy	Outreach Secretary	1/3/77
Hawxwell, Barbara	Media Administrative Assistant	8/7/89
Henry, James	Pastor	9/18/77
Hibbard, Keith	Maintenance Mechanic	10/2/95
Hughes, James	Video Services Technician	6/14/84
Jenkins Jr., Charles	Security Guard	9/21/89
Jennings, Patrick	Director of Food Services	1/24/95
Johnson, Robert Wayne	Assistant Pastor/Media	10/22/73
Keller, Walter	Production Services Assistant	4/3/89
Knight, Viola	CEC Food Service Cook	10/16/81
Knott, James	Associate Pastor	6/3/80
Lawrence, Helen	Print Services Project Secretary	1/30/87
Lear, Paul	First Cook	12/11/95
Lyle, Audrey	Payroll Specialist	8/21/95
Mathews, Stewart	Operations Coordinator	3/25/91
Mathis, Sandra	Executive Assistant to Pastor	3/10/94
Matzick, Richard	Chief Engineer	1/14/88
McClellan, Virginia	Graphics Composer	6/4/90

McKee, Mike	Assistant Pastor/Median/Senior Adults	2/2/92
McKenzie, Donald	Print Services Coordinator	9/21/95
McRae, Katherine	Graphic Artist	7/28/93
Medley, Roland	Lead Steward	12/5/94
Melhem, Euba	Administration Administrative Assistant	10/27/86
Meyer, Mark	Director, Facility Management	11/29/93
Mitchell, Bill	Assistant Pastor/Evangelism/Prayer/Missions	1/1/93
Montgomery, Jerri	Food Service Manager	6/13/94
Moore, Rodney	Maintenance Assistant	4/30/90
Murphy, Art	Assistant Pastor/Children	1/1/85
Nassar Jr., James	Director of Computer Services	5/7/84
Nutting, Nancy	Custodian Lead	10/17/84
Osburn, John	Custodian	5/18/77
Ozuna, Jesus	Custodian	12/19/93
Piercy, William	Custodian Lead	3/8/93
Pinckney, Angela	Custodian	8/10/88
Rauscher, Sherry	Student Assistant	6/19/95
Richardson, Ann	Deacon Secretary/Receptionist	8/6/90
Roberts, Lois Ann	Music Associate	8/16/81
Russo, Dorothy	Accounts Payable Clerk	11/18/85
Sanford, Grace	Pastoral Care Secretary	5/17/82
Seymour, Thomas	Maintenance Mechanic	8/24/89
Shackelford, Pat	Music Administrative Assistant	3/1/76
Silkman, Bill	Business Administrator	8/21/85
Skellenger, Donna	Student Secretary	8/22/91
Slaton, Betty	Associate Pastor's Administrative Assistant	2/22/93
Smith, Joseph	Security Guard	7/30/80
Smith, Steve	Assistant Minister of Media	11/1/94
Somar, Eustace	Assistant Printer	8/14/95
St. Clair, Randy	Maintenance Assistant	3/19/87
Stowell, Helen	Child Enrichment Center Director	5/29/95
Straw, Faye	Assistant Child Enrichment Center Director	7/4/95
Tademy, Darwin	Custodian	1/5/95
Ulvano, Louis	Custodial Supervisor	2/24/92
Vandegriff, Ragan	Assistant Pastor/Music	2/15/78
Wall, Kyle	Assistant Pastor/Students	5/15/95
Walton, Jean	Purchasing/Cash Distribution Clerk	4/1/94
Wassman, Marcia	Young Married Adults Secretary	7/19/93
Wellington, Barbara	Missions/Prayer Assistant	12/21/87
Wellman, Carole	Computer Services Assistant	10/21/85
Wells, Lucy	Controller	2/26/89
Williams, Gloria	Custodian	5/1/89
Winch, Terry	Director of Instrumental Music	8/15/88
Wormack, Jimmy	Custodian Lead	2/20/91

Mildred and Gordon Talton
—Courtesy Mildred Talton

An equal number of part-time staff at First Baptist also greatly contribute to the work of the church.

SOME PAST AND PRESENT MEMBERS

Gordon and Mildred Talton—Both Gordon and Mildred Talton were raised in very strong Christian homes. Gordon's mother and grandmother knew Annie Armstrong. One of his relatives, James Pollard, helped write the WMU's Constitution when that organization was formed from the Southern Baptist Convention. Many other relatives, including the Tyler line, also had early roots in WMU in the Baltimore area. Gordon and Mildred were married in Virginia in 1944 and moved to the Orlando area where Gordon continued his practice of dentistry, and the couple joined First Baptist Church in 1946. They had five children who all became committed Christians. A list of the Talton's involvement at First Baptist would fill several pages. In brief, they were active in working with Juniors (children aged nine through twelve) from 1946 until Gordon's death in 1982. Gordon enlisted several men into work with this age group, such as Mac McCully, Gene Kelsey, Edwin and Charles Moses, and Loren Mallory. Gordon was a deacon for most of those years and was on a number of committees often concentrating in the area of missions. He was one of the original leaders in the forming of Baptist Terrace. Under Dr. Tucker, Gordon led Children's Church on Sunday mornings in Duke Hall. He was the Memorial Committee chairman for the building of the 1961 sanctuary, and he was an active member of Brotherhood. Finally, Gordon was on the state Board of Missions.

Mildred shared in many of her husband's activities and was a busy mother, doing much transporting of their children to various church events. She was also involved in Sunday School and WMU. She was actively involved on the Missions

Committees during the time of the forming of Parkway, McCoy, Maitland, and South Orlando. She joined forces with Harriet Maffett in the writing of the association's history for its one hundredth anniversary celebration. She was the church historian and archivist for twenty-five years and took meticulous notes, which have proved invaluable in the writing of this book. Currently, Mildred is an active member of Downtown Baptist Church and has just completed work with others on the writing of the history of the Greater Orlando Baptist Association for its 125th anniversary. She is that association's historian.

S. A. Newell—From a church bulletin dated June 28, 1925:

> S. A. Newell Leaves for Vacation. This being a common occurrence among our members, some of whom leave every week for a vacation, it would seem passing strange that special mention should be made in the Bulletin of one, and not all. There is a reason for this special notice, in the fact of his loyal and unfailing service over a period of more than twenty years. Brother Newell has kept our books for a long period of time as Church Clerk, has served as Baraca President for many years, as a deacon for all this period, and for more than ten years as Church Treasurer, handling for the church during this period hundreds of thousands of dollars, without one single error ever being detected by the Auditing Committee. For the past two years he has been Financial Secretary of the church. All this work in addition to his arduous duties in the Bank has proven too much for his frail body, so the doctors have ordered him to take several months of complete rest. He, with Mrs. Newell, left last Monday for California, where he will spend a short time in the sanitarium, the remainder of the time visiting with relatives, and touring the Great West. The prayers of all our people follow him. We hope that within a few months he shall be entirely restored and back with us again.

Mrs. Joe Reinertson—From a church bulletin dated June 28, 1925:

> The Passing of Mrs. Joe Reinertson. The beautiful spirit of this godly woman passed to the "happy Summerland of Song" on Thursday afternoon at 3 o'clock. Funeral services conducted in this church yesterday morning, and the body laid to rest in Greenwood Cemetery. Among all the noble band of workers that our great Bible School has had, possibly none has been more faithful than she. Her work in the Beginners' Department will long be remembered, where she served as Secretary for four years without missing a Sunday, spending at least one dollar every Sunday for taxi fare, due to the fact that she was too frail to walk. She has earned the blessed sleep from which none ever wake to weep.

Mattie Hart—She was the Junior Department superintendent in 1931. Barbara Kelsey remembers Mattie Hart as being very forceful. She would have her children recite James 1:22 while she stomped her feet and clapped her hands. Everyone seemed to believe she was "quite a character." Jo Kesler remembers Mattie Hart as working with juniors for thirty to thirty-five years. She described her as very strong and a good dresser. Howard Dobson remembers her when he was nine years old. The Junior Department had classes in the balcony. That way Hart could make sure her "charges" went directly to worship services after Sunday School. Howard also remembers receiving a very fine Bible after a year's worth of correct answers to his Sunday School teacher.

Other Sunday School teachers—Many teachers were called to mind by people filling out the church history questionnaire. Some remembered Mabel Cloud, who worked for thirty to forty years with the primaries. She had a strong heart of service and worked on several committees. Others who were fondly mentioned were Petis Woodward, Charles Titus, Cora Titus, and Virginia Taylor.

Ministers of education—There have been a number of them. Some from the past have been Lee MacDonell, Louie Wilkinson, Mitchell Maddox, Calvin Vice, David Cunningham, and Dan Taylor.

Youth pastors or directors—Some in the past have been H. J. Dominey, Larry Carrol, Jerry Denson, Maynard Tribble, Pat Brademeyer Hanson, Nancy Crider, Ken Hofmeister, Donnette Dunaway, Paul Thomas, Dennis Baw, and Rick Blythe.

Associate pastors—Some in the past have been Walter Brown Knight, C. C. Kiser, Charles Brown, and Bill Curl.

Presidents of the WMU (earlier called WMS)—Some past presidents have been Mrs. N. A. Bailey, Mrs. C. S. Harris, Alice Kimbrough, Mrs. J. L. Empie, Mollie Landrum, Mrs. Stevenson, Mrs. A. G. Fuller, Eunice Delaney, Mrs. C. T. Hungerford, Mrs. F. W. Topliff, Mrs. E. L. Smith, Mrs. M. E. Limerick, Mrs. W. H. Bixby, Mrs. W. H. Brokaw, Mary Richardson, Mrs. J. C. Murchison, Mrs. C. S. Rowe, Mrs. C. T. O'Rork, Mrs. F. F. Bonner, Mrs. J. E. Nobles, Mrs. J. R. Holbrook, Mrs. W. J. Garnett, Mrs. S. W. Shirley, Mrs. George Swain, Mrs. R. M. Martin, Mrs. E. G. Rich, Mrs. W. D. Shedd, Mrs. R. L. Hodges, Mrs. J. F. High, Mrs. Walter Martin, Mrs. L. W. Dockery, Mrs. S. A. Minton, Mrs. T. D. McGraw, Mrs. J. B. Shearouse, Mrs. L. L. Wilkinson, Mrs. Ellis Snipes, Mrs. Ken Snelling, Mrs. Mac McKinney, Mrs. A. Clark, and Patsy Russell.

BTU directors, Sunday School directors, and youth leaders—So many have served through the years. The following are a sampling of these great servants: George W. Phillips, Eugene Reid, Alfred Link, Ethel Weimer, N. T. Barnes, Mabel Ammerman, J. Davis, Charles Bruner, J. C. Wright, Mrs. C. A. Rehberg, Helen Hutchins, Irene Shearon, W. G. Rose, George M. Swain, Fred M. Smith, T. C. Roberts, John Ringsmith, Virginia O'Rork, Nelson Axton, A. G. Graham, Mrs. Hilliard Johnson, H. F. Martin, R. G. Summers, Ona Barfield, Mr. and Mrs. J. C. Ballenger, Bill Hale, Pat Brademeyer, Ralph Clark, Carl Creasman, Joseph M. Pipkin, Pat West, Rick Blythe, Bill Rogers, Lee McDonald, Mabel Starnes, Doris Harper, Alice Price, Mrs. Pat Hanson, and Shirley O'Quinn.

Pastor's assistants—There have been many pastor's assistants, and this title has changed through the years. Some pastor's assistants from 1913 through 1970 have been A. Preston Boyd, Mrs. W. D. Napier, Walter Brown Knight, Mrs. N. T. Barnes, Lee MacDonell, Mabel Starnes, Mrs. Hilliard Johnson, Alice Price, C. C. Kiser Jr., Kenneth Hansen, William Smith, and Jim Wilson.

Brotherhood—One organization in the past of this church was a men's ministry called the Brotherhood. Some officers from 1936 through 1965 have included

E. N. Upshaw, J. B. Bookhart, Robert L. Marrero, Spurgeon Gage, Earl Clay, Charles Luke, William Hale, Marvin Powell, Hewen Lasseter, and Alex Marsh.

Church clerks—The position of church clerk began with W. J. Brack and concludes with the current clerk, who has held that position since 1977, Robert Marrero. Some of the people who came between these two men were S. M. Summerlin, W. B. Hull, S. B. Carter, J. D. Beggs, Ned Rice, A. J. Mostller, W. T. Haizlip, J. A. Rogers, G. L. Stevens, J. W. Prentis, D. D. Kinney, S. A. Newell, R. J. Stevenson, J. A. Stinson, C. M. Tichener, John Bethea, Alex Young, P. L. Woodward, Roger Barber, Roger Clark, Spurgeon Gage, C. L. Durrance, Rufus A. Perry, R. G. Summers, Gene Kelsey III, A. G. Graham, Russell Dobson, W. Ozmint, and H. J. Dominey.

E. H. Gore—Gore came from Michigan on January 21, 1903. He worked for the *Evening Star*. He carried mail, was a partner in a grocery, a post office clerk, and a foreman. He was responsible for collecting most of the factual material for the history of Orlando in his book *History of Orlando: From Florida Sand to "The City Beautiful"* and this church's "History of First Baptist Church 1871–1944." He taught Sunday School for fifty years, working with the juniors and was very active in many other areas in the church.

Lyda Plummer—She was small, thin, busy, humble, and faithful. She served as church librarian and had a gift for knowing just the right book for each person who asked for help. She and Mildred Talton worked on the history of the church.

Mrs. Pauline Tiller—Jo Kesler remembers her as a very well-qualified organist who also directed the church choir, did some counseling, and was a church secretary.

Mr. Henry Symonds—Jo Kesler remembers him as a wonderful, very personable man who wrote hundreds of hymns. He was instrumental in enlarging the choir loft. As has been mentioned earlier, he was a gifted writer of hymns and produced several hymnals.

Mrs. J. B. Shearouse—Jo Kesler remembers her as a wonderful, dedicated choir director who got along very well with everyone. She was almost a "Victorian lady" who was somewhat strict, but people loved her.

Kathy Enfinger—Kathy was a young high school student in the late 1970s when cancer struck her with a vengeance. Through her journey of illness and pain, she became an amazing testimony of the Lord's goodness. She spoke at the Central Florida Fellowship of Christian Athletes on December 18, 1981, at First Baptist Church, Orlando, where multitudes were touched by her witness. Two and a half weeks later, on January 6, 1982, Kathy died. Brother Jim wrote:

> I was with her and her parents when the doctor told her she had the malignancy. We all cried. I asked her parents to leave the room. She shared her concern about not being able to play ball, have a boy friend, etc. We prayed and she seemed to resolve to fight the cancer. She did so in a noble way. I remember two events especially: her testimony before the student body at Oak Ridge shortly before she died. She calmly told them she was dying but knew where she was going and urged them to accept Christ. She sat down to a tremendous standing ovation.

Then, she went with us and the youth to Israel although her arm was fixed in an extended fashion from her shoulder with a steel rod connected to her body for support in keeping it in a raised position. She slept, flew, and rode through Israel in that difficult position without a complaint and with a continued smile.

Glenda Mowdy—Glenda Mowdy suggested the following about teaching children's Sunday school: "Children in grades 1 through 6 are going to be our leaders of tomorrow. If we don't reach them during this critical age, they are hard to reach later."

Marti Albert—Jim Henry wrote the following in an article from the 1988 "Beacon":

> Marti Albert celebrates her 20th year as Pastor's Secretary this month. I know that's not a record, but I also know that it's far above the average! For more than 7,300 days she has handled thousands of phone calls, typed tons of cards and letters, smoothed ruffled feelings, prayed with and counseled broken hearts, encouraged staff and church members with her sweet spirit and ready smile, served as a faithful member of the choir and Sunday School teacher, wept with us and laughed with us. In recent years, her courageous fight against cancer has been an inspiration to all who know how strongly she has waged war against this invisible enemy. Marti has been like a right arm to me. She is swift to see needs before they arise, keep me on schedule, keep tabs on my sermons, illustrations and files, and never complained about any thing I've asked her to do in or above her job responsibilities. She is the consummate executive secretary. She is a friend to our family. She is a prayer warrior. She is loyal beyond question. She relishes her role as mother, wife and grandmother. Marti Albert is a faithful servant of our Lord Jesus Christ, and on this her twentieth year, a grateful church fellowship, staff, and pastor say—"Thanks, Marti! We love you!"

Emmett Browning—Jarlene Montgomery wrote about her father:

> Emmett Browning accepted Christ and was baptized at First Baptist many years ago. He was a member for 43 years. He taught 13 year olds for years, was a deacon, and an usher. He worked on the staff for 13 years retiring at age 85 for health reasons. His main responsibility had been maintaining and keeping the dining room, setting up for meals, weddings, receptions, etc. He made himself a measuring stick just the length he wanted it so that he could have all the tables set up just in the right manner, evenly placed the same distance apart because they were measured in that manner by his stick. He always took great pride in what he did and tried to teach his children that no matter how big or small a job was, to do the best you could. The snack room in Faith Hall is named after him.

Walter Reed—Ralph Edfeldt wrote about Walter Reed:

Walter Reed and his wife Ruth were active in First Baptist for many years. He was a school principal in the public school system. They had one son, George, who went to seminary. Walter taught Sunday School classes, but was *THE* sound man for First Baptist. In the fifties, the sound booth was a converted closet toward the rear of the sanctuary in which Walter had to stand to operate the amplifier, which was about the size of a shoe box. Later, when the new sanctuary (presently Downtown Baptist) was built, he was instrumental in placing and operating a very modern sound board in the balcony, and this became a major part of our church life.

Chaplain H. C. and Mrs. Gober—For a number of years, until health prevented them from attending, Chaplain H. C. Gober and his wife were faithful attendees at church services. A few minutes before the service, Chaplain Gober would be wheeled down to the front in his wheelchair with his beautiful wife walking by his side. Her attention to his needs during the service was apparent to all as they watched this charming couple worship their Lord. One time, during an Easter service, Christ was portrayed at the Second Coming. With tears of joy in his eyes, Chaplain Gober slowing raised himself to his feet for a few unsteady moments of adoration.

Bill and Lucy Pat Curl—Jim Henry wrote about this couple as they prepared to leave for the foreign mission field:

> They've walked with us at First Baptist for eighteen wonderful years. They've been personal friends to me and Jeanette for thirty-four years. Now, they're on their way to Wales as our missionaries to share Christ in that secular land in their winsome way and with their many talents. Wales will rejoice. We will wait! We're sending the very best and we're already missing them.

> "Bill and Lucy Pat"—goes together like ham and eggs. You think of one, you think of the other. Memories: riding their Tandem bicycle . . . Lucy jogging around the church property . . . Bill baptizing so gently . . . Lucy, the accomplished pianist and organist, accompanying all kinds of musicians and doing it with ease . . . Bill keeping twenty things going on at the same time . . . Lucy leading the ladies ensemble . . . Bill and his offertory stories . . . Lucy working at the switchboard and a dozen other jobs around the church . . . Bill and his puns and one-liners . . . Lucy's transparency . . . Bill's mission heart that just kept growing . . . Lucy, the patient and wise mother . . . Bill's ability to be at three meetings at the same time . . . Lucy's love for all people . . . Bill arriving at the meeting; not too early, not too late, somehow being on time . . . Lucy and Bill, young grandparents . . . Bill's agility and finesse in assisting at the Lord's Table . . . his weird costumes for Month of Missions parades . . . his warm hand on your shoulder while you're praying . . . singing his signatory song, "Just Think of Stepping in Space and Finding it Heaven," at dozens of funerals and lifting the soul from grief to joy . . . his singing as he headed for the Prayer Room . . . his ability to counsel wisely . . . the hundreds he and Lucy Pat touched and instructed

in the marriage preparation classes . . . his gentle patience . . . the leadership he gave
to the deacon body . . . his hand signals at the altar during invitation time; something
between a New York traffic cop and a flagman on an aircraft carrier . . . the old cars
he fixed up and kept running . . . their gift of helps that opened their home to many
a missionary, church member, friend, and stranger . . . the rich heritage they received
from godly parents . . . being recycled in their yielded lives . . . Bill's "just right
words" for a thousand different occasions . . . knowing when he took a job or responsibility, you could count on it being done . . . his capability of eating enormous
amounts of food and never gaining weight . . . keeping his hair black past fifty,
(Natural or supernatural? Only his hairdresser knows!) . . . leader in local and state
Baptist work . . . the grace of genuine love which you saw and felt . . . did he ever
get angry at anyone or anything except sin? . . . and did the Holy Spirit give anyone
else more spiritual gifts . . . and won't we miss them? ("Beacon" November 15, 1990)

Fourth and fifth generations—Several of our church families have a rich and
long association with the church. Some go back several generations. We have
listed only those families with one or more generations still active in this church.
Some of these families include:

Beginning Name	Number of Generations
Elsie Belvin	4
Emmett and A. Louise Browning	4
Samuel William and Allyne Cooksley	4
Gladys S. Curl	4
Eugene and Edna Kelsey	4
Edward and Vivian Marrero	4
N. B. and Margaret McGuffey	4
Ivan and Marguerite Morgan	4
Lois H. Murrah	4
Walter F. and Peggy Partin	4
W. K. and Mamie Day Price	5
E. G. and Gennivee Rich	4
Henry and Lucy Symonds	4

Stalwarts of the faith—It is always somewhat risky to list those members of the
church whom others might call stalwart. These valiant saints recorded below are
given as examples of hundreds who might be so described. Preschool worker
Marilyn Avriett loved children, especially the very young ones, and sacrifically gave
her heart and life to them "for the kingdom of God belongs to such as these." Trevor
Hawk loved the story of Easter and, with weak arms, lifted his palm branch and participated in "The Light: The Story of Our Christ" days before his own entrance to
heaven. "There will be no more death or mourning or crying or pain, for the old
order of things has passed away." Helen Jurkuta loved to smile and exemplified a

true saint of God. At Christmastime she wore festive earrings, and the author's little daughter called her "the angel lady" because her "face was like the face of an angel."

Linda Maddox loved the lost and faithfully learned Evangelism Explosion so that she could tell others about her Jesus, for her Lord commanded her to open her eyes and "look at the fields. They are ripe for harvest." Bob Roycroft loved to play his instrument unto the Lord and could be found in his beloved orchestra seat, until just days before his death, lifting his "trumpet call of God." Marsha Shudan loved to sing in the adult choir. She rallied from her bed of pain, and, with choir members supporting her on both sides, she sang "just one more time" on the Singing Christmas Tree. "Sing, all you who are upright in heart!" Gordon Talton loved to work, and when he was diagnosed and told to celebrate Christmas early, he lived another two years. Days before his death, he drove a bulldozer, clearing the land on the new campus. "He who began a good work in you will carry it on to completion until the day of Christ Jesus."

SOME STATISTICS ABOUT FIRST BAPTIST CHURCH

- The parking lots contain a total of approximately three thousand parking spaces on about thirty acres of land.
- The campus contains 450,000 square feet within its buildings (excluding The First Academy).
- The Worship Center contains about one hundred thousand square feet and seats six thousand.
- Membership of the church totals approximately ten thousand.
- The annual budget is approximately $7 million.
- The church baptizes approximately 360 people per year.
- There are over 9,390 people enrolled in approximately 203 age-graded Sunday School classes.
- There are between ninety and one hundred active deacons.
- There are twenty serving committees.
- The church mails out approximately seven thousand newsletters each month.
- There are approximately one hundred full-time and more than one hundred part-time employees.
- The average age of the pastoral staff is forty-four.
- There are over five hundred volunteers for missions each year.
- Nearly $2 million is given annually to mission-related causes and activities.
- The First Academy is a SACS accredited, fully academic, athletic, K–12 coed Christian school, with approximately forty-seven full-time and thirty-four part-time employees serving over eight hundred students.

Bibliography

BOOKS

Adicks, Richard, and Donna M. Neely. *Oviedo: Biography of a Town*. Orlando, Fla.: Executive Press, 1979.

The Annual Register. Vol 113, *1871: A Review of Public Events at Home and Abroad for the Year 1871*. London: Revingtons, 1972.

Armstrong, O. K., and Marjorie Moore Armstrong. *Baptists Who Shaped a Nation*. Nashville: Broadman Press, 1975.

Bacon, Eve. *Orlando: A Centennial History*. Chuluota, Fla.: Mickler House Publishers, 1975.

———. Vol II, *From the City Beautiful to the Action Center of Florida: 1926–1975*. Chuluota, Fla.: Mickler House Publishers, 1977.

Baker, Robert A. *The Southern Baptist Convention and Its People, 1607–1972*. Nashville: Broadman Press, 1974.

"Baptists." *Encyclopedia Americana*. Vol. 3, 1993.

Bishop, Katherine. *Sanford Now and Then*. Sanford, Fla.: Greater Sanford Chamber of Commerce, 1976.

Blackman, W. F. *History of Orange County Florida*. Deland, Fla.: E. O. Painter Printing Co., 1927.

Breakfast, A. G. *Romantic History of Orlando, Florida*. Orlando, Fla.: Pryor, Hyer & Hyer, 1946.

Bulkin, Rena. *Frommer's Comprehensive Travel Guide: Orlando '94*. New York: Prentice Hall Travel, 1994.

Bush, L. Russ, and Tom J. Nettles. *Baptists and the Bible*. Chicago: Moody Press, 1980.

Carter, Clarence E. *The Territory of Florida: 1821–1845*. N.Y., 1973.

Chapin, George M. *Florida 1513–1913*. 2 vols. Chicago: S. J. Clarke Publishers, 1914.

Church Record Book From 3/5/1871 to 12/1893. Book One. First Baptist Orlando.

Cutler, Harry G. *History of Florida: Past and Present, Historical and Biographical*. 3 vols. Chicago: Lewis Publishing Co., 1924.

Florida State Census. Various volumes.

Garrison, Webb. *A Treasury of Florida Tales.* Nashville: Rutledge Hill Press, 1989.

Gore, E. H. *From Florida Sand to "The City Beautiful": A Historical Record of Orlando, Florida.* 2nd ed. Orlando, Fla.: J. M. Cox, 1951.

Harris, Michael H. *Florida History: A Bibliography.* N.J.: Scarecrow Press, 1973.

Henry, Jim. *Heartwarmers: Reading That Makes God Real.* Nashville: Broadman Press, 1977.

Howard, C. E. *Early Settlers of Orange County Florida 1915 Reminiscent—Historic—Biographic.* Orlando, Fla.: C. E. Howard, 1915.

Joiner, Edward Earl. *A History of Florida Baptists.* Jacksonville, Fla.: Florida Baptist Convention Press, 1972.

Kendrick, Baynard H. *Orlando, A Century Plus.* Orlando, Fla.: Sentinel Star Co., 1976.

Marth, Del, and Martha J. Marth. *Florida Almanac 1995–1996.* Fred W. Wright Jr., ed. Gretna, La: Pelican Publishing Co., 1995.

O'Neal, William R. *Memoirs . . . of a Pioneer.* Orlando, Fla.: Orlando Sentinel-Star, Florida Press, Inc., 1932.

Orlando: History in Architecture. Orlando, Fla.: Orlando Historic Preservation Board, 1984.

Richards, John R. *Orange County Gazetter and Business Directory, Vol. 1, 1887.* Jacksonville, Fla.: John R. Richards and Co., 1887.

Robison, Jim, and Mark Andrews. *Flashbacks: The Story of Central Florida's Past.* Orlando, Fla.: The Orange County Historical Society and the *Orlando Sentinel*, 1995.

Rogers, S. B. *A Brief History of Florida Baptists: 1825–1925.* Jacksonville, Fla.: Miller Press, n.d.

Rosser, John Leonidas. *A History of Florida Baptists.* Nashville: Broadman Press, 1949.

Routh, E. C. *Baptists on the March: A History of Baptists.* Shawnee, Okla: Oklahoma Baptist University Press, 1952.

Shofner, Jerrell H. *Orlando: The City Beautiful.* Tulsa, Okla: Continental Heritage Press, 1984.

———. *History of Apopka and Northwest Orange County, Florida.* Apopka, Fla.: Apopka Historical Society, 1982.

Tebeau, Charlton W. *A History of Florida.* Miami: University of Miami Press, 1971.

Thompson, Sharyn. *Florida's Historic Cemeteries: A Preservation Handbook.* Tallahassee, Fla.: Historic Tallahassee Preservation Board, 1989.

Treasures: Historic Architecture of Greater Orlando. Orlando, Fla.: Orlando Landmarks Defense, Inc., 1993.

U. S. Census Population Schedules, Florida. Various volumes.

Webb, Wanton S. *Webb's Jacksonville and Consolidated Directory of the Representative Cities of East and South Florida 1886.* Jacksonville, Fla.: W. S. Webb and Co., 1886.

Willson, Minnie Moore. *The Seminoles of Florida.* Kissimmee, Fla.: Kingsport Press, 1928.

OTHER WORKS, CORRESPONDENCE, AND INTERVIEWS
(Unless stated otherwise, interviews were conducted by the author.)

Andrews, Mark. "Early Orange County Settler Finds Himself in Trouble with the Law." *Orlando Sentinel*. September 11, 1994.

———."Establishing the 1st School District for County Was an Education in Itself." *Orlando Sentinel*. October 2, 1994.

———."Landlocked Central Florida Was State's 1st Seminole Reservation." *Orlando Sentinel*. December 18, 1994.

"Beacon," FBC produced newsletter; various editions.

Bolen, Patricia McNeely. "History of First Baptist Church. Apopka, Florida." (booklet)

———."Foreign-Born Students Learn English Through Church Program." *Southside News*. May 13, 1981.

Carow, Betty. Notes on Kindergarten. May, 1996.

Clark, James C. "Only in Florida. Florida History. 1926 and 1928 Hurricanes Were a Costly and Deadly One-Two Punch for Florida." *Orlando Sentinel, Florida Magazine*. October 16, 1994.

"Cradle Roll Book" of First Baptist Orlando's Sabbath School. 1913.

Curl, Bill. Article in "Beacon" about Missionary Work in Kenya. July 19, 1990.

Davis, Orville R. Personal interview. February 10, 1996.

Deacons Meetings. First Baptist Orlando. Various minutes on microfilm 1929–1960.

Driggers, Darla. Notes about singles with information from Anita Fisher Crews.

Dusek, Shirley. Notes about the Child Enrichment Center.

Edfeldt, Martha. Notes from interview with Jo Kesler.

Edfeldt, Martha and Ralph. Notes from interviews with Bob and Donna Marrero and Dora Mae and Todd Pemberton.

Edfeldt, Ralph. Taped interview with Howard and June Dobson, 1994.

Eidson, George T. Jr. "Paradise Lost." *Orlando Sentinel, Florida Magazine*. "Paradise Lost." August 7, 1994.

Elliot, Brenda. Phone interview. February 20, 1996.

Florida State Library report (included with WPA form). Five pages, dated June 1, 1895.

Gholdston, John. "1st Baptist agrees to a friendly split." *Orlando Sentinel*. June 25, 1985.

Gore, E. H. "History of Florida Baptists. First Baptist Church." 1944 (booklet).

Gouge, Louise. Notes from interviews with Ragan Vandegriff and Wayne Johnson.

Hansen, Carol. Notes from interviews with Ed and Missy Moses, Gennivee Rich, and Don Partin.

Hanson, Pat. Notes on a vast variety of information.

Hastey, Stan L. "Baptists and Religious Liberty." Baptist Heritage Series. Nashville: The Historical Commission of the Southern Baptist Convention, 1979 (pamphlet).

Henry, Jim. Notes about life and various interviews.

Hull Family File Folder. Genealogy Dept. Orlando Public Library.

Hull, William Benjamin. "By an Old Settler." *South Florida Sentinel*. July 1, 1885.

"Impressive Ceremonies Attended by 400 Persons." *Orlando Sentinel*. March 28, 1924.

Kesler, Jo. Phone interview. Summer 1995.

King, Jean. Phone interview. February 20, 1996.

Ladies Aid Society of the First Baptist Church Orlando Florida, Record Book 1919–1921.

Locke, Don and Nellie. Notes. 1995.

Logsdon, Donna G., comp. "Discover Orlando! A Student Walking Tour." Orlando, Fla.: Orlando Landmarks Defense, Inc., 1992.

Mallory, Loren. Notes from interview with F. Ray Dorman. Other notes on Tom Gurney, Dr. Parker, missionaries and journeymen, jail ministry, thrift shop, annointing ministry, and shut-ins.

May, Lynn E. Jr. "The Baptist Story." Baptist Heritage Series. Nashville: The Historical Commission of the Southern Baptist Convention, 1979 (pamphlet).

McBeth, H. Leon. "Baptist Beginnings." Baptist Heritage. Nashville: The Historical Commission of the Southern Baptist Convention, 1979 (pamphlet).

McKinney, Beverly C. ("Mac"). "The Real Scoop on Ragan: The Story of Ragan Vandegriff on the 15th Anniversary of the Beginning of His Ministry at FBC of Orlando." (Adapted from an article in the 1986–1987 adult choir yearbook with Debbie Helander Derrick as editor.) February 21, 1993.

Meehan, Mary. "The New Face of the Religious Right." *Orlando*. December, 1994: 44–52.

Meiner, Emily. Notes from Bonnie McNutt, Jim Wilson, and Virginia Taylor.

Morgan, Doris. Notes from interview with Jim Wilson.

Moses, Ed. "Destitute Refugees Lead a Triumphant Parade." N.d. publication unknown.

———. Phone interview. May 1996.

Murrow, Murl. Notes and help from Alex Marsh, Karick Price, Bruce Ogden, Basil and Nancy Hull, Kitty Denson, Robert McFarland, Helen Lawrence, Pat Hanson, and Barbara Hawxwell.

New Wind publication. (Musical group from First Baptist, Orlando). n.d.

One Sacred Effort: 150 Years of Southern Baptist History and Life (video). Nashville Historical Commission, SBC., 1995.

"Orange County, A Ripe Old Age of 150." *Orlando Sentinel*. January 29, 1995.

Orange County Citizen. Orlando, Fla. Wednesday, April 15, 1914.

Orange County Reporter. February 1884.

Orlando Morning Sentinel. January 28, 1950.

"Orlando Natives Luncheon." May 5, 1990, Dubsdread Country Club (video).

"Orlando Natives Luncheon." April 11, 1992, Dubsdread Country Club (video).

Parker, Henry A. "Autobiography of Henry A. Parker." N.d.: Self published.

———. "Our Church: Past, Present, Future." Sunday sermon January 16, 1977 (tape).

Parker, Virginia. Telephone interview. April, 1996.

"Pioneer Churches of Central Florida." *Pioneer Days Magazine*. The Pine Castle Center of the Arts. Fall, 1980: 16–19.

Poole, Kathleen. "Built on an Orange Peel" (newspaper from The Orange County Historical Museum), n.d.

Reddick, Linda, and Mac McKinney. "In The Beginning . . ." Choir History Booklet, 1984.

Reiman, Jean. "Dr. Henry Parker's Five-Minute Sermons. A Little Extra Support to Meet the Day's Inevitable Challenges." *Orlando Sentinel*. August 28, 1966.

Robison, Jim. "More Than Just the Spice of Life, Salt Meant Life Itself for Early Florida Homesteaders." *Orlando Sentinel*. April 17, 1994.

Roycroft, Fran. Notes about Bob Roycroft and the First Baptist Church orchestra.

Shackelford, Pat. Notes about Terry Winch and the First Baptist Church orchestra.

Shaw, Mrs. Dorothy H. Letter. May 15, 1995.

Shearouse, George. Phone interview. February 15, 1996.

Shofner, Jerrell H. Phone interview. May 2, 1996.

Shurden, Walter B. "Crises in Baptist Life." Baptist Heritage Series. Nashville: The Historical Commission of the Southern Baptist Convention, 1979 (pamphlet).

"Spanish Flu Symptoms." *Orlando Morning Sentinel*. October 8, 1918.

Stoll, James H. "Pocket History of Orlando, Florida." Orlando Centennial 1875–1975. Chuluota, Fla.: Mickler House Publishers, 1975 (booklet).

Strickland, Dixon Nadine. "Cracker Girl." *Florida Living*. July 1994: 14–15.

Symonds, Henry S. Letter within Centennial Album. First Baptist Orlando Archives, n.d.

Talton, Mildred. Two black binders, n.d.

———. Various notes, folders, and personal and phone interviews.

Tate, Sharon. Phone interview. April 1996. Later photocopies from Powell Bible and notes.

Taylor, Virginia. Phone interview. May 20, 1996.

Thigpen, Barbara. Phone interview. February 13, 1996.

Truex, Dot. Personal interview. May 21, 1996.

Tucker, George. Phone interview. May 20, 1996.

Vickery, Bob. Phone interview. May 2, 1996.

"We Dedicate." Dedication program for the new sanctuary. May 14–16, 1961.

Wekiwa Baptist Association, various published minutes.

Williams, Andy. "Baptist Wind Up 3-Day Conference." *Orlando Sentinel*. January 16, 1976.

WMU meeting notes on microfilm. Beginning January 6, 1901.

Yothers, Jean. Phone interviews and correspondence, various times.

Index

Index

(Bold page numbers refer to photographs.)